Radical Whigs
and
Conspiratorial Politics
in
Late Stuart England

Frontispiece of *Argumentum AntiNormannicum*

Melinda S. Zook

Radical Whigs and Conspiratorial Politics in Late Stuart England

The Pennsylvania State University Press
University Park, Pennsylvania

Library of Congress Cataloging-in-Publication Data

Zook, Melinda S.
   Radical whigs and conspiratorial politics in late Stuart England /
Melinda S. Zook.

       p.   cm.
   Includes bibliographical references and index.
   ISBN 0-271-02841-6 (alk. paper)
   1. Great Britain—Politics and government—1660–1688.
   2. Protestants—England—Political activity—History—17th century.
   3. Great Britain—History—Revolution of 1688—Causes.   4. Political
science—England—History—17th century.   5. Great Britain—Kings
and rulers—Succession.   6. Conspiracies—England—History—17th
century.   7. Radicalism—England—History—17th century.   8. Whig
Party (Great Britain)—History.   I. Title.
DA435.Z66   1999
320.942′09′032—dc21   98-41057
                                                                      CIP

It is the policy of The Pennsylvania State University Press to use acid-free paper for
the first printing of all clothbound books. Publications on uncoated stock satisfy the
minimum requirements of American National Standard for Information Sciences—
Permanence of Paper for Printed Library Materials, ANSI Z39.48-1992.

Frontispiece: Frontispiece of *Argumentum AntiNormannicum.* Used by permission of
The Folger Shakespeare Library

Contents

Acknowledgments   vii

Abbreviations   ix

Introduction: Rethinking Exclusion   xi

1. Mapping the Radical Whigs: A Cultural and Social Biography   1

2. Resisting the Future: Secularism and the Debate over Exclusion   37

3. Refiguring the Past: Constitutionalism and the Debate over History   63

4. Creating Revolution: Robert Ferguson and the Rye House Plot   87

5. Making Martyrs: Rye House Legacies and Monmouth's Manifesto   115

6. Revolution Justified: The Radical Response to 1688   149

Conclusion: Radical Whig Legacies   173

Appendix: Radical Whig Careers   195

Bibliography   203

Index   228

For Bernard Charles and Elinore Anne Zook

Acknowledgments

I received generous funding from Georgetown University, supporting my graduate work and my first research trip to England. I am particularly thankful to Jo Anne Moran and James Collins who devoted their time and talent to my education as both teachers and scholars of history. Much of my initial research was completed at the Folger Shakespeare Library, and I would like to thank the entire library staff for their assistance, support, and kindness during my many months there. I would also like to thank the Folger Institute Center for the History of British Political Thought. The center's steering committee at that time, Lena Orlin, John Pocock, Gordon Schochet, and Lois Schwoerer, inspired, encouraged, and supported my research. I am indebted to the center for my approach to political texts.

My research at the Huntington Library, California, in 1992, was funded by a grant from the Andrew W. Mellon Foundation and the North American Conference on British Studies (NACBS). I am also grateful to the NACBS for awarding me a dissertation fellowship that supported my research in England. The latest stages of research and writing were made possible by two Purdue Faculty Incentive and Research grants and two Purdue Research Foundation grants. I would like to thank John Contreni and Nancy Gabin for the supportive atmosphere they have provided for me since my arrival at Purdue University in 1993, and my colleagues, particularly Susan Curtis, James Farr, Michael Morrison, and Whitney Walton, who have read and critiqued various papers and proposals of mine.

I am grateful to Mark Knights for identifying radical Whig petitioners for me. My debt to his work is abundantly clear in Chapter 1. I would like to express my thanks to R. J. Q. Adams, Robert Bucholz, Janelle Greenberg, Newton Key, Hilda Smith, Janet Todd, Daniel Woolf, and

Elizabeth Zelensky for their support, friendship, and encouragement. Readers will also recognize that my work owes much to recent scholarship by Richard Greaves, Mark Goldie, Tim Harris, and Gary De Krey. Last, and most important, I would like to thank Lois G. Schwoerer, my mentor, teacher, and friend, for encouraging me and challenging me to write this work. My debt to her as a scholar is great.

Finally, allow me to express my gratitude to my husband, Michael G. Smith, a true and loyal friend. This work is dedicated to my parents, Elinore and Bernard, who gave me, my sister, and my brother such a loving and supportive start in life.

Abbreviations

Add.	Additional Manuscripts, British Library, London
AHR	*American Historical Review*
BDBR	*Biographical Dictionary of British Radicals in the Seventeenth Century.* Eds. Richard L. Greaves and Robert Zaller. 3 vols. Brighton: Harvester Press, 1982–84
BIHR	*Bulletin of the Institute for Historical Research*
BL	British Library
Burnet	Gilbert Burnet, *History of His Own Time.* 6 vols. Oxford, 1833.
Carstares Papers	*State Papers and Letters Addressed to William Carstares . . . to which is prefixed the Life of Mr. Carstares.* Edinburgh, 1774.
CHJ	*Cambridge Historical Journal*
CSPD	*Calendar of State Papers, Domestic*
Dalrymple	John Dalrymple, *Memoirs of Great Britain and Ireland.* 2 vols. London and Edinburgh, 1771–73
DNB	*Dictionary of National Biography*
EHR	*English Historical Review*
Grey's Confession	Lord Ford Grey, *The Secret History of the Rye House Plot and Monmouth's Rebellion,* 1685, rpt. 1754
Grey, *Debates*	Anchitel Grey, *Debates of the House of Commons from the Year 1667 to the Year 1694.* 10 vols. London, 1763
Harl.	Harleian Manuscripts, British Library
History of Parliament	*The History of Parliament: The House of Commons, 1660–1690.* Ed. B. D. Henning. 3 vols. London:

	The History of Parliament Trust, Seeker and Warburgh, 1983
HJ	*Historical Journal*
HMC	*Historical Manuscripts Commission*
Hume	Patrick Hume, *Narrative of Occurrences in the Expedition of the Earl of Argyle in 1685*, in George Rose, *Observations of the Historical Work of the Right Honourable Charles James Fox*. London, 1809
JBS	*Journal of British Studies*
Luttrell	Narcissus Luttrell, *A Brief Historical Relation of State of Affairs from September 1678 to April 1714*. 6 vols. Oxford, 1857
P & P	*Past and Present*
POAS	*Poems on the Affairs of State: Augustan Satirical Verse, 1660–1714*. Eds. George de F. Lord and others. 7 vols. New Haven: Yale University Press, 1963–75
PRO	Public Record Office
Roberts	George Roberts, *The Life, Progresses, and Rebellion of James, Duke of Monmouth*. London, 1844
Somers Tracts	*A Collection of Scarce and Valuable Tracts [belonging to Lord Somers]*. Ed. Sir Walter Scott. 13 vols. London, 1809–15
State Trials	*A Complete Collection of State Trials*. Ed. T. B. Howell. 22 vols. London, 1816
TRHS	*Transactions of the Royal Historical Society*

Introduction: Rethinking Exclusion

Actions receive their tinctures from the times
—Daniel Defoe, *Hymn to the Pillory* (1703)

"Imagine you see the whole town in a flame . . . you behold troops of papists ravishing your wives and daughters, dashing your little children's brains out against the walls, plundering your houses and cutting your throats by the name, heretick dogs." So reads an anonymous tract warning the English in 1679, of the dangers before them should the king's brother, a Catholic, ascend the throne. The graphic images, shrill tone, and harsh language employed in *An Appeal to the Country from the City* were not atypical of seventeenth-century anti-Catholic propaganda. In the late 1670s and early 1680s, radicals used such propaganda to galvanize popular support in their battle to exclude James, duke of York, from the royal succession. Their propaganda and public demonstrations further teased and heightened popular fears already set on edge in the late summer of 1678, by tall tales of popish plotting. The Popish Plot, the story of a sinister scheme by Jesuits to poison the king and lead a Catholic uprising in Ireland and England, may have sounded fantastic to some people, including Charles II. But those few were vastly outnumbered by the many, who felt that any minute their city would be set ablaze, their wives raped, their babies skewered on pikes. "We were all of us alarmed with terrible apprehensions and possessed with a dreadful expectation of having our throats cut by papists in a sudden insurrection, which was to be made and assisted with an invasion of the French," reported an Oxford cleric. "Such was the terror and consternation which the generality of the nation was upon the discovery of the plot."[1]

---

1. [Charles Blount] *An Appeal from the Country to the City* (1679), reprinted in *State Tracts* (1689), 401–3. On antipopery during the Restoration, see John Miller, *Popery and Politics in England, 1660–1688* (Cambridge: Cambridge University Press, 1973). BL, Add. 27,440, fol. 11, for the quotation from the Oxford cleric Charles Allestree.

It was within this strained political climate that the Whig exclusion movement began. From 1678 to 1681, Whigs concentrated on parliamentary and propaganda campaigns to resolve what historians have traditionally labeled, "the Exclusion Crisis." Although various proposals for dealing with the problem of a Catholic heir apparent were put forth, most Whigs sought to exclude the "popish successor" from the throne completely. In Parliament, Whig attempts to legislate the exclusion of the duke of York were thwarted by the king. Legal methods having failed, the radicals among them resorted to more drastic measures. In 1682 and 1683, they concocted various plots to overthrow Charles II or simply force him to accept the exclusion of his brother. The most extreme became known as the Rye House Plot. The machinations behind this conspiracy were discussed and debated by a circle of Whig lords and gentlemen, and by a lower cabal of lawyers, soldiers, artisans, Dissenting preachers and Whig scribblers. At one point, it was agreed that the royal brothers would be ambushed and assassinated at Rye House Mill as their coach returned from Newmarket. The plot, however, was exposed, and those plotters who did not escape abroad were rounded up and tried for treason, including prominent Whig leaders who were executed.

Scholars have traditionally examined the Exclusion Crisis within these strict parameters, closing off the crisis either with the dissolution of Charles II's last Parliament in 1681, or with the trials and executions that followed the discovery of the Rye House Plot in 1683.[2] But the Whig drive for exclusion did not end in 1681 or 1683. In fact, the Whig exclusion movement became increasingly more exclusive, more determined, and more radical in the years that followed. Those who continued to fight for the alteration of the royal succession I have chosen to

---

2. For a long time, the standard work on this period was J. R. Jones, *The First Whigs: The Politics of the Exclusion Crisis, 1678–1683* (Oxford: Oxford University Press, 1961). Jones believed that the Whigs had formed a political party, organized under the leadership of the earl of Shaftesbury as early as 1678. Exclusion was their issue, and they declined rapidly after the demise of the Oxford Parliament, the death of Shaftesbury, and the discovery of the Rye House Plot. Mark Knights's more recent study, *Politics and Opinion in Crisis, 1678–81* (Cambridge: Cambridge University Press, 1994), cautions readers against regarding the first Whigs as an organized party; nor does he think it appropriate to use the word "Whig" before 1680–81. Moreover, he reminds us that exclusion was not the only divisive issue of the period. I believe that the label "Whig" can be used as early as 1678, though I do not believe the Whigs formed a coherent party. On the other hand, I do think that exclusion was the central issue behind the activities of radical Whigs throughout the 1680s.

call "Whig radicals"; they are the subjects of this study. I distinguish them from other Whig exclusionists by their willingness to use and justify violence to obtain their ends. Between 1679 and 1685, their goal was to bar the Catholic James from the throne. As the London City Whig Sir Patience Ward succinctly put it before the Convention Parliament in January 1689, "The prospect of a popish successor was that which laid all the plots against the life of late King Charles," who so resolutely opposed all Whig attempts to alter the succession.[3]

In 1685, Charles's brother, James, did ascend the throne. Radicals, many now fugitives in Holland, turned their attention and hopes to Charles's bastard son, the duke of Monmouth. In the early 1680s, Whigs had raised Monmouth's ambitions by putting him forward as a possible Protestant heir apparent. Monmouth had earlier participated in the Rye House conspiracy and was thereafter banished to Europe by his father. But upon Charles II's death, Monmouth was persuaded by fellow Whigs to attempt to take the Crown from James II by force. The Battle of Sedgemoor on July 6 ended his vain hopes, and he was brought back to London and executed. Many of his followers suffered a worse fate under the direction of James's new lord chief justice, George Jeffreys. Jeffreys's western assizes saw to the hanging and quartering of approximately 250 tradesmen, artisans, and peasants who had followed Monmouth. Following this defeat, radical activity reached a low ebb, but it did not die. Books and pamphlets were smuggled in from the Continent and antipapist and Whig ideology continued to be sold at London bookstores. Moreover, Whig radicals came out in force in November 1688, after the prince of Orange invaded the country. Those abroad accompanied the prince's army; those in England joined his march to London. For radical Whigs, the 1680s had been one long exclusion crisis.

In the course of their years of struggle, radical Whigs formulated an ideology worthy of justifying their aims and activities, one that not only played upon long established fears of popery but also promoted an alternative political settlement for the country. After all, if radicals meant to meddle with the royal succession, they had to show the proper cause. They consequently framed their political principles in the very English story of the ancient constitution, and through it propagated an ideology that vindicated the people's right to alter the succession. Radical Whigs also asserted that government was man-made, a historical

3. Grey, *Debates*, 9:27.

construction particular to the nation that conceived it. There was no divine blueprint to be followed, no legacy from the first man, Adam. They believed that government was contracted between the people and their chosen leader. They believed in the supremacy of the law, and most important for their movement, they believed in the people's right of resistance. When the law was violated by those entrusted to uphold it, violence was justifiable.

In 1688, radical Whig ideology was best expressed by Robert Ferguson, known as "the Plotter," in his *Brief Justification of the Descent of the Prince of Orange*, arguably the true manifesto of the Glorious Revolution. The ever pragmatic Ferguson knit together several strands of Whig argumentation developed in the course of the 1680s. The end result was a secular, contractarian theory of government, which resonated with political sentiments, opinions, ideas, and visions already in circulation and familiar to the public. Radical Whig ideology not only justified the conspiracies of Whig radicals in the decade before 1688, but also fed what I see as a broader "revolution culture." This culture, in turn, made up of the ideas and adventures of these Whig desperadoes—set forth in tracts, weeklies, newsletters, manifestos, dying speeches, crude broadsides, and satiric songs—helped create the atmosphere that made the Glorious Revolution of 1688–89 possible.

Because the Glorious Revolution has often been portrayed as a rather tame event, over which little blood was spilt and which occasioned little actual change,[4] we forget that during the preceding decade a prolonged cycle of violence between Whig radicals and the Stuart government took place. The Exclusion Crisis, the Rye House Plot, Monmouth's Rebellion, and the Revolution of 1688—episodes that historians have often examined separately[5]—were for radicals all part of one long struggle over which many of their brethren lost their lives. Survivors even created

4. Conservative interpretations of the Revolution are found in J. R. Jones, *The Revolution of 1688 in England* (New York: St. Martin's Press, 1972), and J. P. Kenyon, *Revolution Principles: The Politics of Party, 1689–1720* (Cambridge: Cambridge University Press, 1977). More recently, Tony Claydon's revisionist study, *William III and the Godly Revolution* (Cambridge: Cambridge University Press, 1995), has questioned the constitutional nature of the Revolutionary Settlement of 1689.

5. Both Richard Greaves, *Secrets of the Kingdom: British Radicals from the Popish Plot to the Revolution of 1688–89* (Stanford: Stanford University Press, 1992), and Richard Ashcraft, *Revolutionary Politics and John Locke's Two Treatises of Government* (Princeton: Princeton University Press, 1986), deal with these events together. However, while Greaves's book provides an excellent narrative of the events, it is short on interpretation. Ashcraft's book centers on John

a set of martyrologies after the Revolution to remember the many radicals who ended their careers on the scaffold and the gallows. If we take the entire decade of the 1680s into account, the Glorious Revolution begins to look less glorious, less smooth and bloodless, and more like other modern revolutions. This study, with its focus on the revolution culture of the radical exclusionists, attempts not only to desacralize the Revolution but also to begin to provide a cultural context for the revolutionary experience in England, an objective not unlike that which scholars of cultural history have already achieved for the French Revolution.[6]

If studying the exclusion movement of the 1680s compels us to rethink traditional assumptions about the Glorious Revolution, it further prompts us to question the prominence of the political theorists who have long been associated with the grand event. John Locke's *Two Treatises of Government*, published in August 1689, was once paired with the Revolution and commonly portrayed as its finest vindication, a founding document of political liberalism. But since Peter Laslett's landmark study of the text, in which he placed its actual composition in the early 1680s, composed as a response to Sir Robert Filmer's *Patriarcha* (1680), scholars have been forced to rethink its significance. For Locke's goal had been not to justify the Revolution but to counter Filmer's absolutist principles, then popular among royalists, particularly the Anglican clergy. Fearful of the punitive arm of the Stuart state, Locke waited until after the Revolution to publish the work, and then only anonymously. When the *Two Treatises* did appear in print, as the important work of John Dunn has shown, it received only a mild reception and generated few responses, far less than the anti-Filmer propaganda of the Whig polemicists studied here. Richard Ashcraft's work has recontextualized Locke, transforming the once aloof, apolitical theorist into a scheming Whig activist. But even so, Locke was not a

---

Locke, who I argue was not nearly as prominent a conspirator or as infamous a polemicist as the Whig radicals under investigation here.

6. Recent works in French cultural history have provided scholars with a fuller awareness of the functions of revolutionary propaganda, from iconography to ritual. See, for example, Lynn Hunt, *Politics, Culture, and Class in the French Revolution* (Berkeley and Los Angeles: University of California Press, 1984); Vivian Cameron, "Political Exposures: Sexuality and Caricature in the French Revolution," in Lynn Hunt, ed., *Eroticism and the Body Politic* (Baltimore: Johns Hopkins University Press, 1991); and Mona Ozouf, *Festivals and the French Revolution*, trans. Alan Sheridan (Cambridge: Harvard University Press, 1988).

very prominent partisan; certainly nowhere near as notorious as the Robert Ferguson or the Reverend Samuel Johnson in the 1680s or even the 1690s. Nor were Locke's political ideas widely familiar to the reading public until the eighteenth century. Recent work on Locke has further questioned Ashcraft's designation of him as a "revolutionary." John Marshall depicts Locke's political thought as essentially conservative, appealing to the Whiggish country gentry, who cherished what they understood to be England's ancient constitution.[7]

This study reasserts the centrality of what have traditionally been labeled "Lockean ideas," including the foundation of government through the consent of the governed and the ultimate right of revolution. But it argues that these ideas were most powerfully expressed and disseminated by radical Whig propagandists before the Revolution. These individuals have received little or no attention from scholars of political thought, who have often been obsessively focused on Locke. Although the propagandists under investigation here may not always have written either eloquently or concisely enough to please modern minds, they did attract the attention of their contemporaries. In fact, their ideas, coupled with their escapades, made them difficult to ignore. Even burning their books, as Oxford loyalists did in 1683, did not halt their dissemination and influence. Moreover, these Whig writers grappled with the critical constitutional and historical issues of their day, which Locke avoided. They most often posited their ideas through the familiar discourse of the ancient constitution.[8] Locke's strict use of the language of natural law, as both John Pocock and Martyn Thompson have pointed out, made his work unique rather than representative of Whig thinking in the late seventeenth century.[9] This study reacquaints

7. John Locke, *Two Treatises of Government*, ed. Peter Laslett (1960; Cambridge: Cambridge University Press, 1988 [student edition]); John Dunn, *The Political Thought of John Locke* (Cambridge: Cambridge University Press, 1969); Ashcraft, *Revolutionary Politics*; and John Marshall, *John Locke: Resistance, Religion, and Responsibility* (Cambridge: Cambridge University Press, 1994).

8. I agree with Glenn Burgess who, following John Pocock, reminds us that the "common law mind," from which the discourse of ancient constitutionalism arose, was no longer a "hegemonic *mentalité*" after the Civil Wars. It was one among several political languages including that of natural law. However, I am arguing that it remained a powerful mode of expression and was used far more frequently by radical Whig polemicists than natural law. Glenn Burgess, *The Politics of the Ancient Constitution* (University Park: Pennsylvania State University Press, 1992), 230–31.

9. Pocock, "The Myth of John Locke and the Obsession with Liberalism," in J. G. A. Pocock and Richard Ashcraft, eds., *John Locke: Papers Read at the Clark Library Seminar, 10 December 1977*

us with the actual voices people heard and pondered during this era. What readers will find here is essentially a history of early Whig ideology without John Locke.

A crucial element within the revolution culture propagated by radicals was religion. That radicals most often spoke of their aims as the "Protestant cause" reminds us just how intrinsically religious fears, beliefs, and bigotries were linked with politics in the late Stuart era. These fears motivated political action. Antipopery was not simply a Whig harangue or bogey meant to stir the masses. The nightmarish scenarios of papists burning London, cutting Protestant throats, and ravishing wives and daughters, as portrayed in Whig propaganda, represented what were for many very real fears: fears of foreign influence and French-style absolutism; fears of the loss of elite and freeborn rights and privileges; and fears of the extirpation of English Protestantism. It was not without reason that there were those "who perpetually raved about with the words 'popery, French and arbitrary government' flaming out of their mouths." Religious concerns, as Leopold von Ranke pointed out long ago, were at "the very kernel of the political" in seventeenth-century England.[10] In fact, the two were one and the same. To the English mind, Catholicism and absolutism were indistinguishable.

Dissenters from the Church of England—Presbyterians, Independents, Baptists, Quakers, and others—played vital and leading roles in this Protestant cause. Already harassed and persecuted by the Restoration Church, they saw themselves as the first to suffer should a Catholic succeed to the throne. Most radical Whigs were themselves nonconformists or were strongly sympathetic to nonconformity. Many others were "occasional" or "partial" conformists, individuals who sometimes took the sacrament in the Anglican Church but who frequented Dissenting conventicles.[11] While not all Whigs were nonconformists, Dissent was a powerful and important ingredient in the radicalism of the 1680s, helping to unify and stiffen Whig resolve.

(William Clark Memorial Library, University of California, Los Angeles, 1980), 3–23; Martyn Thompson, "Significant Silences in Locke's *Two Treatises of Government:* Constitutionalism, History, Contract, and Law," *HJ* 32 (1987): 275–94.

10. Roger North, quoted in *State Trials*, 9:190, and Leopold von Ranke, *A History of England principally in the seventeenth century* (Oxford, 1875), 4:348, for the quotes.

11. John D. Ramsbottom, "Presbyterians and 'Partial Conformity' in the Restoration Church of England," *Journal of Ecclesiastical History* 43 (1992): 249–70.

Who were the creators of revolution culture? This study examines four of the most prolific and influential Whig polemicists of the pre-Revolution era, along with their legacies in the 1690s and early eighteenth century: the lawyers, Thomas Hunt and William Atwood; the Anglican cleric, the Reverend Samuel Johnson; and the Independent preacher, Robert Ferguson. Each vigorously and continuously engaged in the controversies of their era, which spanned from the bishops' rights debate and the dispute over the origins of Parliament, to notions of divine right kingship and Sir Robert Filmer's patriarchalism. These ideologues produced the most sophisticated pro-exclusion literature. They formulated theories of government, which were based on popular consent and which affirmed the right of resistance. Their tracts went into multiple editions, were translated into foreign languages, were plagiarized, and were often met by floods of responses both negative and positive. These individuals were on the front lines of ideological battle in the 1680s. They not only promoted a Protestant succession, their political principles were used to justify the violent overthrow of the Stuart monarchy, as plotted by the Rye House conspirators in 1683, and by the duke of Monmouth and his followers in 1685. Ferguson, Atwood, and Johnson (Hunt had died), also wrote in adamant support of the Glorious Revolution. Their ideas, particularly those of Robert Ferguson, influenced the Revolutionary Settlement of 1689. They continued to reiterate their principles, formulated in the violent years of the 1680s, during the more stable political climate of the 1690s. The gentleman and scholar James Tyrrell, who helped to make radical Whig ideology more respectable in calmer times, joined them.

Hunt, Atwood, Ferguson, and Johnson may have been some of the most important radical polemicists, but they did not write in isolation. They were surrounded by fellow radicals—publishers, scribblers, soldiers, lawyers, merchants, artisans, and aristocrats—the like-minded men and women who together composed the exclusion movement in the 1680s. These people knew and supported one another. They were the activists and propagandists, the conspirators and the scribblers, who made up a radical Whig network in the 1680s. The political principles of Hunt, Atwood, Ferguson, and Johnson were hardly the product of the philosopher's study, but rather that of the smoky tavern, the noisy coffeehouse, the London prison cell, or the Amsterdam safe house. Radical Whig ideology cannot be understood separately from the conspiratorial politics of that decade. As in the case of Ferguson, the propagandist and plotter were often one and the same. Ideas and actions, thoughts and deeds, words and events were intimately linked.

Historians have created numerous labels for these conspirators and polemicists active in the late Stuart era, among them, "Republicans," "commonwealthmen," "first Whigs," "true Whigs," and "radical Whigs."[12] The Whigs examined in this study were not republicans or commonwealthmen. This was not the "good old [republican] cause reviv'd" or "forty-one over again," a rehashing of the politics of rebellion that led to the bloody civil wars at midcentury.[13] The Reverend Samuel Johnson, William Atwood, and others repudiated the label of republican heaped on them by their enemies. Kingship was an essential part of the political thinking of Atwood, Johnson, Ferguson, and Tyrrell. The ancient constitution demanded as much. Restoration ideology was no mere regurgitation of Leveller and republican ideas from the 1640s and 1650s. The cries of "forty-one all over again" that have enamored historian Jonathan Scott were essentially Tory caterwauling. For historians to envision 1681 as a simple copy of 1641 is to be won over by royalist propaganda.[14] Certainly the dark shadow of the civil wars casts itself over Restoration thought, but as J. G. A. Pocock has written, it was precisely because of those wars and the chaos they created "that the English were above all else determined not to repeat the experience."[15] This was as true of the court's supporters as it was of the opposition who, by and large, did not see themselves as the descendants of Cromwell or Pym, but were more apt to look back to Protestant sufferers like the

12. Jonathan Scott, among others, labeled many of these individuals "republicans," in *Algernon Sidney and the Restoration Crisis, 1677–1683* (Cambridge: Cambridge University Press, 1991); Caroline Robbins has called them "seventeenth-century commonwealthmen," in *The Eighteenth-Century Commonwealthman* (Cambridge: Harvard University Press, 1959); J. R. Jones named them "first Whigs," in *The First Whigs*; Mark Goldie referred to some of them as "true Whigs," in "The Roots of True Whiggism, 1688–94," *History of Political Thought* 1 (1989): 195–236; Richard Greaves called them "radicals," in *Secrets of the Kingdom*; and Richard Ashcraft identified them as "Whigs, Dissenters, and Radicals," in *Revolutionary Politics*, 9.

13. John Dryden, *Absalom and Achitophel*, part 1 (1681), line 82, and Roger L'Estrange, *Observator*, no. 77 (December 3, 1681), for the quotations.

14. Scott, *Algernon Sidney and the Restoration Crisis*, 6. As Mark Knights points out in *Politics and Opinion*, the past was "manipulated for partisan reasons and we must be careful not to accept the assertions of a prejudiced contemporary press at face value" (11).

15. See his review article, "England's Cato: The Virtues and Fortunes of Algernon Sidney," *HJ* 37 (1994), 932.

Marian martyrs, or medieval heroes like the barons of 1215, for legitimizing models.[16]

Though not republican, the thinking of the Whig ideologues under examination was radical within its context. The ideas of these individuals sought to repudiate the existing order and legitimate a new one. Parliamentary politics and public pressure were the means they used prior to 1681; after the abortive Oxford Parliament, they validated the use of revolutionary violence as a political tool in their struggle. The term "radical," as scholars have pointed out, was anachronistic to the seventeenth century, but I have chosen it as the most descriptive and meaningful of all the possible alternatives.[17] Resorting to terms contemporaries did use is not helpful; while "disaffected," "seditious," and "factious" do describe the individuals under study here, they may also be applied to numerous other seventeenth-century folk with numerous other kinds of grievances. The domain in which I am using the term "radical" is the political. We cannot simply call these people "exclusionists," since the desire to exclude the duke of York from the throne defined nearly all Whigs, at least prior to 1685. But not all Whigs were willing to promote the use of violence to force a Protestant succession. Radicals were and many did.

Naturally, radical Whigs posed as restorers, bent on restoring England's ancient constitution, applying what Conal Condren has called "a tradition-centered rhetoric of change" while accusing their enemies of using "a rhetoric of innovation and upstart or false tradition." The Tories, Whigs claimed time and again, were the real innovators, or as the Reverend Samuel Johnson put it, patriarchal and divine right theories were the "new-fangled opinions of a few mischievous and designing innovators."[18] In fact, both sides employed arguments used since the

---

16. A prominent example of the former is John Tutchin's modeling of his Whig martyrologies, written in the post-Revolution era, on Foxe's *Acts and Monuments*, wherein from the outset he compared his Whig and Dissenter heroes and heroines of the 1680s with the Marian martyrs. See his preface to *The Western Martyrology, or The Bloody Assizes* (1705).

17. My thinking about this term is indebted to Gary De Krey, "Rethinking the Restoration: Dissenting Cases for Conscience, 1667–1672," *HJ* 38 (1995), 53–83; Richard Greaves, *Deliver Us from Evil: The Radical Underground in Britain, 1660–1663* (New York: Oxford University Press, 1986), 5–7; J. C. Davis, "Radicalism in a Traditional Society: The Evaluation of Radical Thought in the English Commonwealth, 1649–1660," *History of Political Thought* 3 (1982): 193–213; and Conal Condren, *The Language of Politics in Seventeenth-Century England* (New York: St. Martin's Press, 1995), 140–67.

18. *The Language of Politics*, 153, 158; and *Julian the Apostate* (1682), 82, for the quotations.

beginning of the Stuart era and earlier. Radical Whig discourse, drawn predominantly from history and common law, was not novel. On the other hand, its descriptions of the venerable ancient constitution bore little resemblance to the English polity, past or present. Radicals hoped to manipulate the past in order to refashion the political future. Theirs, in short, is a story of storytellers: of individuals who revised the English past to create their own version of the ancient constitution, who were continuously revising their own stories of daring, debacle, and death, weaving narratives of Catholic conspiracy and Whig heroism. Their stories were heard and sometimes acted upon in the 1680s. Whig exploits and propaganda combined to make a powerful impression on the English public. The pope-burning processions, the "monster" petitions, the progresses of the duke of Monmouth, the spectacular trials and executions, the Battle of Sedgemoor, the "bloody assizes"—these scenes played upon the English consciousness. Whig goals, slogans, visions, aspirations were widely disseminated through an increasingly powerful print culture. Their revolution culture smoothed the way for the Protestant succession of the prince and princess of Orange.

In 1689, the exclusion movement came to an end. But if the radical network faded away, the political tropes and principles it constructed lived on. The drama of the 1680s continued to be important in the political dialogue of the 1690s. The Whigs now rewrote the history of their movement, mythologizing, sanctifying, and sanitizing their exploits, nursing tales of the "bloody assizes" and the "glorious revolution" that became part of the English historiographical tradition. Antipapist rhetoric, songs, and satire still poured forth from the presses.[19] Atwood and Johnson applied ideas of the 1680s to issues of the1690s. Tyrrell made it his life's task to reiterate radical Whiggism in various polemical genres. But these ideas were now bigger than their creators; they took on lives of their own, infused the Whig newspapers, plays, pamphlets, and poetry of the 1690s and early eighteenth century. Their violent birth forgotten, they became part of mainstream Whig rhetoric, seeding the political philosophy based on contract and consent known as liberalism.

19. Lois G. Schwoerer, "William, Lord Russell: The Making of a Martyr, 1683–1983," *JBS* 24 (1985): 41–71; Blair Worden, "The Commonwealth Kidney of Algernon Sidney," *JBS* 24 (1985): 1–40; Melinda Zook, "The Bloody Assizes: Whig Martyrdom and Memory After the Glorious Revolution," *Albion* 27 (1995): 373–96; and *The Muses Farewell to Popery and Slavery* (1689).

1

Mapping the Radical Whigs: A Cultural and Social Biography

Your *Lawless Tongues,* and *Arbitrary Juries?*
Your *Burlesques Oaths,* when one *Green-Ribbon-Brother*
In Conscience will be *Perjur'd for another?*
Your *PLOTS, Cabals;* Your *Treats, Association,*
Ye Shame, Ye very Nuisance of the Nation
— Aphra Behn, *Prologue to Romulus* (1684)

In the 1680s, a network of radical Whigs attempted to refashion the English polity. Their efforts at political persuasion, like those of their opponents, took numerous forms and guises and went far beyond the machinations of Whitehall and Westminster. London was infused with a new political culture—one both furious and fluid, anxious and angry, powerful and ever present. This political culture knew no bounds. It crossed class, gender, and religious divides; it spread out from the metropolis to the manor house, to the village parish, and to the country inn. Whig radicals helped create this political culture, disseminating their aims through pamphlets, street processions, weeklies, and newsletters. But when political persuasion failed, they took political action and formulated a political theory that vindicated their deeds. The desperadoes and conspirators, rebels and revolutionaries, plotters and propagandists—those who justified political violence and those who participated in it—are the focus of this chapter.

Together these individuals constituted a radical fringe of the Whig party, a network of men and some women who knew each other and were bound together by one powerful motive. Their desire, prior to 1685, was to bar the succession of the Catholic James, duke of York; and after 1685, to overthrow James II. To this aim, various lesser causes and concerns attached themselves, but for all these diverse individuals it was the common goal of diverting or disrupting James's reign that tied them together. The network's efforts, legal and illegal, official and seditious, met with failure after dismal failure until the Glorious Revolution: a revolution that was not of their making alone, but which bore the stamp of their ideals and sacrifices.

Radicalism throughout the 1680s remained a diverse and dynamic movement. It encompassed members of all castes, from London merchants and country gentlemen to craftsmen, soldiers, and lawyers, as well as members of various confessional affiliations, from Anglican divines to Independent preachers. This chapter discusses the cultural climate in which radicalism formed and constructs a social profile of the network during the era of the Popish Plot and the Exclusion Crisis (1678–83). It also delineates the patronage, professional, regional, religious, and familial ties that connected radicals to one another.

Identifying the shared social and cultural connections among radicals is not possible without first identifying the individuals themselves. The appendix lists ninety-four radical Whigs. The list identifies individuals who were members of the Green Ribbon Club, who signed either the 1679 or the 1680 Whig petitions, who actively supported the bill to exclude the duke of York from the royal succession, who participated in the Whig conspiracy known as the Rye House Plot in 1682–83, and who promoted or participated in either Monmouth's or Argyle's rebellions in 1685 or in the Revolution of 1688–89. The appendix also tracks those who fled to Europe, either following the disclosure of the Rye House Plot or after the failure of the 1685 rebellions. And finally, this list records the known "fates" of Whig radicals. Some were rewarded for their deeds and suffering in defense of the Protestant cause by William and Mary following the Revolution. Others did not live to see it. Nineteen of the ninety-four radicals listed were executed or killed in battle in the course of the Whig exclusion movement of the 1680s.

Naming names is always a dangerous business. On the one hand, I have tried to be as comprehensive as possible, gathering information on the first Whigs from a vast range of sources.[1] On the other hand, when it came to actually identifying individuals as "radical," I tried to be as selective as possible. I named only those who, through their words or their actions or both, promoted a violent solution to the problem of the royal succession; and only those who readily subverted justice for the radical cause, as, for example, *ignoramus* jurors or participants in the shrieval riot of 1682. Moreover, among this latter group, I listed only those who had a consistent history of radical politics.

This list is not exhaustive. It certainly does not identify every radical in late Stuart England. It does not include women such as the printer Jane Curtis or the Anabaptist Elizabeth Gaunt, both of whom were active in radical Whig circles. Women are excluded from the list because of the dearth of information on them. They were not signatories of the various Whig petitions. They were not listed as members of the Green Ribbon Club or as Rye House plotters or as soldiers in Monmouth's ragtag army. Various women may have consorted with Green Ribbon brothers, been privy to the machinations of the Rye House conspirators, or donned breeches and joined Monmouth's army, but their actions as well as their words are, for the most part, absent from the records.

Though not exhaustive, the appendix does identify those at the center of radicalism in the 1680s, many of whom led sustained careers as radical Whig propagandists or conspirators or both. These individuals knew each other. They met at coffeehouses, conventicles, taverns, prisons, and safe houses. They entertained each other, dined together, drank healths at public feasts together. They drew up political tracts and declarations together. They fled in exile together. Many became court Whigs after the Revolution of 1688–89. Some continued to relive the 1680s, churning out radical propaganda or pursuing conspiratorial politics as Jacobites. The fallen became the martyrs whose pictures illustrate the frontispieces of the Whig martyrologies, reminding us of the hazards radicals faced in the 1680s.

Throughout the 1680s, the size and character of this network of Whig

---

1. For much of the information that went into compiling this list, I am indebted to the following printed sources: *DNB*; *BDBR*; W. MacDonald Wigfield, *The Monmouth Rebels, 1685* (New York: St. Martin's Press, 1985); J. R. Woodhead, *The Rulers of London, 1660–1689* (London: London & Middlesex Archaeological Society, 1965); *A Dictionary of the Printers and Booksellers Who Were at Work in England, Scotland, and Ireland from 1641 to 1725*, ed. Henry R. Plomer (Oxford University Press for the Bibliographical Society, 1922); and A. G. Matthews, *Calamy Revised* (Oxford: Clarendon Press, 1988).

radicals changed. This was partly due to the highly fluid nature of politics in pre-Revolution England. Political alliances and allegiances shifted rapidly. Even many of the most hardened radicals could be seduced into serving Charles II's or James II's government, particularly after yet another Whig debacle. Still, Jonathan Scott's remark that "1678's 'Whigs' *were* 1681's 'Tories'" exaggerates the fluidity between the political parties.[2] The dissolution of the Oxford Parliament in 1681, only stiffened the resolve of most radicals. Of the network, not one member had repented their former Whig ways until after the discovery of the Rye House Plot in June 1683. The most significant point of conversion for many dissidents was James II's own policy shift in 1687, when the king courted and rewarded Whigs and Dissenters with offices and favors. In return, he expected their support for his assault on the penal laws against Catholicism and nonconformity. Many of them joined his administration. Yet one year later, most of these individuals remained true to their Whig principles and, as we shall see, with few exceptions, they readily supported the invasion of Prince William.

When radical numbers diminished, it was usually not a result of ideological conversions but because Whig activities were highly dangerous. Lives and fortunes were placed on the line, and many were lost. The discovery of the Rye House conspiracy resulted in the loss of much of the radical aristocratic leadership. The defeat of the duke of Monmouth's army two years later completed that loss and seriously diluted the numbers of the rank and file. If we add to the death toll the series of imprisonments, whippings, deportations, public humiliations, and devastating fines that many radicals incurred, the true cost of revolutionary politics rises even higher.

London Radicalism and Political Culture

> The City's a grumbling, lying, dissatify'd City
> and no wise or honest Man regards what it says.
> —Aphra Behn, *The City Heiress* (1682)

London was the incubus of radicalism. In the late 1670s and early 1680s, London's political culture offered Whigs numerous avenues through which to assert their aspirations and goals. Parliament, bookstores, play-

---

2. *Algernon Sidney and the Restoration Crisis*, 47.

houses, coffeehouses and taverns, London streets, and civic politics all became arenas in which radical politics fomented and fought its first battles. Scholars have long understood that the political atmosphere of London became increasingly strident and disputatious in the late 1670s.[3] The series of political and religious crises that began with the Popish Plot in 1678, and continued through the controversy over the royal succession, produced a highly volatile political climate. Politics became the topic of discussion in the new coffeehouses and the traditional taverns. Politics became theater on the stage, where Tory and Whig playwrights satirized one another, and on the streets among the bonfires, processions, and petition signings.[4] Politics also became conspiratorial, whispered on street corners, contrived in rented rooms and jail cells.

This new political culture produced a vast array of printed products through which the controversies, crises, and news of the day, both foreign and domestic, could be disseminated, scrutinized, debated, and satirized. Whig radicalism propagated its slogans and ideology and answered its opponents through print, particularly the political tract but also through newsletters, weeklies, satiric verse, broadsides, almanacs, drama, and doggerel. The Tory opposition responded in kind, creating a war of words. The influence of print on this new political culture was significant. The government certainly considered its use by Whigs and Dissenters a very serious threat. The harassment of Whig printers and booksellers, the suppression of Whig newspapers in May 1680, and the Oxford book burning in July 1683, all speak to the persuasive power of the press and to official concerns about that power.[5]

3. Tim Harris, "The Problem of 'Popular Political Culture' in Seventeenth-Century London," *History of European Ideas* 10 (1989): 43–58; Gary De Krey, "The London Whigs and the Exclusion Crisis Reconsidered," in A. L. Beier, D. Cannadine, and J. M. Rosenheim, eds., *The First Modern Society: Essays in English History in Honour of Lawrence Stone* (Cambridge: Cambridge University Press, 1989), 457–82; Dan Beaver, "Conscience and Context: The Popish Plot and the Politics of Ritual," *HJ* 34 (1991): 297–327; John Miller, "Public Opinion in Charles II's Reign," *History* 80 (1995): 359–81; and Steven Zwicker, introduction to *Lines of Authority: Politics and English Literary Culture, 1649–1689* (Ithaca: Cornell University Press, 1993), 1–8.

4. Shelia Williams, "The Pope-Burning Processions of 1679, 1680, and 1681," *Journal of the Warburg and Courtuald Institutes* 21 (1958): 104–18; Tim Harris, *London Crowds in the Reign of Charles II* (Cambridge: Cambridge University Press, 1987), 96–129; Knights, *Politics and Opinion*, 153–99; George W. Whiting, "Political Satire in London State Plays," *Modern Philology* 28 (1930): 29–43; Robert Hume, *The Development of English Drama in the Late Seventeenth Century* (Oxford: Clarendon Press, 1976), 340–77.

5. J. Walker, "Censorship of the Press during the Reign of Charles II," *History* 35 (1950): 219–38; Timothy Crist, "Government Control of the Press After the Expiration of the Printing Act in 1679," *Publishing History* 5 (1979): 49–77; James Sutherland, *The Restoration Newspaper and Its Development* (Cambridge: Cambridge University Press, 1985); and Lois G. Schwoerer,

London coffeehouses were commonly seen as dens of sedition where, as Aphra Behn put it, Whigs would "rail for the cause against the government." Even in smaller towns, coffeehouses were reported to be places where "disaffected persons . . . intermeddle with state affairs, reflect on their superiors and debauch the affections and loyalty of liege people."[6] In polemics of the 1670s and 1680s, coffee itself was often identified as "puritanical," "seditious," and "Whig," whereas ale or tea was often seen as "conformist," "loyal," and "Tory."[7] It was in the coffeehouses that Whig newsletter writers sold their handwritten broadsheets. Newsletters such as those written by Giles Hancock, known as "a little penny-post pocket devil" by his detractors, were stridently Whig, notoriously unreliable, and deliberately sensational. Still, they fulfilled a demand for domestic news and comment—particularly after the Whig newspapers disappeared—and despite official harassment and intervention, they continued to flourish.[8]

Radical Whigs produced and participated in all forms of the new political culture at every level of London society. They met their friends and foes in coffeehouses and taverns. They formed political clubs to advance their agenda. They sought to demonstrate their numbers and forward their demands through petition drives and street theater. They promoted their goals and protected one another by attempting to control London City politics. Whig clubbing, petitioning, and civic

---

"Liberty of Press and Public Opinion, 1660–1695," in J. R. Jones, ed., *Liberty Secured? Britain Before and After 1688* (Stanford: Stanford University Press, 1992), 199–230.

6. Aphra Behn, epilogue to *The Second Part of the Rover* (1681), for the first quotation, and Presentation of the Grand Jury of Kent, *CSPD*, 24:103, for the second. On coffeehouses in the Restoration, see Steve Pincus, "'Coffee Politician Does Create': Coffeehouses and Restoration Political Culture," *Journal of Modern History* 67 (1995): 807–34.

7. See, for example, the pro-Whig tract, *A Dialogue between Tom and Dick over a Dish of Coffee, Concerning Religion and the Government* (London,1680), and the Tory response by Roger L'Estrange, *Citt and Bumpkin in a Dialogue over a Pot of Ale, Concerning matters of Religion and Government* (London, 1680). Also see the broadside poem *Rebellious Antidote: Or A Dialogue Between Coffee and Tea* (London,1685), wherein "Coffee" expresses Whig concerns and "Tea" represents royalist positions.

8. Bryant Lillywhite, *London Coffee Houses: A Reference Book of Coffee Houses of the Seventeenth, Eighteenth, and Nineteenth Centuries* (London: Allen & Unwin, 1963), 19; Peter Fraser, *The Intelligence of the Secretaries of State and Their Monopoly of Licensed News, 1660–1688* (Cambridge: Cambridge University Press, 1956), 114–23; and Henry L. Snyder, "Newsletters in England, 1689–1715, with Special Reference to John Dyer—A Byway to the History of England," in Donovan H. Bond and W. Reyonds McLeod, eds., *Newsletters to Newspapers: Eighteenth-Century Journalism* (Charlottesville: West Virginia University, 1977), 3–19.

politics in the late 1670s and early 1680s attracted radicals of diverse social backgrounds. Each of these activities was an early effort to unify and forward Whig demands. While successful for a time, each was eventually met by a powerful royalist reaction. By 1683, Whig clubbing had all but disappeared, their petition movement had failed, and Whig control of London was lost, increasing Whig frustration and a sense of desperation.

The most notorious political club, active between 1678 and 1681, was the Green Ribbon Club, which met at the King's Head Tavern on the corner of Fleet Street and Chancery Lane. The Green Ribbon Club orchestrated antipopery, effigy-burning processions, sponsored petition drives, disseminated antipapist and anti–duke of York literature, and provided Whigs of all social levels with a place to meet, converse, and conspire. It boasted around 150 members.[9] The club's members included storekeepers and artisans, like Zachery Bourne the brewer and William Hone the joiner, and aristocrats, like Barons William Howard of Escrick and Ford Grey of Werk. Numerous lawyers and gentlemen, along with many of those active in London civic politics, were also members of the club. While the club's members—plebeians, lords, and professionals alike—focused on legalistic and theatrical politics in the years of the club's importance, these same men went on to organize more extravagant and violent political action in the 1680s. Forty of the ninety-four radicals listed in the appendix belonged to the Green Ribbon Club. They are represented in Table 1. Twenty-four of the Green Ribbonites were later implicated in the Rye House conspiracy; fourteen participated in or supported Monmouth's Rebellion.[10] Mem-

9. The Green Ribbon Club is discussed in George Sitwell, *The First Whig* (Scarborough, 1894), 74–93; J. R. Jones, "The Green Ribbon Club," *Durham University Journal* 49 (1956): 17–20; and O. W. Furley, "Pope-Burning Processions of the Late Seventeenth Century," *History* 44 (1959): 16–23. Also see *The Procession: or, The Burning of the Pope in effigie in Smithfield-Rounds on 17 November 1681* (1681), which describes a pope-burning procession sponsored by the Green Ribbon Club. The club also gave financial aid to promoters of the Protestant cause in need. In 1680, it took up a collection for the antipapist polemicist Henry Care to support him during his imprisonment for seditious libel (Pepys Library, Magdalene College, Cambridge, ms. 2,875, 484). There are three member lists for the Green Ribbon Club, with most of the members appearing on all three. Two of the lists, from Thomas Dangerfield, *Particular Narrative of the Late Popish Design* (1679), and Nathaniel Wade's Confession, BL, Harl. 6,845, fols. 266–72v, were published in Sitwell, *The First Whig*, 197–202. The third list is in PL, ms. 2,875, 465–91. My information is collated from all three lists.

10. Green Ribbonite John Ayloffe joined the Scottish earl of Argyle's invasion. Twelve Green Ribbonites later participated in the Glorious Revolution.

bers of the Green Ribbon Club remained in contact long after the club itself disappeared. Through the club they discovered one another, highborn and low, and learned organizational and propaganda tactics. The King's Head Tavern may well have posed as a school in opposition politics and training ground for future conspirators.

Richard Ashcraft believes the club served "as a kind of party head-quarters for the Whigs." He may overstate the club's importance; there were at least twenty-eight other Whig clubs in the 1680s.[11] Many of the Whig lords and leaders belonged to Colonel Blood's club, which met at a chandler's shop in Westminster.[12] The duke of Buckingham, an important Whig leader in the House of Lords, kept a club at the Salutation Tavern. Two clubs formed and met in the interest of the earl of Shaftesbury at the Angel and the Queen's Arms. City Whig Slingsby Bethel chaired the club at the Queen's Arms, where in 1682, radicals proposed to arm themselves against the growth of arbitrary government. There were also important Whig clubs in cities with large Dissenting populations, such as Bristol.[13] Still, no other club was nearly as notorious or active as the Green Ribbon Club. Tory scribblers constantly refer to it, suggesting that it was the Green Ribbonites whom they were most frightened by. True enough, in the course of the 1680s, Green Ribbon brothers went far beyond barroom plotting and public spectacle and turned to more incendiary activities.

The Whig petition movement that began in 1679 has often been linked to Whig clubs and particularly the Green Ribbon Club. Green Ribbonites helped sponsor the Whig petition drives, using coffeehouses and taverns as places to procure signatures. The recent work of Mark Knights on the petitioning movement demonstrates that the socioeconomic makeup of the petition subscribers reflected that of the Green Ribbon Club and Whig radicalism as a whole. Radicals of a diverse range

---

11. Ashcraft, *Revolutionary Politics*, 144; Harris, *London Crowds*, 100; PRO SP 29/417, fol. 277.

12. The earls of Shaftesbury and Essex, the duke of Monmouth, Lord Grey of Werk, Sir William Waller, and Sir Thomas Armstrong were all named as members of Colonel Blood's club at Westminster by Thomas Dangerfield in his *Particular Narrative*. Dangerfield also lists the members of the clubs at the Green Dragon Tavern (Fleet Street) and Sun Tavern (behind the Royal Exchange). For lists of other Whig clubs and taverns, see David Allen, "Political Clubs in Restoration London," *HJ* 19 (1976): 561–80, and *CSPD*, 21:296.

13. *CSPD*, 23:236–37; 25:165–66.

Table 1. Green Ribbon Brothers

Name	Activities	Occupation
Arnold, John (c. 1635–1702)	Exclusion MP Convention 1689	Gentleman
Ayloffe, John (1645–85)	Propagandist Rye House plotter Argyle rebel	Lawyer
Bethel, Slingsby (1617–97)	City Whig	Merchant
Bettiscomb, Christopher (d. 1685)	Rye House plotter Monmouth rebel	Law student
Blaney, Robert	Rye House plotter	Lawyer
Blount, Charles (1654–93)	Propagandist	Gentleman
Booth, Henry, Lord Delamere (1652–94)	Exclusion MP Rye House plotter Active in Revolution of 1688	Gentleman
Bourne, Zachary	Rye House plotter	Brewer
Dare, Thomas (d. 1685)	Monmouth rebel	Goldsmith
Freke, John	Propagandist Rye House plotter	Lawyer
Goodenough, Francis (d. 1685)	Rye House plotter Monmouth rebel	Lawyer
Goodenough, Richard (d. 1689)	Rye House plotter Monmouth rebel	Lawyer
Grey, Ford, Baron of Werk (d. 1701)	Exclusion MP Rye House plotter Monmouth rebel	Peer
Hone, William (d. 1683)	Rye House plotter	Joiner
Hooper, James	Monmouth rebel	Unknown

MP = member of Parliament.

9

Table 1. Green Ribbon Brothers (*continued*)

Name	Activities	Occupation
Howard, William, Baron of Escrick (d. 1694)	Exclusion MP	Soldier
Ireton, Henry	Rye House plotter Rye House plotter (?) Monmouth rebel	Lawyer
Jenks, Francis	Rye House plotter	Merchant
Lee, Thomas	Rye House plotter	Dyer
Nelthorpe, Richard (d. 1685)	Rye House plotter Monmouth rebel	Lawyer
Norton, Edward (1654–1702)	Exclusion MP Rye House plotter Active in Revolution of 1688	Lawyer
Peyton, Sir Robert (d. 1689)	City Whig	Soldier
Prideaux, Edmund (1634–1702)	Exclusion MP Monmouth supporter	Lawyer
Row, John	Rye House plotter	Former sword bearer of Bristol (otherwise unknown)
Rumsey, Colonel John	Rye House plotter Monmouth rebel	Soldier
Smith, Aaron (d. 1699)	Rye House plotter	Lawyer
Speke, Charles (d. 1685)	Monmouth supporter	Filacer at the King's Bench
Speke, George (1623–89)	Exclusion MP Monmouth supporter	Gentleman
Speke, Hugh (b. 1656)	Propagandist Active in Revolution of 1688	Lawyer
Speke, John (d. 1728)	Exclusion MP Monmouth rebel	Lawyer

MP = member of Parliament.

Name	Activities	Occupation
Starkey, John (d. 1699)	Rye House plotter	Bookseller
Tily, Joseph	Rye House plotter	Lawyer
	Monmouth rebel	
Trenchard, Henry (d. 1694)	Exclusion MP	Lawyer
	Convention, 1689	
Trenchard, Sir John (1649–95)	Exclusion MP	Lawyer
	Rye House plotter	
	Active in Revolution of 1688	
Trenchard, William (d. 1713)	Exclusion MP	Gentleman
	Active in Revolution of 1688	
Waller, Edmund (1652–1700)	Rye House plotter (?)	Lawyer
	Convention, 1689	
Waller, Sir William (d. 1699)	Exclusion MP	Gentleman
	Rye House plotter (?)	
	Active in Revolution of 1688	
West, Robert	Rye House plotter	Lawyer
Yonge, Sir Walter (1653–1713)	Exclusion MP	Gentleman
	Convention, 1688	

MP = member of Parliament.

of castes and confessions signed these petitions, demonstrating once again the vertical social nature of the network.[14]

The first petition, the so-called peers petition of December 1679, asking Charles II to call Parliament, was signed by seventeen peers, including the earl of Shaftesbury.[15] Future petitions, which usually called for Parliament and an expedient redress of the nation's grievances, were far more popular campaigns. The May 1679 petition presented to London's Court of Aldermen was a product of the atmosphere of fear and suspicion created by the Popish Plot. Signatories affirmed their belief in the plot and recognized Parliament's "pursuance of divers methods, means, and ways" of preserving the king's safety and the security of the Protestant religion. The petition was signed by 1,536 men.[16] The "monster petition," presented to Charles II in January 1680, contained sixteen thousand signatories. This petition also asserted that "your Majesty's most sacred person, the protestant religion, and the well-established government of this your realm" were in "imminent danger" due to the "horrid villainies" of the popish plotters.[17]

All of the radicals listed in the appendix, with four exceptions, signed either the May 1679 or the January 1680 petition. Forty-seven signed the 1679 petition, and approximately another forty-seven signed the 1680 petition.[18] Charles Bateman, the earl of Shaftesbury's surgeon later implicated in the Rye House Plot, signed both. This information, like that of the membership of the Green Ribbon Club, speaks to the

---

14. The link between the Whigs, coffeehouses, and petitioning is portrayed in L'Estrange, *Citt and Bumpkin in a Dialogue* (1680), 1. I am grateful to Mark Knights for identifying those radical Whigs who signed the May 1679 or January 1680 petition. Much of the following information is culled from his three articles on the petition movement and his book. See his "Petitioning and the Political Theorists: John Locke, Algernon Sidney, and London's 'Monster Petition of 1680,'" *P & P* 138 (1993): 94–111; "London Petitions and Parliamentary Politics in 1679," *Parliamentary History* 12 (1993): 29–46; "London's 'Monster' Petition of 1680," *HJ* 36 (1993): 39–67; and *Politics and Opinion*, 227–56. Also, on the Tory response to Whig petitioning, see Philip Harth, *Pen for a Party: Dryden's Tory Propaganda and Its Contexts* (Princeton: Princeton University Press, 1993), 31–33, 73–75, 81–82.

15. Knights, *Politics and Opinion*, 229; Harth, *Pen for a Party*, 31. The December 1679 petition is printed in *The Domestick Intelligence*, no. 45 (December 1679).

16. Knights, "London Petitions," 32–37.

17. Knights, "London's 'Monster' Petition," 43, passim.

18. The four exemptions were John Arnold, William, Lord Russell, the duke of Monmouth, and John Hicks. Many of the names in the appendix appear several times on the 1680 petition. They are marked (X?), since there is no way of knowing, for example, whether one of the "Samuel Johnsons" who signed the petition was the Reverend Samuel Johnson who penned the pro-exclusion tracts discussed in Chapter 2.

incredible diversity and vertical social nature of the Whig movement. Whig clubbers and non-clubbers alike signed the petitions. Anglican churchmen like the Bishop Gilbert Burnet and the Reverend Samuel Johnson, subscribed. Nonconformists, including the Independent preachers Robert Ferguson, Matthew Mead, and Nathaniel Hooke, signed. Prominent City Whigs and country gentlemen, brewers and booksellers all subscribed to one petition or another. These were the "Cits," whom the dramatist Edward Ravenscroft satirized as "trudging, drudging, cormudging, *petitioning* citizen(s)."[19]

Mark Knights has appropriately described the 1680 petition as "the roll-call of the discontented." He has also asserted that the Whig petition movement was basically a failure that Charles II "successfully weathered." As the earl of Conway observed in April 1682, "The Whigs have got so little advantage by their former petitions for a parliament that I cannot see any great advantage they propose to themselves by continuing it."[20] Failure to move the government was becoming the hallmark of early Whiggism. Little wonder so many of the Whig petitioners resorted in time to far more extreme activities to obtain their goals. Forty-four petitioners were later implicated in the Rye House conspiracy; thirty-four promoted Monmouth's futile rebellion; and of those who lived to see it, twenty-seven supported the overthrow and abdication of James II in the winter of 1688–89.

Whig petitioners also held positions in London's corporate government. Between 1679 and 1682, Whig efforts to maintain control of several key positions within the City government were often successful.[21] In the era of the Popish Plot and Exclusion Crisis, as Henry Horwitz has observed, connections between civic and national politics became increasingly tightened and intertwined. A Whig agenda could not be forwarded without their presence within the City governance. Though Whigs were a minority within the Court of Aldermen, they

19. *The London Cuckolds* (1681), 1.2.11, emphasis mine.

20. Knights, *Politics and Opinion*, 231; Knights, "London's 'Monster' Petition," 66; and the earl of Conway to Secretary Jenkins, *CSPD*, 23:154, for the quotations.

21. On City politics in the early 1680s, see Gary De Krey, "The London Whigs and the Exclusion Crisis Reconsidered"; Henry Horwitz, "Party in a Civic Context: London from the Exclusion Crisis to the Fall of Walpole," in Clyve Jones, ed., *Britain in the First Age of Party* (London: Hambledon Press, 1978), 173–94; Margaret Priestley, "London Merchants and Opposition Politics in Charles II's Reign," *BIHR* 29 (1956): 205–19; and Reginald R. Sharpe, *London and the Kingdom*, 3 vols. (London, 1894), 2:456–502.

consistently received strong support from the far larger Common Hall and Common Council, particularly from Dissenters.[22] In 1680 and 1681, the Common Hall returned Whig sheriffs and elected four Whig members of Parliament to each of the three Exclusion Parliaments. Whigs also held the lord mayor's office in 1679 and 1680.[23]

Whig control of the shrievalty and mayoral offices had no small effect on national and cultural politics. The shrievalty was particularly important. Whig sheriffs ignored implementation of the penal laws against unlicensed preaching and conventicles. They were even known to harass and imprison those who informed on the meetings of Dissenters.[24] Nor did they pursue the scribblers or publishers of pro-exclusion and antigovernment libels. Instead they actively sought to thwart court efforts to prosecute Whig booksellers, newsletter writers, and propagandists.[25] Little wonder that at the Queen's Arms, members of Slingsby Bethel's club agreed, "that their principal care was to have always the sheriffs in the City of their own friends."[26]

Whig sheriffs also controlled whom the courts punished and, more important, whom they did not, by selecting jurors sympathetic to Whig and Dissenting interests. "Whig justice" meant that those who committed minor infractions, such as the case of the spinster Katherine Johnson, who reportedly stated that "the king is a papist and the duke of York is a popish dog," were found not guilty by a London jury in July 1682. But a year later, after Whigs had lost control of the shrievalty, a constable, James Holby, was convicted for saying that the "law for suppressing conventicles is against the law of Christ," fined a hundred pounds, and committed to New Prison until he could pay.[27]

22. Horwitz, "Party in a Civic Context," 178; De Krey notes that in 1681, 50 percent of the Whig common councilmen were nonconformists ("The London Whigs and the Exclusion Crisis Reconsidered," 462). For a chronological list of aldermen in these years, see Alfred B. Beaven, *The Aldermen of the City of London* (London, 1908), 301–3. For a list of common councilmen and their religious and political affiliations, see PRO SP 29/418, fols. 138–48.

23. The four Whig MPs were Sir Thomas Player, Sir Robert Clayton, Thomas Pilkington, and William Love. The sheriffs were Henry Cornish (1680–81), Slingsby Bethel (1680), Pilkington (1681), and Samuel Shute (1682). The Whig mayors were Sir Robert Clayton (1679) and Sir Patience Ward (1680).

24. A newsletter for June 1682 reported that in London, "Several informers against conventicles held in this City were severely treated last Sunday and one of them committed to prison" (*CSPD*, 23:272).

25. Crist, "Government Control of the Press," 63–67.

26. The Information on Oath of Samuel Oates, junior, *CSPD*, 23:236.

27. *Middlesex County Records (Old Series)*, 4 vols., ed. John Cordy Jeaffreson (London: Greater London Council, 1972), 4:162, 191.

More important for national politics were the big publicity cases in 1681, of Stephen Colledge, a Whig activist and scribbler accused of sedition, and John Rouse and the earl of Shaftesbury, prominent Whigs who were both accused of treason. In each case, London juries empanelled by Whig sheriffs all came back with *ignoramus* verdicts. News of Rouse's verdict made Charles II himself declare that it was "a hard case that I am the last man to have law and justice in the whole nation." The joyous street scenes that took place following news of Shaftesbury's acquittal stiffened the king's resolve to regain control of London by challenging the City's charter. Tory polemicist John Northleigh neatly summarized the situation: "if we find a factious city, then a factious sheriff; if a factious sheriff, then a factious jury; if a factious jury, then all the factious fellows are acquitted."[28]

These factious aldermen, sheriffs, and jurymen were Whigs, several of whom were deeply involved in radical activity. Most of them belonged to a small but powerful circle of wealthy London merchants whose attraction to Whig politics was motivated by ideological as well as economic considerations.[29] Fifteen of the radicals identified in the appendix held positions within London's corporate government during this period. They are listed in Table 2, along with several other prominent City Whig leaders and their professions, the City offices they held, and their confessional affiliation if known. With the exception of Sir Robert Clayton, all of these men were nonconformists. Thomas Pilkington, for example, was an important member of the Skinner's Company and ally of leading Whig lords. At the first Exclusion Parliament in 1679, he suggested that the duke of York be impeached of high treason. In June 1681, he was elected sheriff and continued the Whig device of packing grand juries. A year later when the royalist lord mayor Sir John Moore secured the appointment of two Tory sheriffs, in order to prevent the further empanelling of Whig juries, Pilkington led a street riot in protest.[30] Pilkington was allied with London's most notorious lord

28. K. H. D. Haley, *The First Earl of Shaftesbury* (Oxford: Clarendon Press, 1968), 672, for the Charles II quotation; John Miller, "The Crown and the Borough Charters in the Reign of Charles II," *EHR* 100 (1985): 71, on the challenge to the City's charter; and John Northleigh, *The Parallel: or, the New Specious Association an Old Rebellious Covenant* (1682), 33, for the Northleigh quotation.

29. For their economic concerns, see Margaret Priestley, "London Merchants and Opposition Politics," 205–19.

30. *DNB*; *BDBR*; J. R. Jones, *The First Whigs*, 65–66, 203–5; Greaves, *Secrets of the Kingdom*, passim.

mayor in these years, Sir Patience Ward. Ward was the second son of a Yorkshire squire who rose to the forefront of London mercantile society after the Restoration. He had become a master of the Merchant Taylor's Company in 1671, and was knighted in 1675. Ward's strident antipapism was so well known in London that Tory playwright Aphra Behn modeled the title character of her satiric comedy about city Whigs, *Sir Patient Fancy*, after him. In 1680, as London's lord mayor, Ward made several inflammatory antipapist speeches, accusing papists of burning the City in 1666; murdering the Middlesex magistrate, Sir Edmundbury Godfrey, who was one of the first officials to hear the Popish Plot tales of Titus Oates; and plotting to assassinate the king.[31] Ward was infamous for adding an inscription on the monument commemorating the London fire of 1666, which blamed papists with having "begun and carried on that most dreadful burning of this Protestant City."[32]

But Whig control of London politics was ephemeral. In 1682 and 1683, the court launched a concerted drive to regain control of the City. In the summer of 1682, the struggle spilled onto the streets over the contested shrieval appointments made by the royalist lord mayor. Whigs Thomas Pilkington, Slingsby Bethel, Henry Cornish, Sir Thomas Player, Richard Goodenough, Francis Jenks, Samuel Shute, and the Whig leader, Lord Grey of Werk, staged a riot at the Guildhall in protest.[33] But the Guildhall riot, like the Whig campaign in 1682 and 1683 against the court's quo warranto proceedings, which ended with the loss of London's City charter, were but rearguard actions that ended in failure. The Tory backlash not only regained control of the city but also sought to destroy prominent City Whigs. Lives and fortunes were ruined in the process.

In 1682, Thomas Pilkington was sued by the duke of York for supposedly exclaiming, in 1679, that the duke "hath burnt the city and is come to cut our throats." The Tory jury awarded the duke a large sum that Pilkington could not pay; he languished in prison for four years. Sir

31. *The Speech of . . . Sir Patience Ward, Lord Mayor Elect, at Guildhall, London, September 29, 1680* (1680); *The Speech of the Right Honourable Sir Patience Ward, Kt., The Present Lord Mayor of London* (1681).

32. C. E. Whiting, "Sir Patience Ward of Tanshelf," *The Yorkshire Archaeological Journal* 34 (1939): 245–72; F. M. Fry, *The Pictures of the Merchant Taylor's Company* (London: Chapman & Hall Ltd., 1907), 83.

33. See their trial for riot, assault, and battery in *State Trials*, 9:187–222; also see the Tory satire on the riot, *Massinello: or, A Satyr Against the Guild-hall Riot* (1683).

Table 2. City Whigs

Name	Occupation	City Offices	Religion
Barnardiston, Sir Samuel (1620–1707)	Merchant	Exclusion MP *Ignoramus* juror	Presbyterian
Bethel, Slingsby (1617–97)	Deputy Governor, East India Company		Independent
	Merchant	Sheriff (1680)	
Clayton, Sir Robert (1629–1707)	Financier, merchant	Exclusion MP (London) Alderman (1670–83) Lord mayor (1679–80)	Anglican
Cornish, Henry (d. 1685)	Merchant (haberdasher)	Alderman (1680–83) Sheriff (1680–81)	Presbyterian
Dubois, John (1622–84)	Merchant (weaver)	Common Council (1674–82) City auditor (1679–80) Exclusion MP (Liverpool)	French Protestant
Goodenough, Francis (d. 1685)	Lawyer	Under sheriff (1680–81)	Dissenter
Goodenough, Richard (d. 1689)	Lawyer	Under sheriff (1680–81)	Dissenter
Jenks, Francis	Merchant (draper)	Common Council (1672–82)	Dissenter
Love, William (d. 1689)	Merchant (draper)	Exclusion MP (London)	Independent
Papillon, Thomas (1623–1702)	Merchant (mercer)	Exclusion MP (Dover)	French Protestant
	Deputy governor, East India Company	*Ignoramus* juror Common Council (1681)	
Peyton, Sir Robert (d. 1686)	Soldier	Exclusion MP	Dissenter
Pilkington, Thomas (d. 1691)	Merchant (skinner)	Exclusion MP (London) Sheriff (1681) Common Council (1667–80)	Presbyterian

Note: I have used the generic label "Dissenter" for all the individuals I knew were nonconforming Protestants but whose exact confessional affiliation I could not determine.

MP = member of Parliament.

Table 2. City Whigs (*continued*)

Name	Occupation	City Offices	Religion
Player, Sir Thomas (d. 1686)	Merchant (haberdasher)	Exclusion MP (London) City chamberlain (1672–83) Common Council (1672–82)	Dissenter
Shute, Samuel (d. 1685)	Merchant (draper)	Common Council (1682–83) Sheriff (1682)	Independent
Starkey, John (d. 1699)	Bookseller	Common Council (1682)	Dissenter
Ward, Sir Patience (1629–96)	Merchant (tailor)	Alderman (1670–83) Exclusion MP (Pontefract) Lord mayor (1680–81)	Independent

Note: I have used the generic label "Dissenter" for all the individuals I knew were nonconforming Protestants but whose exact confessional affiliation I could not determine.

MP = member of Parliament.

18

Samuel Barnardiston suffered a similar fate. A deputy of the East India Company, he was an *ignoramus* juror at the trial of Shaftesbury. In 1684, he was found guilty of libel for asserting in a series of private letters that the Whig conspiracy known as the Rye House Plot was a "sham plot staged by the government to discredit the exclusionists." Barnardiston refused to pay damages and was imprisoned until June 1688. Thomas Papillon, a master of the Mercer's Company and a staunch Protestant of Huguenot descent, was also hauled before a jury in 1685, and heavily fined. Sir Patience Ward was found guilty of perjuring himself in the Pilkington trial. He was sentenced to the pillory and a fine of five thousand pounds but absconded to Holland.[34] The court had effectively ended the reign of "Bethelite Sheriffs and Barnardiston juries."[35] The loss of the City charter in 1683, discussed in Chapter 4, allowed the king to handpick City aldermen and common councilmen. Pilkington, Barnardiston, Papillon, Ward, and other City Whigs, like Sir Robert Clayton and Sir Robert Peyton, were fortunate enough to witness the Glorious Revolution, and many made triumphant returns to civic politics. Others were not so lucky. The alderman Henry Cornish was tried and executed in 1684, on perjured testimony for his supposed participation in the Rye House Plot. The under sheriff Francis Goodenough was killed at the Battle of Sedgemoor in 1685.[36]

---

34. *The Tryal and Conviction of Sir Samuel Barnardiston, bt. for High Misdemeanor* (1684). There is some information on the Barnardiston family in John Shower, *Memoirs* (1716), passim. Also see the entry for Barnardiston in the *DNB*. The entry in the *History of Parliament* contains errors. For Thomas Papillon, see the entries in the *DNB*, *BDBR*, and *History of Parliament*. Also see Alexander Papillon, *Memoirs of Thomas Papillon of London, Merchant* (London, 1887), and David Ormond, "Puritanism and Patriarchy: The Career and Spiritual Writings of Thomas Papillon, 1623–1702," in *Studies in Modern Kentish History* (Maidstone: Kent Archaeological Society, 1983), 123–37. For Ward, see *The Proceedings at the Tryal of Sir Patience Ward, Kt.* (1683).
35. Nathaniel Thompson, preface to *A Collection of Eighty-Six Loyal Poems* (1685).
36. Pilkington was knighted and elected lord mayor of London in 1689. He died in 1691. Barnardiston was elected MP from Suffolk and Ipswick in 1690. Papillon became a court Whig under William III, serving in a variety of positions until his death in 1702. Ward sat at the convention in 1689, and was active in City politics until his death in 1696. Clayton was also at the convention and was appointed commissioner of customs in 1689; he remained active in City politics throughout the 1690s. Peyton, a member of the Haberdasher's Company, who had been outlawed for high treason in 1685, took part in William of Orange's invasion. He died in May 1689. Henry Cornish, further discussed in Chapter 5, was a City alderman and wealthy merchant. As sheriffs, he and Bethel Slingsby had packed the grand juries that set Shaftesbury and others free. See the article on Cornish in the *DNB*, and John Hawles, *Remarks on the Tryals of . . . Stephen Colledge, . . . The Lord Russel, Collonel Sidney, Henry Cornish* (1689). Francis Goodenough and his brother Richard were deeply engaged in Whig conspiratorial politics in

By 1681, Whigs and Dissenters were not only losing their grip on London, they were losing the cultural and political initiative as well. They had seized that initiative in 1678 and 1679, with their antipapist propaganda campaign, clubbing, and petitioning, but by 1681, they were on the defensive. Losing control of the judicial system not only led to a number of imprisonments, exiles, and executions of prominent radicals, it also removed the shield from the Whig press. The court began to successfully close the operations of several of the most notorious Whig booksellers. This did not mean an end to Whig propaganda, which still flowed forth from the presses for several more years, although it was more often anonymously authored and anonymously printed. But it did mean that propagating the radical voice became far more dangerous. Moreover, as Tory forces rallied in 1682 and 1683, Whig polemic was more often answered and challenged in the press. The more sophisticated Whig tracts were often met by four or five equally strong Tory responses. Tory stage plays appropriated the theater. Their satirical weeklies and broadsides on "Whig-land" became far more numerous and far more shrill. The playhouse and press increasingly became their territory.

This legal and cultural onslaught served to further radicalize Whig politics. Under siege, Whig propagandists reformulated and honed their ideas, particularly the right of active resistance. Whig politicians became Whig plotters, meeting in secrecy, stockpiling arms, formulating demands and declarations, seeking ever more drastic means to their ends. With the legal and semilegal routes that they had pursued since 1678 effectively closed to them, both with the dissolution of the last Exclusion Parliament in 1681, and with the loss of the City charter in 1683 (and hence control of civic politics and the press), Whig radicalism went underground.

The Network: Patronage, Professions, and Family

Conspiratorial politics and radical ideology in the 1680s was the work of men and women who were linked to one another not only by religious

---

the 1680s. They were both members of the lower echelon of Rye House plotters, and both participated in Monmouth's Rebellion. See Wigfield, *The Monmouth Rebels, 1685*, 70.

and political beliefs but also by the professional services that they provided for one another, and quite often by blood and marriage ties as well. Whig leaders patronized Whig theorists. Whig publishers sold their propaganda. Whig lawyers represented fellow Whigs in the courtroom. Whig brothers, fathers, and sons sat in Parliament together, met in clubs and cabals together, and eventually marched onto the battlefield together. There were certainly no strict patterns of organization among the members of this radical network. They were not a disciplined unit, cell, or party. But Whig radicals did form a nexus of individuals who knew each other, who supported and advised one another, and whose families intermarried.

This network not only made the conspiratorial politics of the 1680s possible, it supported the development of a radical ideology and the dissemination of a revolution culture. Without patrons and booksellers, the radical voice would not have been heard. Without the window of opportunity between 1680 and 1682, provided by Whig sheriffs and *ignoramus* juries, Whig propaganda would have been muffled far sooner. The glue that held this diverse web of individuals together was, first and foremost, fear of popery and fear for England's future under the "popish successor." Protestant Dissent further emboldened and unified radicalism.

In the early 1680s, Whig leaders, among them aristocrats, country gentlemen, and urban oligarchs, patronized numerous like-minded men of lesser standing. The services clients provided were various and numerous. Many served as their master's spy, informer, and messenger, gathering and passing information along London streets and in bookstores and coffeehouses.[37] Others, usually former soldiers, served as their master's bodyguards. Sir Thomas Armstrong, "the Bully Whig," was the duke of Monmouth's constant companion and henchman. Armstrong's son-in-law, Captain Edward Matthews, served Monmouth in like manner after Armstrong's execution in 1684. After Monmouth's death, Matthews became Sir John Trenchard's "bully and pensioner" while the two lived in exile in Amsterdam. Colonel John Rumsey and

37. For example, the London magistrate Edmund Warcup was frequently met at coffeehouses and taverns by Whig clients seeking information for their masters. Robert Ferguson went to Warcup to query him for information the court might have against his patron, the earl of Shaftesbury. William Petyt represented the earl of Essex's interests to Warcup. See *Diaries of the Popish Plot*, comp. Douglas C. Greene (Delmar, New York: Scholar's Facsimiles & Reprints, 1977), 107, 100.

Captain Thomas Walcot served the earl of Shaftesbury in a similar fashion.[38]

Still others, men of the universities and the Inns of Court, articulated their master's politics into political theory and set these ideas in writing. John Locke, William Petyt, the Reverend Samuel Johnson, and Robert Ferguson all served the aristocratic leaders of the Whig party in various ways. Locke tutored the earl of Shaftesbury's grandchildren, Petyt was the earl of Essex's barrister, Johnson was Lord Russell's chaplain, and Ferguson was Shaftesbury's paymaster of Whig hacks. But their most important function was as propagandist.

The story of John Locke's association with the earl of Shaftesbury is well known.[39] William Petyt, a leading Whig constitutionalist, served the earl of Essex and his family, giving the family legal and business advice throughout the 1670s. In the 1680s, he turned to propaganda and dedicated his most influential tract, *The Ancient Right of the Commons of England Asserted* (1680), to Essex in order to "publickly shew my humble gratitude for the many favors your Lordship has been pleased to confer upon me."[40] The Reverend Samuel Johnson was employed as the domestic chaplain to William, Lord Russell. Russell admired Johnson's learning and his "zeal for the legal polity of his country."[41] Johnson became nearly as famous as his master when in 1682, he published an

---

38. Sir Thomas Armstrong, "the Hector for the Whigs' cause," was notorious for his dueling, dicing, and hard drinking. See the Tory broadside, *The Bully Whig or, The Poor Whores Lamentation for the Apprehending of Sir Thomas Armstrong* (1684). Lord Fountainhall referred to Armstrong as "Hector," in Sir Walter Scott, ed., *Chronological Notes of Scottish Affairs from 1680 till 1701, being chiefly taken form the Diary of Lord Fountainhall* (Edinburgh, 1822), 36. There are entries on Armstrong in the *DNB* (and under "corrections and additions") and in the *History of Parliament*, 1:544–45. There is very little information on Captain Edward Matthews. He is mentioned in John Evelyn, *The Diary of John Evelyn*, ed. E. S. de Beer, 6 vols. (Oxford: Clarendon Press, 1955), 4:452, and there is scattered information on him in Grey's and Wade's confessions and in the Middleton Manuscript Collection. He is referred to as John Trenchard's "bully and pensioner" in BL, Add. 41,818, fol. 206. On Rumsey's association with Shaftesbury, see *State Trials*, 9:415–16; *Carstares Papers*, 9; and Ashcraft, *Revolutionary Politics*, 134. On Walcot, see Thomas Sprat, *A True Account and Declaration of the Horrid Conspiracy against the Late King* (1685), 21.

39. See Maurice Cranston, *John Locke: A Biography* (London: Longmans, Green, and Co., 1957); Haley, *Shaftesbury*; and Ashcraft, *Revolutionary Politics*.

40. Corrine Weston and Janelle Greenberg, *Subjects and Sovereigns: The Grand Controversy Over Legal Sovereignty in Stuart England* (Cambridge: Cambridge University Press, 1981), 189–99; William Petyt, dedication to *The Ancient Right of the Commons of England Asserted* (1680), pages unnumbered.

41. Samuel Johnson, "Some Memoirs," in *The Works* (1713), iv.

elaborated defense of the right of resistance, *Julian the Apostate*, which is discussed in Chapter 2. The most infamous Whig plotter and propagandist, Robert Ferguson, served many patrons. In the 1670s, he attached himself to the City Whig and deputy governor of the East India Company, Thomas Papillon. Ferguson dedicated one of his first theological tracts, *The Interest of Reason in Religion* (1675), to Papillon, declaring "The interest you have in me by an entail of peculiar kindness gives you a right to my studies and the fruits of them."[42]

By 1679, Ferguson was an intimate of the earl of Shaftesbury and served his new master in various ways. Ferguson was the earl's chaplain, his chief scribbler, and his envoy and spy around London. Shaftesbury "perused and corrected" as well as paid Ferguson for his Whig propaganda. In July 1681, he commissioned Ferguson to turn a manuscript he had previously written into a polemic on the life and reign of Charles II, which was to be distributed to the members of the Oxford Parliament. The following year, Ferguson accompanied Shaftesbury into exile where, according to Sir John Dalrymple, Shaftesbury died in Ferguson's arms.[43] During their exile in Amsterdam, Ferguson wrote to his wife of Shaftesbury's "fatherly love and care" for him. "The person with whom I came hither treats me as his son as well as his father." Ferguson was later dismayed to learn Shaftesbury had left him a legacy of only forty pounds.[44]

Ferguson was also the creature of the earl of Essex in the early 1680s. After Essex's death in 1683, Ferguson wrote, "he did me the kindness to own and befriend me at a junction when I was in no small hazard from the malice of very powerful as well as considerable persons." In exile, following the discovery of the Rye House conspiracy, Ferguson attached himself to the duke of Monmouth. In the spring of 1685, he drew up the *Declaration* that accompanied Monmouth's futile invasion of the western counties and also served as the Duke's army chaplain.[45] After the death

---

42. Dedication to *The Interest of Reason in Religion* (1675), pages unnumbered. In 1680, Ferguson wrote *A Treatise concerning the East India Trade* at Papillon's house under the Whig merchant's supervision.

43. The tract was never printed as far as I can discern (*CSPD*, 25:439; PRO 30/24/43/63, fol. 215). The story that Shaftesbury died in Ferguson's arms is probably specious; see Dalrymple, 2:25.

44. *CSPD*, 24:23, 58; 25:90.

45. *An Enquiry into and Detection of the Barbarous Murther of the late Earl of Essex* (1689), 5, for the Ferguson quotation; this tract was first printed in 1684. Ferguson's role in Monmouth's Rebellion and his *Declaration* are discussed in Chapter 5.

of Monmouth, Ferguson lived in penury in Holland until the Glorious Revolution reversed his fortunes.

Lawyers played a leading role in revolutionary politics in the 1680s. They composed Whig propaganda, both sensationalist satire and sophisticated constitutional theory; they provided legal advice and counsel for one another; and, in desperation, they became Rye House conspirators in 1682–83, and Monmouth rebels in 1685. Of the ninety-four radical Whigs listed in the appendix, twenty-four were lawyers, by far the largest occupational group represented.[46] They are identified in Table 3, where I have also noted whether they were conspirators, propagandists, or both. That these men were many of the Whig movement's most active and learned theorists is not particularly surprising. Nor was it strange that Whiggism attracted men of the Inns of Court. The lawyers and party pens, such as William Atwood and William Petyt, saw themselves as the true defenders and restorers of England's ancient constitution. The common law was a bulwark against the intrusion of popery and arbitrary government. As men trained in the law, they believed themselves to be its most appropriate interpreters and guardians. Whig lawyers were often highly anticlerical. They were concerned by what they saw as clerical meddling in the affairs of state. Politics, Whigs like Atwood asserted, was not the business of the gownmen, but rather that of learned men steeped in legal tradition. Patent rolls, writs, charters, and jurist opinion were their authorities, not Scripture.

Radical Whig lawyers were not only some of the most articulate spokesmen of Whig theory in print and Parliament, they also served as counselors to various members of the network, including one another, in the courtroom. As royalists cracked down on seditious libelers and booksellers and began prosecuting Whig leaders in Parliament and City politics in the early 1680s, Whigs were nearly as often side by side at the Court of King's Bench as they were at the King's Head Tavern. While Whig sheriffs were able to pack London juries, Whig lawyers successfully

---

46. In addition to the twenty-five practicing lawyers listed in the appendix, James Tyrrell and Christopher Battiscomb had studied law. On law and lawyers during the Restoration, see Michael Landon, *The Triumph of Lawyers: Their Role in English Politics, 1687–89* (Tuscaloosa: University of Alabama Press, 1970); Howard Nenner, *By Colour of Law: Legal Culture and Constitutional Politics in England, 1660–1689* (Chicago: University of Chicago Press, 1977); Lois G. Schwoerer, "The Role of Lawyers in the Revolution of 1688–89," *Fortsetzung Umschlagseite* 3 (1987): 473–98; and David Lemmings, *Gentlemen and Barristers: The Inns of Court and the English Bar, 1680–1730* (Oxford: Clarendon Press, 1990).

Table 3. Whig Lawyers

Name	Role
Atkyns, Sir Robert (1621–1707)	Propagandist
Atwood, William (d. 1705)	Propagandist
Ayloffe, John (1645–85)	Propagandist
Blaney, Robert	Conspirator
Cooke, Edward	Propagandist
Freke, John	Propagandist
Goodenough, Francis (d. 1685)	Conspirator
Goodenough, Richard (d. 1689)	Conspirator
Hunt, Thomas (d. 1688)	Propagandist
Ireton, Henry	Conspirator
Matthews, Captain Edward	Conspirator
Nelthorpe, Richard (d. 1685)	Conspirator
Norton, Edward (1654–1702)	Conspirator
Petyt, William (d. 1707)	Propagandist
Prideaux, Edmund (1634–1702)	Conspirator
Smith, Aaron (d. 1699)	Conspirator
Speke, Hugh (b. 1656)	Propagandist and conspirator
Speke, John (d. 1728)	Conspirator
Tily, Joseph	Conspirator
Trenchard, Henry (d. 1694)	Conspirator
Trenchard, Sir John (1649–95)	Conspirator
Wade, Nathaniel (d. 1718)	Conspirator
Waller, Edmund (1652–1700)	Conspirator
Wallop, Richard (1616–97)	—
West, Robert	Conspirator
Wildman, Major John (1623–93)	Propagandist and conspirator
Williams, Sir William (1634–1700)	—

defended their clients. John Ayloffe, a Whig barrister and poet, collaborated with Aaron Smith in the legal defense of the earl of Shaftesbury in October 1681. Smith and Robert West counseled the "Protestant joiner," Stephen Colledge, during his trial for sedition in August 1681. Both times, London jurors brought back *ignoramus* verdicts. But Whig control of the judicial system was short-lived. Ayloffe, Smith, and West, all committed radicals, later participated in the Rye House Plot. Robert West was caught and turned king's evidence. Smith, "a violent monster" according to Roger North, was imprisoned until March 1688.[47] Ayloffe escaped abroad, joined the earl of Argyle's invasion of Scotland in 1685,

47. *BDBR*, s.v. "West, Robert." The information he gave against his fellow Rye House plotters was published in *State Trials*, 9:389–412. On Aaron Smith, see the articles in the *DNB*

and was captured and sent back to London. He and fellow lawyer and Monmouth rebel Richard Nelthorpe were executed in October 1685, for their part in the Rye House Plot. Each was hanged, drawn, and quartered outside of the Inns of Court, where they had formerly studied law, as a warning to all lawyers who meddled in sedition.[48]

The most numerous courtroom battles, which pitched Whigs against the government in the early 1680s, were over seditious libel. This was the result of a conflation of several factors. The first was the lapsing of the Licensing Act in 1679, which placed control of the press under no other restrictions than the haphazard restraints of royal prerogative. Without legislative restrictions in place, control over the press was limited for the most part to royal proclamations or prosecution for seditious libel. At the time, the Popish Plot revelations, the battle over the succession, and several other related issues led to a virtual flood of partisan weeklies, broadsides, and pamphlets. Mark Knights has estimated that between five and ten million printed items were in circulation between 1679 and 1681.[49]

Most of the cases of seditious libel in these years did not bring the authors of the tract or broadside in question before judge and jury. Rather, the booksellers, many of whom were committed radicals, stood accused. These were the men and women who made the radical voice possible. Their politics often shaped what they sold. They daringly published the highly incendiary works of Shaftesbury's host of Whig hacks, as well as the constitutional theorists whose work challenged patriarchal and divine right theories of kingship. Radical booksellers also composed and published their own thoughts on the current crises by way of Protestant weeklies, satires, and doggerel.

These men and women were not simply auxiliaries to the radical network. They were very much a part of it. The majority, not surprisingly, were Dissenters. The Baptist Benjamin Harris began the first Whig weekly, *Domestick Intelligence,* in 1679, which he was able to keep running for two years despite official harassment.[50] Fellow Baptist Francis Smith,

and the *BDBR;* Roger North, *Lives of the Norths,* ed. Augustus Jessopp, 3 vols. (London, 1890), 1:189; and Haley, *Shaftesbury,* 664–65.

48. *A True Account of the Proceedings against John Ayloffe and Richard Nelthorp* (1685).

49. *Politics and Opinion,* 168.

50. Crist, "Government Control of the Press," 53–59; Sutherland, *The Restoration Newspaper,* 13–25.

known as "Elephant Smith" because his shop was at the sign of the
Elephant and Castle, began publishing *Smith's Protestant Intelligence* in
1681, though it lasted for only two and half months before being closed
down. Harris's and Smith's weeklies, along with others like Langley
Curtis's *True Protestant Mercury* and Richard Janeway's *Impartial Protestant
Mercury*, fanned the flames of antipopery and demonized the duke of
York. Their papers reported the explosive speeches of City Whigs like
Sir Patience Ward and the every move of their Protestant hero, the duke
of Monmouth. They advertised Whig pamphlets, petitions, and the
dying speeches of their fallen comrades.[51]

Naturally, booksellers were keenly interested in London City politics
since they could only count on protection as long as Whigs controlled
the judiciary. John Starkey, another Dissenting bookseller, was a Green
Ribbonite and sat on the Common Council. As a councilmen, Starkey's
politics were described by a royalist in 1682 "as bad as maybe." In 1683,
Starkey fled from England after having reprinted Nathaniel Bacon's
antimonarchical *Historical Discourse*.[52] In Amsterdam he became a
burgher to protect himself from being hauled back to England and
associated with the growing number of English and Scottish dissidents.
Fellow Whig bookseller John Dunton hailed Starkey as "a brave asserter
of English liberties to his last breath."[53]

Radical booksellers played a major role in the Whig petition movement. They printed the petitions, exhibited them in their shops, helped
circulate them, and were themselves signators. Benjamin Harris printed
each of the petitions in his *Domestick Intelligence* and reported on the
progress in the countryside of the signature collection for the "monster"
petition of 1680. Their promotion of Whig petitions was not without
danger. John Dunton reported that Harris was fined five hundred
pounds and sent to the pillory for selling one.[54] Francis Smith was
accused of using his shop to display two petitions calling for Parliament,
for which he was collecting signatories. When asked by the king himself
if the accusation were true, Smith replied, "Yes, and please your Majesty

---

51. There is information on Smith, Curtis, and Janeaway in Plomer, ed., *A Dictionary of the
Booksellers*, and Sutherland, *The Restoration Newspaper*. Also see the *BDBR* entry on Smith.

52. PRO SP 29/418, fol. 145v; *CSPD*, 23:236, 608.

53. John Dunton, *The Life and Errors of John Dunton* (London, 1705), 289.

54. Sutherland, *The Restoration Newspaper*, 162–64; Dunton, *Life and Errors*, 293–94. For
information on Harris, see David Knott, "The Booksellers and the Plot," *The Book Collector* 23
(1974): 194–206.

with all my heart . . . I could not do Your Majesty and my country better service."[55]

Bookselling was a family business. Francis Smith's son, wife, and daughter all published books, and each at one time or another was tried and fined for having printed and sold seditious work.[56] Bookselling afforded women, as the widows, wives, sisters, and daughters of publishers, their most active and conspicuous role in Whig politics. Mary Thompson, the wife of the publisher Nathaniel Thompson was taken into custody for dispersing the infamous *Appeal from the City to the Country* in 1679.[57] Elinore Smith, Francis Smith's daughter, was fined ten pounds in 1683, for publishing *The Second Part of the Ignoramus Justices*.[58] But the most notorious female publisher, dragged before the chief justice on numerous occasions, was Jane Curtis, the wife of Langely Curtis. Jane was not only responsible for keeping her husband's Whig weekly, *True Protestant Mercury*, before the public during his many absences, she also sponsored the publication of several seditious tracts, including another edition of the Reverend Samuel Johnson's *Julian the Apostate* and the anticourt satire entitled *The Perplexed Prince*. The latter, authored by one "T.S." and dedicated to Whig leader William, Lord Russell, championed the "legitimate" heir to the throne, the duke of Monmouth, and vilified the scheming, ambitious duke of York.[59] Curtis was prosecuted successfully for seditious libel in February 1680. Apparently it was not always true that Roger L'Estrange, the Crown's most active censor, "would wink at unlicensed books if the printer's wife would but smile on him."[60]

The royalist backlash, beginning in 1681, and accelerating in 1683, with the loss of London's City charter, took its toll on the radical voice.

55. Quoted in Crist, "Government Control of the Press," 59.

56. *CSPD*, 23:564; 24:178; 26:214.

57. The Thompsons' political allegiances were not readily discernable. Nathaniel may have been the first to publish the highly seditious pro-exclusion tract, *An Appeal from the Country to the City* (1679). On the other hand, his weekly, *The True Domestick Intelligence*, was a royalist foil to Harris's *Domestick Intelligence*. See *The Tryal of Benjamin Harris on an Information for Printing an Appeal from the Country to the City* (1680), and Knights, *Politics and Opinion*, 161.

58. *CSPD*, 24:178.

59. The Information of Richard Crowder (a journeyman to Mrs. Curtis), in *CSPD*, 24:37–38; T.S., *The Perplexed Prince* (1682); Greaves, *Secrets of the Kingdom*, 46–47.

60. Dunton, *Life and Errors*, 266. For further information on Jane Curtis and Elinore Smith, see Maureen Bell, "Women and the Opposition Press after the Restoration," in John Lucas, ed., *Writing and Radicalism* (London: Longman, 1996).

The price of authoring, printing, selling, or simply saying seditious words became increasingly costly and dangerous. Stephen Colledge's hanging in 1681, for seditious words and actions, was just the beginning. Benjamin Harris was pilloried and fined in 1680, Francis Smith in 1684.[61] John Starkey went into exile. The City Whig Sir Samuel Barnardiston was imprisoned for denying the existence of the Rye House Plot in private correspondence; Hugh Speke and Laurence Braddon were jailed for rumoring that the Whig grandee, the earl of Essex, had been murdered in the Tower. In 1685, the Reverend Samuel Johnson was defrocked and whipped through London streets for writing a seditious tract, and the preacher William Disney was hanged and quartered for printing the duke of Monmouth's *Declaration*.[62]

William Disney was an active participant in the radical network and an ejected minister who was probably eking out a living as a nonconformist preacher before his death.[63] Dissenting preachers played important roles as both propagandists and conspirators within the radical network. Robert Ferguson, an Independent preacher, archplotter, and prolific polemicist is the most notorious example. But there were many others. The Congregationalists Matthew Mead and Stephen Lobb preached in London conventicles. They were both periodically harassed by the authorities for unlicensed "teaching and preaching." Mead's meetinghouse was wrecked in 1682. Both were arrested on suspicion of complicity in the Rye House Plot.[64]

Ultimately, Mead fled to Amsterdam, where he was surrounded by numerous other dissidents: City Whigs, country gentlemen, and other Dissenting preachers as well, many of whom staked their lives on Monmouth's bid for the Crown in 1685. John Shower, a Presbyterian minister, helped fund Monmouth's tiny band and preached to his men as they departed Amsterdam. Nathaniel Hooke, an Independent, served as Monmouth's private chaplain; Robert Ferguson, was the army

---

61. *CSPD*, 27:80.

62. *The True Account of the Behavior and Confession of William Disney esq.*, . . . *His Last Dying Words*, 1685, reported that Disney was captured on June 15, 1685, with nothing but a shirt on and "his maid in his bed." He was sentenced by Jeffreys and executed on June 29. Braddon's, Speke's, and Johnson's run-ins with the law are discussed in Chapter 5.

63. Matthews, *Calamy Revised*, 165. Information on Disney is very spotty. On the Essex matter, see BL, Lansdowne Collection, 1152A, fol. 266; concerning Monmouth, see Greaves, *Secrets of the Kingdom*, 19.

64. *Middlesex County Records*, 4:166, 182, 184; Gorden Alexander, *Freedom After Ejection* (London, 1917), 311, 304.

chaplain. John Hicks, a Presbyterian minister, joined Monmouth's army upon its landing in western England, as did fellow preacher Stephen Lobb. Hooke and Ferguson managed to escape back to Holland after Monmouth's failure at Sedgemoor. Lobb was eventually pardoned, but John Hicks was not so fortunate. One of the many victims of Jeffreys's "bloody assizes," he was hanged and quartered at Wells with little ceremony.[65]

Both Protestant Dissent and radical politics ran in families, and John Hickes's family is a good example. Hickes had married the sister of the prominent Presbyterian preacher John Howe. Howe had been Cromwell's domestic chaplain, and in the mid-1680s he was the confidant of Lady Rachel Russell, the Whig martyr's widow, and City Whigs Thomas Papillon and Sir Patience Ward. Hickes's daughter married the future Whig martyrologist and radical journalist John Tutchin, who supported Monmouth in 1685. In 1688, Hickes's son joined the invading prince of Orange during his march to London.[66]

Interconnections between radicals by way of marriage and kin were common. Fathers and sons, uncles and nephews, brothers, brothers-in-law, and cousins acted together to fight what they believed to be the forces of popery and arbitrary government. In the case of the Spekes of White Lackington in Illminster, the entire family, including mother and daughters, was infamous for its support and involvement in oppositional politics. But they were not alone. The Trenchards of Dorsetshire and the Hampdens of Buckinghamshire, as well as several others, also made radical religion and politics a part of the family tradition.

Gentry families like the Spekes, Trenchards, and Hampdens remind us of the vital link between country and City politics. While London was the focus of Whig efforts, particularly in the days of the Popish Plot and Exclusion Crisis, much of the money and brain power that went into creating oppositional politics came from gentry families in the counties. Most of those families lived in the southwest, where nonconformity was strongest. The sons and fathers of these families joined the Green Ribbon Club, supported the Exclusion Bill in the House of Commons, defended Whig clients in trouble with the law, and reportedly stockpiled

---

65. Wigfield, *The Monmouth Rebels*, 83, 88, 105, 155.

66. Henry Rogers, *Life and Character of John Howe* (London, 1836), 144–49. There are articles on Tutchin in the *DNB* and *BDBR*. On Hickes's son, see J. R. Jones, *The Revolution of 1688 in England*, 294.

weapons at their estates. Those who were among the boldest supported Monmouth in 1685, with money, men, and arms.[67]

Whig gentry families had much in common. They often intermarried. The Spekes were related through marriage to the Pyes of Farringdon, the Trenchards of Bloxworth, and the Prideaux of Ford Abbey. Most of these families had a tradition of Dissenting politics and religion. Their grandfathers, fathers, and uncles had heartily supported the Long Parliament in the civil wars. They were Puritans in the 1650s and Dissenters after the Restoration. Many patronized nonconformist preachers and maintained conventicles on their estates. Edmund Prideaux's house was known as a "receptacle of all fanatics."[68] These families were usually but not always Presbyterian. The Spekes intermarried with Quakers; William Trenchard sheltered a Baptist conventicle. The men in these families were usually trained in London's Inns of Court, served their local communities in various offices, and represented them at Westminster.

Family attraction to opposition politics in the 1680s was probably due to a combination of factors, including a strident loathing of papism and fear of further persecution of Dissent; an anxiety over French influence at court; and concern regarding arbitrary kingship, with an accompanying loss of their freeborn liberties and privileges. There also seems to have been a kind of puritanical-country disgust with the libertinism of Charles II's court.[69] For the most part, country gentlemen and their sons became Whigs for conservative reasons: to conserve what they believed was their English heritage from the infectious diseases disseminated from France and Rome, and to practice their Protestantism freely.

67. For a statistical map of Dissent in England and Wales showing the strength of nonconformity in the southwest, see *English Historical Documents, 1660–1714*, ed. Andrew Browning (New York: Oxford University Press, 1953), 424. There were various reports that Whigs had arms "sent into the West" (*CSPD*, 23:246). Numerous members of the Whig gentry had their houses searched, sometimes repeatedly, for arms, suggesting not only royalist fears about the stockpiling of weapons but the real possibility that some Whigs were hoarding arms. For example, in May 1683, new muskets were found at Lord Grey's house that authorities believed were bought at the time of the Oxford Parliament (BL, Add. 28,875, fol. 275).

68. The Spekes and Trenchards began intermarrying in the sixteenth century. See Bernard Burke, ed., *Royal Families of England, Scotland and Wales*, 2 vols. (London, 1851), 2:cix. *CSPD*, 23:26, for the quotation on Prideaux's house.

69. J. R. Jones noted that Charles II's court was "increasingly isolated and out of touch with the nation. . . . [I]ts frivolity, luxury, culture, immorality, and ostentatious corruption . . . [and its] affiliations and sympathies with France" alienated and disgusted the country gentry (*The First Whigs*, 5).

Many of these families championed the "Protestant duke," Monmouth, as an alternative to the Catholic duke of York. The route of Monmouth's progress to the west country, in the summer of 1680, was dictated by his visits to the manor houses of many of the most disaffected gentry families. Monmouth was joyously greeted and entertained by the Spekes of White Lackington, the Strodes of Barrington Court, the Prideaux at Ford Abbey, and the Yonges of Colyton Great House among others. When Monmouth landed at Lyme Regis in Somerset with his tiny army in 1685, he looked to these gentry families for support. He was soon disappointed. Advanced warning of Monmouth's invasion led to an official dragnet that swept up the disaffected, including men like Walter Yonge and other "such private gentlemen as were obnoxious to the censure of the court." The brothers William and Edmund Strode both sent Monmouth money but did not come out themselves. Edward Prideaux also sent the duke money, and after Monmouth's defeat at Sedgemoor had to bribe the merciless Lord Chief Justice Jeffreys nearly fifteen thousand pounds to save himself from execution.[70]

The aftermath of Monmouth's Rebellion was devastating in the west country. Jeffreys's bloody assizes left behind a trail of severed heads, arms, and legs perched on steeples, lampposts, and pikes. Charles Speke was hanged in Ilminster Square. Several gentlemen, like John Trenchard and John Speke, went into exile for a time, though they eventually reconciled with the government of James II and came home. Many others silently retired to their estates. A few were seduced by James II's promises of toleration for Dissent and joined his government. Yet almost all of them were early supporters of the prince of Orange in 1688. They joined his march to London, sat at the convention, and quite often became trusted and powerful Williamite Whigs.

The gentry, of course, were not the only caste of society that made conspiratorial politics a family affair. The radical network included several pairs of brothers, fathers and sons, and cousins, men of lesser status. The Goodenough brothers, Richard and Francis, the Rumbold brothers, Richard and William, and the Wade brothers, Nathaniel and William, were all involved in the conferences of the lower echelon of Rye House plotters in 1682–83. All six escaped abroad following the

---

70. Ralph Thoresby, *The Diary*, ed. Joseph Hunter (London, 1830), 180; *History of Parliament*, 3:288; Edward Parry, *The Bloody Assize* (New York: Dobb, Mead & Co., 1929), 260.

plot's disclosure. The Goodenoughs and Nathaniel Wade were made captains in the duke of Monmouth's army. Francis was killed, but Richard and Nathaniel were captured and ultimately saved their own lives by naming others.[71] William Rumbold provided money for Monmouth's invasion; his brother, Richard, joined the Scottish earl of Argyle's invasion of Scotland in 1685, and was captured and executed.[72] Richard was cruelly treated after his capture; his sons avenged him by murdering the man who arrested him.[73] Fathers and sons were also engaged in conspiratorial activity together. Major John Manley and his son, Izaack, as well as Major Abraham Holmes and his son, Blake, joined Monmouth in 1685. While both Manleys escaped, Blake Holmes was killed in battle during the rebellion, and Abraham was captured and executed.[74]

The contribution of women in radical politics—most often the wives, sisters, and daughters of Whig conspirators—is difficult to gage since the deeds of women are often missing from the sources. There were a few extraordinary women who, by virtue of their class, are present in the records. The most conspicuous example is the Lady Rachel Russell. Her recent biographer, Lois Schwoerer, has demonstrated the extent to which she defended her husband during his treason trial in 1683, and her efforts to establish a cult of his martyrdom after his execution. She also helped to maintain the Whig propagandist, the Reverend Samuel Johnson, and saw that Johnson was rewarded after the Revolution.[75]

Even more active in radical politics and religion, although less well known, was Mary Speke of White Lackington. She seems to have been the driving force within her family, behind the involvement of her husband, sons, and daughters in Whig activities. Mary kept a Presbyterian conventicle at White Lackington and was known for frequenting

71. *State Trials*, 9:351–491, passim; BL, Add. 6,845, fol. 274; Greaves, *Secrets of the Kingdom*, passim.

72. *BDBR*, s.v. "Richard Rumbold." William Rumbold was implicated in the Rye House Plot by James Holloway (see *State Trials*, 10:23). On his activities in Holland and his support of Monmouth's Rebellion, see BL, Add. 41,810, fol. 59, and Wade's Confession, BL, Harl. 6,845, fol. 270.

73. BL, Add. 35,508, fol. 74; Fountainhall, *Chronological Notes*, 64.

74. *BDBR*, s.v. "Manley, John." Manley and his son were spotted in the Hague after the rebellion (see BL, Add. 41,818, fol. 200). On Abraham Holmes and his son, see Roberts, 253, 262, and the articles on Abraham in the *DNB* and *BDBR*.

75. Schwoerer, *Lady Rachel Russell: One of the Best Women* (Baltimore: Johns Hopkins University Press, 1988), passim.

Dissenting meetings throughout Somerset with her children in tow.[76]
Her movements were closely watched by the bishop of Bath and Wells,
Peter Mews, who warned Secretary Jenkins in 1683, when Mary visited
London that, "there is not a more dangerous women in the west than
she, and what her sons are I need not tell you." "I need give you no
character of their family," Mews wrote later, "I suppose it is well known
how actively of late years they have all appeared against his Majesty's
interest, especially the mother and the son, Hugh. . . . It is a wonder that
Whitelackington house is not searched by particular order, not only for
arms but papers for the lady keeps great correspondence, and her
son-in-law, Trenchard, is her darling."[77] Mary's eldest son, John, and her
son-in-law, John Trenchard, spent most of James II's reign in exile, living
among other radicals and Dissenters in Holland. Her second son,
Hugh, landed in prison in 1684, for his Whig activities, described in
Chapter 5; and her youngest son, Charles, was a victim of Judge
Jeffreys's "bloody assizes" in the west following Monmouth's Rebellion.
For their support of Monmouth, Mary, her husband, George, and her
daughter Mary Jennings were all excepted from James II's General
Pardon of March 1686.[78]

Mary Speke disappears from the records after the Revolution. Her
position as the wife and mother of a gentry family gave her a certain
amount of influence and standing in Somerset. Certainly the aristocrat
Lady Russell had power, money, and influence at her disposal, and
women like the publisher Jane Curtis had the press. But most of the
wives and widows of Whig radicals played far less conspicuous roles in
the promotion of the Protestant cause. The records give us only
glimpses of these women, usually after their husband's activities have
been discovered. The wife was a fellow sufferer in her husband's
captivity, a supplicant for his life or a mourner at his execution. Sarah
Hampden and Phillipa Trenchard both stayed with their husbands,
John Hampden and John Trenchard, while they were held as close

76. *Original Records of Early Nonconformity Under Persecution and Indulgence*, 3 vols., ed. G.
Lyon Turner (London, 1911), 2:111–12,1:7; Emanuel Green, *The March of William of Orange
through Somerset and a notice of other local events in the time of James II* (London, 1882), 53.

77. PRO SP 29/427, part 1, fol. 20; PRO SP 29/429, fol. 178. John Trenchard of Bloxworth
married Phillipa Speke. He was a Green Ribbonite, an active supporter of the Exclusion Bill,
and a participant in the Rye House Plot.

78. Hugh Speke is discussed in Chapter 4. James II's General Pardon is printed in Roberts,
2:258–60.

prisoners in the Tower following their arrests in July 1683.[79] Phillipa Trenchard followed John to Amsterdam as did the wives of many other radicals, both high and low.[80] Daughters and sisters also suffered with their fathers and brothers. Sir Thomas Armstrong's daughter, Jane Matthews, attended him at his trial at King's Bench Court on June 14, 1684. Despite his daughter's desperate pleas, Armstrong was sentenced by Judge Jeffreys to death for outlawry. Jane and her mother, Katherine Armstrong, later appealed to Jeffreys and Lord Keeper Francis North but to no avail.[81] Hannah Hewling, the sister of Monmouth rebels William and Benjamin Hewling, pleaded with James II to spare her brothers after their capture. Both were executed. Hannah, however, was able to save them from the quartering and give them Christian burials.[82] She later married the grandson of Oliver Cromwell.

Not all of the women who assisted the plotters and propagandists of the 1680s were kin. One Mrs. Lee, a friend of Titus Oates who was known to authorities as a "pernicious woman," gave the money that enabled William Disney to print the duke of Monmouth's manifesto in 1685. Mrs. Lee was also believed to have given Whig lawyer Laurence Braddon money in his quest to bring out the truth of the earl of Essex's "murder" in the Tower in 1683.[83] Elizabeth Gaunt of London was burned alive at Tyburn in 1685, for harboring a Monmouth rebel. Elizabeth and her husband, William, were Anabaptists and were deeply involved in London Whig politics, escorting dissidents back and forth between London and Amsterdam. In Amsterdam their contact was one Mrs. Smith, a wealthy English widow living in Amsterdam.[84] She not only lodged Scottish and English conspirators but funded both Monmouth's and Argyle's rebellions.[85]

Conspiratorial politics, then, was the work of a diverse group of com-

---

79. No small sacrifice considering that "close" prisoners were shackled arms and legs (*CSPD*, 25:16, 25, 189, 220, 249; BL, Add. 41,804, fol. 78).

80. BL, Add. 41,817, fols. 237–38.

81. *DNB*, s.v. "Sir Thomas Armstrong"; *State Trials*, 9:993–94. Another Armstrong daughter was beaten by his guard when she tried to approach her father to receive his blessing.

82. Roberts, 205–9.

83. BL, Add. 41,804, fol. 26.

84. Parry, *The Bloody Assizes*, 267–69, 279; BL, Add. 41,817, fols. 219, 225.

85. Mrs. Smith's husband was a rich sugar baker and a friend of Whig conspirator Abraham Holmes, who in turn was connected to the earl of Argyle. The Smiths probably left England for religious reasons. See Greaves, *Secrets of the Kingdom*, 105; BL, Add. 41,817, fols. 219, 225, 237; and Cranston, *John Locke*, 151–52.

mitted men and women, tied to one another by their struggle to achieve a Protestant succession. The Whig network contained a cross section of London's social hierarchy: lords, gentlemen, lawyers, merchants, preachers, booksellers, soldiers, and artisans—they intermingled, shared services, and together promoted a Whig agenda. They had their own coffeehouses and taverns, newspapers, newsletters, and bookstores. They had their own clubs and public feasts as well as their own pamphleteers, poets, and playwrights to supple them with songs, satire, plays, and most important the ideological underpinnings of their cause.

In the late 1670s and early 1680s, these cultures, royalist and Whig, could still afford to be relatively fluid. Exchange and dialogue between the court and its supporters, and the Whigs and theirs, was still more characteristic of this time than any sort of strict dividing line between the two. Whigs and Tories could still frequent each other's taverns and enjoy each other's plays. But as the tension of the times increased and the tenor of propaganda reached new heights, particularly following the dissolution of the Oxford Parliament and the royalist backlash against the City, these divisions sharpened. Resistance and force became realistic options to those Whigs who feared England's future under a Catholic monarch. Radical ideology formed in this increasingly divisive atmosphere.

2

Resisting the Future:
Secularism and the Debate over Exclusion

Then Johnson wrote his Patron's Creed
A Doctrine straight from Hell
'Twas Christian-like to disobey
And Gospell to Rebell
—"New Narrative of the Old Plot" (1683)[1]

On July 21, 1683, William, Lord Russell was beheaded at Lincoln's-Inn-Fields. His crime was high treason for conspiring against the life of the king. On that same summer's day in Oxford, the university decreed that certain "pernicious books and damnable doctrines destructive to the sacred persons of princes" should be burned.[2] Most of the books committed to the flames on that day were products of the civil war era and earlier. Only two, Thomas Hunt's *Mr. Hunt's Postscript for rectifying some mistakes in some of the Inferior Clergy* (1682) and the Reverend Samuel Johnson's *Julian the Apostate* (1682), were written during the Exclusion Crisis.

In the minds of contemporaries, the burning of Hunt's and Johnson's

---

1. "A New Narrative to an Old Plot" was handwritten on the back of another satiric poem, *The Newcastle Associators* (1683), Verney Cambridge Collection, Sel. 2, 120.

2. *The Judgement and Decree of the University of Oxford, pass'd in their Convocation, July 21, 1683, against certain Pernicious Books and Damnable Doctrines, Destructive to the Sacred Persons of Princes, their State and Government, and of all Human Society* (1683).

dangerous doctrines and the execution of Lord Russell for his alleged role in the Rye House Plot were by no means unrelated events. Royalists claimed that the ideas of Hunt and Johnson—both of whom defended the right of resistance—had inspired and justified the kind of conspiratorial politics that led to the assassination and insurrection designs of 1682–83. The Tory press vilified the Whig lawyer Hunt for sowing the seeds of sedition by reviving those "damnable doctrines" that had led to the tragedy of the civil war. Hunt's "managed mongrel" was none other than Lord Russell's chaplain, the Anglican cleric Samuel Johnson, who was responsible for first poisoning that "unfortunate gentleman [Russell] with that seditious maxim" that vindicates rebellion against princes.[3] "Julian [Johnson's nickname] and Hunt make that which the government calls rebellion," Roger L'Estrange blasted, "consistent with our laws, liberties and religion." "I look upon *Julian* [*the Apostate*]," L'Estrange continued, "with a respect to this conspiracy only as the rule to the example."[4]

The scholars and clerics at Oxford University who burned the *Postscript* and *Julian the Apostate* apparently agreed with L'Estrange and other court supporters that "this Huntscrapt" and "Julian [were] at the bottom on't."[5] "Yesterday, the whole university met in convocation," Oxford's vice-chancellor wrote to Secretary Jenkins, "where the principles and positions thought to have given rise to, produced, and carried on the late most horrid conspiracy were by unanimous consent censured and condemned."[6] While the Exclusion debate generated nearly two hundred titles for and against prohibiting the duke of York from the royal succession, the authorities at Oxford chose only these two contemporary tracts to be immolated alongside the works of Buchanan, Hunton, Milton, and Hobbes.[7] That the works of Hunt and

3. Edward Pelling, *The Apostate Protestant* (1682), 39; John Northleigh, *Remarks upon the Most Eminent of our Late Antimonarchical Authors and their Writings* (1685), 410; Roger L'Estrange, *Considerations Upon a Sheet entitled the Speech of the Late Lord Russell* (1683), 52.

4. *Considerations*, 22, 52.

5. Edward Rawlins, *Heraclitus Ridens: Or, a Discourse between Jest and Earnest*, 1681–1682, 2 vols. (1713), 1:127; L'Estrange, preface to *Considerations*.

6. Dr. John Lloyd, vice-chancellor, to Secretary Jenkins, July 22, 1683, *CSPD*, 25:185.

7. The figure of two hundred comes from O.W. Furley, "The Whig Exclusionists: Pamphlet Literature in the Exclusion Campaign, 1679–1681," *CHJ* 13 (1957). Jonathan Scott has noted that the Verney Collection of Popish Plot and Tory Reaction pamphlets at Cambridge University Library contains fewer than thirty tracts on the Succession or Exclusion Crisis. This collection, however, is not representative of the total press output between 1679 and 1683.

Johnson were singled out attests to the power of their poison. The public spectacle of their burning and that of Lord Russell's execution made a powerful impression on the minds of contemporaries and reminds us that the words and deeds of the radical Whig network were closely linked.

Russell's execution in 1683 also reminds us just how desperate and just how radical the politics of Whig leaders became in their effort to resist the future—a future in which they believed popery would be reestablished, Protestantism annihilated, and French-style absolutism introduced; a future in which an Englishman's life, liberty, and property would all be subject to the precarious whims of an untrammeled tyrant. This future stared back at them in the face of James, duke of York. Prior to the plotting of 1682 and 1683, Whig leaders, activists, and ideologues still hoped that words could convince, and even change the course of the future, through peaceful means.

Thomas Hunt

We know very little about the life of Thomas Hunt; much of the scanty information that is available about him comes from hostile sources. Hunt was born in London and educated at Cambridge, where he was a fellow at Queen's College. According to Anthony Wood, "he was esteemed a person of quick parts and of ready discourse, but withal too pert and forward." Hunt entered Gray's Inn in 1650, and became proficient in municipal law. From 1660 to 1683, he practiced law in Banbury and worked as a steward for the estates of the dukes of Buckingham and Norfolk.[8]

Betty Behrens was correct when she asserted that the production of pamphlet literature for the period between 1678 and 1683 was "so enormous" that it had no parallel except for the civil war era. Nor was she referring simply to tracts dealing with the earl of Danby and arbitrary government as Scott asserts, but rather with the entire constitutional debate that arose around the Exclusion Crisis. Scott, *Algernon Sidney and the Restoration Crisis*, 21; Behrens, "The Whig Theory of the Constitution in the Reign of Charles II," *CHJ* 7 (1941), 45–46. J. G. A Pocock has also questioned Scott's "counting" of pamphlet literature. See his critique of Scott in "England's Cato," 923.

8. Anthony Wood, *Athenae Oxonienses*, 2 vols. (1721), 2:728; *BDBR* and *DNB*, s.v. "Hunt, Thomas."

Hunt began his polemical career in 1679, but not in the service of the Whig opposition. His first contributions to party polemic concerned a controversy sparked by the downfall of Charles II's lord treasurer, Thomas Osborne, the earl of Danby, and the king's effort to pardon his long-time minister. In 1678, just before it was abruptly dissolved, the Cavalier Parliament had begun impeachment proceedings against Danby over his secret negotiations with the French. Danby's assertion of kingly prerogative, his efforts to build a "court party" within Parliament, and his strict enforcement of the penal laws against Dissenters had long incurred the wrath of the growing opposition. The earl of Shaftesbury pushed to continue the proceedings at the Parliament of 1679, but in March, Charles II announced that he had granted Danby a full pardon, which he hoped would save his minister and end the controversy.[9]

Instead it raised constitutional issues. Since impeachment proceedings had already begun, the king's pardon was seen as interfering with the judicial powers of Parliament. On the other hand, if Parliament ignored the pardon and pursued the prosecution of Danby, one of the king's prerogatives (the right to pardon) was jeopardized. In the Commons the opposition to Danby was fierce. A day after the king's announcement, Algernon Sidney wrote, "The King's pardon is found defective in every point . . . the House of Commons doth not acknowledge that it could exempt one impeached by them from being brought to justice."[10] The Commons voted the pardon illegal and passed a bill of attainder against Danby.

After much debate, the Lords decided to vote upon the Commons' bill of attainder. The Whig opposition led by the earls of Shaftesbury, Essex, and Denzil, Lord Holles, struggled to see the king's pardon fail and the bill pass. Their strategy was to remove the bishops, who were strong defenders of Danby and the kingly prerogative, from the vote. Shaftesbury argued that since a man's life was in balance, the bishops should withdraw from the vote. Historically, he asserted, the Lords Spiritual could not vote in capital cases. If the bishops withdrew from the proceedings, the Whigs hoped to have enough support to throw out Charles's pardon and agree upon a bill of attainder. Six bishops with-

9. Andrew Browning, "Parties and Party Organization in the Reign of Charles II," *TRHS*, 4th ser., 30 (1948): 21–36; Henry Horwitz, "Protestant Reconciliation During the Exclusion Crisis," *Journal of Ecclesiastical History* 15 (1964): 202; BL, Add. 28,046, fols. 30–31v.

10. Sidney's letter of March 23, 1678–79, in *Original Letters of John Locke, Algernon Sidney, and Anthony, Lord Shaftesbury*, ed. T. Forster (London, 1847), 11.

drew; seven remained to vote against the bill. It passed by a narrow margin.[11]

Danby was committed to the Tower, where he languished for the next five years. Though he was out of sight, the controversy raised in the House of Lords over the bishops' rights in Parliament continued to provoke a heated discussion in the press. There the debate took the form of a quest into the history of Parliament and the presence of the bishops during proceedings for capital offenses.[12] Thomas Hunt published one of the first pamphlets on the subject in 1679, followed by three more over the next three years, all of which argued in favor of the bishops' rights.[13] This was a curious beginning for one of the leading Whig ideologues of the early 1680s. In 1679, Hunt even attacked the Whigs and Dissenters: "'Tis not unknown to any in our English Israel that there are yet here amongst us some remainders of the men of '42 and that the disease sticks close to them."[14]

Hunt never repudiated his pro-bishops argument. He continued to assert their rights even after he began writing for the Whigs. But sometime in 1680, he changed his mind about the powers and sanctified nature of kingship; and about the "fanatical party," which he had once believed would "throw down episcopacy" and lay their "wicked hands in His [Charles II's] most sacred blood."[15] Royalists charged that Hunt's conversion to the opposition came in 1681, when he published yet another pro-bishops piece that pleased Charles II so much that he

11. Haley, *Shaftesbury*, 509–10; Bodleian, Carte 81, fols. 561–68; Andrew Browning, *Thomas Osborne, Earl of Danby, and Duke of Leeds, 1632–1712*, 3 vols. (Glasgow: Jackson, Son & Co., 1951), 1:336; Burnet, 2:216–19; Mark Goldie, "Danby, the Bishops, and the Whigs," in Tim Harris, Paul Seaward, and Mark Goldie, eds., *The Politics of Religion in Restoration England* (Oxford: Basil Blackwell, 1990), 90–91.

12. In addition to Hunt's contributions to the debate cited in note 13 of this chapter, see Thomas Barlow, *A Discourse of the Peerage and Jurisdiction of the Lords Spiritual in Parliament* (1679); Edward Stillingfleet, *The Grand Question concerning the Bishops Right to Vote in Parliament in Capital Cases* (1680); and Henry Briggs, *Considerations touching that question, whether prelates have the right to sit among the Lords and vote with them in Parliament in capital cases* (1682).

13. *The Honours of the Lords Spiritual Asserted* (1679); *The Rights of the Bishops to Judge in Capital Cases in Parliament Cleared* (1680). Hunt republished these two tracts in a single volume, *Two Books in Defense of the Bishops Voting in Capital Cases in Parliament*, in 1680. In 1682, he published *An Argument for the Bishops Right in Judging Capital Cases*, which came out in a second edition the same year with Hunt's famous "postscript" attached. The same year, he also published *An Apology for the Government of England . . . Upon a Question of the Bishops Right of Judging Capital Cases*, which was later reprinted in 1686.

14. *The Honours*, "To the Reader."

15. *The Honours*, "To the Reader."

nominated Hunt for the position of lord chief baron of the exchequer in Ireland. The duke of York, however, intervened and Hunt lost the position.[16] In bitterness, so the story goes, Hunt reissued the same 1681 pro-bishops tract a second time, adding a "postscript" for "rectifying some mistakes that are mischievous and dangerous to our government and religion." Those mistakes, according to Hunt, were such absurd notions as the divine right of kings and an unalterable hereditary succession that were preached and propagated by the "utterly ignorant" lower clergy. This was his revenge upon the duke of York and his clerical supporters.[17]

The royalist story of Hunt's disappointment, a tale of sour grapes leading to his conversion to the Whig cause, was spurious. For reasons that remain mysterious, Hunt had already had a change of heart, and, in fact, though this was not immediately apparent to royalists, he had begun writing in support of the Exclusion Bill in 1680. That year he published a powerful and sophisticated argument in favor of excluding the Catholic duke of York from the throne entitled, *Great and Weighty Considerations Relating to the Duke of York or the Succession of the Crown . . . Considered.*[18] Yet, it was Hunt's celebrated "postscript" that made him infamous as a hero to the Whigs and that earned him the nickname, "Postscript Hunt." Riding a wave of success, Hunt made no effort to hide his authorship of the tract, reissuing it separately in 1682 as *Mr. Hunt's Postscript.*

The power of Hunt's arguments was immediately apparent to his court supporters; five hostile replies to the *Postscript* were published between 1682 and 1685.[19] In addition, Roger L'Estrange vigorously attacked Hunt and the *Postscript* in his weekly, the *Observator.* Hunt

16. This story was probably created by Roger L'Estrange. See his *Lawyer Outlaw'd, Or A Brief Answer to Mr. Hunt's Defense of the Charter* (1683), 1; and *Observator,* no. 276 (January 22, 1682); also see Northleigh, *Remarks upon the Most Eminent,* 351. Wood repeated the story in *Athenae Oxonienses,* 2:728, and it appears in the *DNB* and the *BDBR.*

17. *Mr Hunt's Postscript for rectifying some mistakes in some of the inferior clergy* (1682), 2d ed., 50, and preface. The postscript was originally published as part of *An Argument for the Bishops Rights in Judging Capital Cases.* Though the only surviving versions of *An Argument for the Bishops Rights* with the postscript attached are dated 1682, the tract was first published in 1681. It is advertised in Richard Janeways's *Impartial Protestant Mercury,* no. 66 (December 6–9, 1681), and the *London Gazette,* no. 80 (December 1681).

18. *Great and Weighty Considerations* (1680) was also reprinted by Hunt in 1682 and 1686.

19. Walter Williams, *An Answer to Sundry Matters contained in Mr. Hunt's Postscript* (1682); Thomas Long, *A Vindication of the Primitive Christians . . . with an Appendix being a more full and distinct Answer to Mr. Hunt's Preface and Postscript* (1683); William Assherton, *The Royal Apology*

"philosophizes upon . . . the mysteries of state," wrote L'Estrange, "throws off [royalist apologists] Sir Rob.[ert] Filmer and Dr. Brady with as much contempt and indignation as a gamebull would do a couple of whelps . . . He casts off the D.[uke] of Y.[ork], settles the succession . . . Smiles upon the clergy with one side of his mouth and shews his teeth at them on the other." Not satisfied with assailing Hunt in public alone, L'Estrange wrote to Secretary Leoline Jenkins, informing him that the *Postscript* was "one of the most scandalous libels against the royal family, the succession, the clergy, the King's interest and party that has yet come out." The Tory Walter Williams described it as "a mere heap of confused, scandalous rubbish," which he then went on to refute point by detailed point.[20]

Hunt not only became a major defender of Whig politics in the early 1680s, he also became active in Whig circles. He frequented Whig taverns and lodgings, including the residence of the notorious Titus Oates, architect of the Popish Plot, and was on friendly terms with Whig historian William Petyt and with the Reverend Samuel Johnson.[21] He also softened his stance toward Dissenters and argued for comprehension. He asserted that England's peace and security were at stake so long as Protestants remained divided over what were often trivial, indifferent issues. "Peace in the Church is better than precise and nice orthodoxes," wrote Hunt, "Union is to be preferred before unnecessary truth." In 1683, officials reported that Hunt, "a dangerous fellow," kept a great correspondence with many "strong fanatics." They also believed that "several traitorous persons were haboured" at his house.[22]

In January 1683, Hunt promoted another Whig cause and established himself as the champion of the City of London's liberties with the publication of a fierce, impassioned diatribe against the court's quo

---

(1684) (see "the parallel" in the conclusion); Edward Pelling, *The Apostate Protestant* (1685); John Northleigh, *Remarks upon the Most Eminent* (1685).

20. *Observator,* no. 80 (December 14, 1681); *CSPD,* 22:627; and Williams, preface to *An Answer to Sundry Matters,* for the quotations.

21. According to his own admission, Hunt met London Whig leader Sir William Waller at the Dog Tavern (*State Trials,* 8:364). His name also appears on a list of Whigs who frequently visited Titus Oates. See William Smith, *Intrigues of the Popish Plot Laid Open* (1685), 29. William Petyt supplied Hunt with historical documents for his tract defending London's City charter; see Weston and Greenberg, *Subjects and Sovereigns,* 199. The relationship between Hunt and Johnson is discussed below.

22. *Mr. Hunt's Postscript,* 91; *CSPD,* 25:242.

warranto proceedings that threatened to take away London's City charter. Hunt's *Defense of the Charter* lashed out against the duke of York and his papist minions. Once the popish successor became king, Hunt asserted, the governments of all the once corporate towns, whose charters were lost, would be put into the hands of the papists. Their ultimate aim was nothing less than the extirpation of the Protestant religion.[23] Hunt's *Defense of the Charter* earned him further notoriety. Whigs celebrated it and royalists set out to refute it.[24]

Hunt's *Defense of the Charter* also contained an attack on the playwrights John Dryden and Nathaniel Lee. Hunt claimed that their play, *The Duke of Guise* (1682),[25] was a political parallel, wherein the character of the duke of Guise, portrayed as "a turbulent, wicked, and haughty courtier," represented the champion of the Protestant cause, the duke of Monmouth. But Monmouth, asserted Hunt, was really an "innocent and gentle Prince as well as brave and renowned for noble achievements; a Prince that hath no fault, but that he is the King's son, and the best too of all his sons." Dryden and Lee's play, Hunt claimed, "encouraged" the assassination of Monmouth.[26] Dryden, a royalist, published a response in defense, declaring that while "there was no parallel intended," his play did present a "glass, which has showed them [the Whigs] their own faces." The lawyer Hunt, quipped Dryden, must certainly be "cracked and if he should return to England . . . his only prison might be bedlam."[27]

Indeed, Hunt had left England. On January 15, 1683, only two days after his *Defense of the Charter* was registered at the stationer's office, all copies of it were confiscated from Hunt's publisher, Richard Baldwin. By

23. *A Defense of the Charter and the Municipal Rights of the City of London* (1683), 5–6. The battle over the City charter is described in Chapter 4.

24. See, for example, L'Estrange, *The Lawyer Outlaw'd* (1683).

25. *The Duke of Guise* (1683) was the work of both John Dryden and Nathaniel Leed, though it was Dryden that Hunt attacked. Hunt was not alone in believing that the play was meant as a political parallel. The Whig playwright Thomas Shadwell argued along similar lines in *Some Reflections upon the Pretended Parallel in the Play called the Duke of Guise* (1683).

26. *A Defense of the Charter,* 27. About Dryden, Hunt wrote, "His province is to corrupt the manners of the nation and lay waste their morals, his understanding is clapt, and his brains vitiated, and he is the rot of the age" (30).

27. *The Vindication; or, the Parallel of the French Holy-League and the English League and Convenant turn'd into a Seditious kibell against the King and His Royal Highness by Thomas Hunt* (1683), 14, 42. For a discussion of *The Duke of Guise* in its political context, see Harth, *Pen for a Party,* 188–205.

January 31, Hunt had absconded to Holland.[28] He had made the right decision. In April, a warrant was issued for Hunt's arrest for seditious libel concerning his *Defense of the Charter*. His house was searched for further culpable evidence. A second warrant was issued in August (this time for the *Postscript*) and his house searched again. A year later, L'Estrange was convinced that Hunt was in some way involved in the Rye House conspiracy and wrote to Secretary Jenkins to that effect: "beyond dispute Hunt is privy to the conspiracy."[29]

In Holland, Hunt took the alias "Mr. Briggs" and was known to associate with Rye House conspirators, future Monmouth rebels, and the equally notorious Whig scribbler, Robert Ferguson.[30] He seems to have made a trip incognito to England in the spring of 1686. One of the English envoy's spies reported that, "Mr. Hunt, a lawyer . . . inclinable to their own party . . . is gone to England." His mission was to gather information about James II's General Pardon for those participants in the failed Monmouth's Rebellion living in the United Provinces. Hunt was to determine whether "this pardon was chiefly intended for them and their like." Nothing more is known of Hunt's activities in Holland other than a report that he had visited Germany with the City Whig Slingsby Bethel.[31] He died in Utrecht in 1688, only a few weeks short of the prince of Orange's invasion.

Hunt's Assault on Filmer

Hunt's polemical career was as explosive as it was short. While his output was small in comparison with the other major Whig ideologues of the 1680s examined in this study, his two tracts on the Exclusion debate, *Great and Weighty Considerations* and the *Postscript*, had a powerful impact on the development of Whig thinking in the late seventeenth century. His concept of the secular origins of government, his stance on the right

---

28. *A Transcript of the Registers of the Worshipful Company of Stationers from 1640–1708* (London, 1913) 3 vols. 3:19; *CSPD*, 24:17; Luttrell, 1:247. Edward Warcup "delivered Baldwyn's information against Hunt about the defense of the citty charter" to Secretary Jenkins on January 18, 1683 (*Diaries of the Popish Plot*, 118).

29. *Observator*, no. 328 (April 27, 1683); *CSPD*, 25:242; 26:219.

30. BL, Add. 41,817, fol. 265; 41,818, fol. 17; 41,820, fol. 87.

31. BL, Add. 41,804, fol. 158; 41,819. fol. 272.

of resistance, his thoughts on toleration, and his rebuttals to Filmerian principles—all became standard arguments in the political discourse of the first Whigs. Some of Hunt's ideas took directions more radical than the other Whig theorists were willing to follow. In the final outcome, the Whigs' historicist vision of government was not built on Hunt's rationalism. Yet Hunt's secularism laid the groundwork for the Whig thinkers who followed, and his assault on Filmer also served early Whig ideology as a wrecking ball—a destroyer of primary royalist principles.

Though Hunt had begun his polemical career as a defender of the upper clergy, his *Postscript* launched a fierce attack on the lower clergy. Hunt asserted that its purpose was to expose the fallacies so often disseminated from the pulpits of the parish divines. The lower clergy, he explained, were corrupted by the very popish principles that had started the civil wars. The preservation of the church, the nation, and "the rights of the people" were once again at stake. Like "apes and parrots," these young churchmen "were perpetually repeating" the destructive tenets that had torn the nation asunder in the late troubles.[32]

Those destructive tenets, now being revived and spread by an ignorant clergy, were the basic pillars of royalist ideology in the 1680s. The divine appointment of kings, an unalterable hereditary succession, and the obligation of subjects to obey their sovereigns in all things—these were the positions clung to and reiterated in royalist polemic and high Anglican sermons. They were extreme positions, taken up by royalists in response to the Whig propaganda offensive that had begun in the late 1670s, particularly Whig efforts to bar the duke of York from the royal succession. The Exclusion Bill represented the negation of all these principles. Charles II so hotly opposed it that to pursue its passage was to openly defy the will of the king, an act of rebellion in and of itself. Moreover, excluding the duke of York would mean human intervention into that which royalists claimed was divinely ordained. Even if the reign of James were to result in the worst tyranny and suffering imaginable, so supporters of passive obedience asserted, the people would have no recourse but to suffer in silence, weep, and pray.

Divine-right kingship and passive obedience were certainly not the inventions of Restoration courtiers and clerics. As Hunt was well aware, such notions had been promoted and challenged throughout the first

32. Preface to *Mr. Hunt's Postscript.*

half of the century.[33] But the Whig promotion of the Exclusion Bill in both Parliament and print, together with the so-called "Protestant plots" against the government, both real and imagined, made the court's defenders believe that the propagation of these principles was urgent and essential to the survival of the monarchy and to the prevention of another civil war. They were greatly assisted in their task by the republication of the books of the staunch royalist Sir Robert Filmer, as well as his previously unpublished manuscript, *Patriarcha*, in 1680.

Patriarcha was the longest and strongest statement of Filmer's patriarchalist political thinking.[34] It was an essay on the origins of government according to Scripture and a description of a divinely devised, indivisible, omnipotent sovereignty. Filmer was heavily indebted to the work of the French lawyer and scholar Jean Bodin, whose *Six Livres de la Republique* (1576) was translated into English in 1606. Like Bodin, Filmer posited a concept of absolute and irresistible sovereignty and, like Bodin, Filmer saw the power to create law as the hallmark of sovereignty.[35] Yet Bodin's sovereign had limitations that Filmer's did not. For Bodin, the sovereign could not interfere in the family unit or arbitrarily assert authority over private property; nor could Bodin's sovereign tax at will. Filmer's "omnicompetent" sovereignty, on the other hand, was "unrestricted, unlimited, unbound, from which there is no appeal and within which there is a radical simplicity, an undiluted singleness of will." Undoubtedly, it was this "radical simplicity" of Filmerian sovereignty that made it so appealing in the 1680s.[36]

Filmer's theories were also appealing because they were based on a biblical theory of the origins of government. According to the Book of Genesis, God made the first man, Adam, monarch of all the earth. All those who came after him, his wife and his children, were born unfree, unequal, and under Adam's absolute dominion. By the right of primogeniture, Adam's descendants inherited his power. Absolute monarchy with a lineal succession, then, was the universal model set up for mankind by God. Monarchy was the only government divinely or-

---

33. J. P. Sommerville, *Politics and Ideology in England, 1603–1640* (New York: Longman, 1986), 9–50.

34. J. P. Sommerville, introduction to Robert Filmer, *Patriarcha and Other Writings* (Cambridge: Cambridge University Press, 1991), ix.

35. Sommerville, introduction to *Patriarcha*, xvi–xvii; James Daly, *Sir Robert Filmer and English Political Thought* (Toronto: University of Toronto Press, 1979), 20–23.

36. Daly, *Filmer*, 20–23, 13.

dained, instituted by God himself. Filmer also equated sovereignty with fatherly authority. As fathers have absolute authority within the family, so kings have patriarchal power over their subjects; and as kings hold the power of life and death over their subjects, so fathers may dispose of disobedient children howsoever they choose.[37]

In Filmer's own lifetime, patriarchal ideas were commonplace. James I's *True Law of Free Monarchies* (1603), which Filmer often quoted, used the family-state analogy and proclaimed that kings were accountable to God alone; this view was also held by the midcentury clergymen Lancelot Andrews and Thomas Jackson, who also espoused patriarchalist ideas.[38] But in the era of the Exclusion controversy, nowhere was patriarchalism more cogently and forcefully argued than in Filmer's *Patriarcha*. Filmer's principles epitomized royalism in the 1680s, and as Gordon Schochet writes, "The Filmerian position very nearly became the official state ideology"—or more appropriately, the official court ideology.[39]

Hence it was Filmer whom Hunt and other Whig exclusionists had to answer. When Hunt attacked the Anglican clergy, he did so for their mimicry of Filmerian ideas—which were not only false—"there are no footsteps in the records of the Old Testament to verify his hypothesis"—but also exceedingly dangerous. Hunt struck out against the lower clergy for preaching the absolute authority and divine right of kings from their pulpits. He proclaimed that the propagation of such ideas was "a forerunner to our late unnatural war and is now again revived by the republishing of Sir Robert Filmer's books." By asserting that the basic positions of royalist ideology were responsible for the "parliamentary war," Hunt turned the tables on his opponents, who consistently maintained that ideas such as popular sovereignty and the right of resistance had resulted in the bloodshed and chaos of the civil wars. But Hunt insisted that patriarchalism misled kings as to the true nature of their power and authority. Charles I was deluded by a sycophantic clergy; he abused his powers and hence the parliamentarians were forced to take up arms to defend themselves. For the ideas that caused

---

37. Filmer, *Patriarcha*, 7–20.
38. Sommerville, introduction to *Patriarcha*, xix, xviii.
39. Gordon Schochet, *Patriarchalism and Political Thought* (Oxford: Basil Blackwell, 1975), 193.

so much suffering and bloodshed in the recent past to be reasserted once again was nothing less than treason.[40]

Hunt also asserted, as did many Whigs, that concepts of divine right and passive obedience were popish ideas, and that they led to the kind of arbitrary government that many English identified with France, particularly with the government of Louis XIV, "the personification of absolutism."[41] The papists, Hunt claimed, "have corrupted some of our churchmen with principles that subvert our government and betray the rights of our people." The solution, Hunt proclaimed, was Protestant unity: "Our enemies will be destroyed merely by our uniting."[42]

So powerful were the ideas of these enemies, able to delude kings and courtiers, laymen and clerics, that Hunt, like many Whig polemicists, fought royalist principles through every argument at his disposal, including reason, law, history, and, to a lesser degree, Scripture. Hunt manipulated and exploited English history when it suited his needs. He attached "A Short Historical Collection touching the Succession of the Crown" to his 1680 version of the *Great and Weighty Considerations*, in which he showed that the Crown was the gift of the people bestowed on a king of their choosing and that throughout English history the Crown rarely descended in a lineal succession. The English government was a matter of consent, not divine appointment: "The succession of the crown is the right of the whole community, their appointment, their constitution . . . and [is] alterable."[43]

Hunt often cited, and reprinted in *Great and Weighty*, the act of

---

40. *Mr. Hunt's Postscript*, 59, 35, for the first two quotations; 52–54, on "parliamentary war." Hunt's treatment of the "late unnatural war" was unique. Most Whig polemicists avoided the subject of the civil war. If they mentioned it at all, they almost always condemned it in no uncertain terms, often referring to Charles I as "our Late King of Blessed Memory." The exception was the Reverend Samuel Johnson, who had an irreverent view of nearly everything (see his comment about Charles I in note 72 of this chapter). Hunt condemned the war itself, but he offered a pro-parliamentary explanation of its causes that he presented in a rational, matter-of-fact tone.

41. J. R. Jones, *The First Whigs*, 5.

42. Preface to *Mr. Hunt's Postscript*.

43. *Great and Weighty*, 32. Edward Pelling believed that Hunt had simply plagiarized *A Conference About the Next Succession to the Crown of England*, which was originally published in 1594, by a Jesuit priest, Father Robert Parsons (1546–1610). *A Conference*, published under the pseudonym, R. Doleman, argued that the succession was not divinely ordained. The tract was republished throughout the seventeenth century, appearing in 1681, amid the Exclusion Crisis. Hunt was probably influenced by Parson's tract, but he did not plagiarize it. Pelling, *The Apostate Protestant*, 21.

Parliament, 13 Eliz., I., which determined that it was treason to declare that another person had a right to the Crown within Elizabeth's lifetime, and that the queen and Parliament would ultimately determine the succession. Hunt claimed that it was just as treasonous and dangerous to assert that the duke of York was the next successor in Charles II's lifetime. Not only had Charles's successor not as yet been determined by Parliament, but Hunt as well as other Whigs saw the assumption of James's succession to the throne as tantamount to licensing Charles II's death warrant, since eager papists might expedite the process of crowning James.

Hunt rarely quoted Scripture, but he did find an apt passage for his purposes: "Submit yourselves to every ordinance of man for the Lord's sake: whether it be to the king, as supreme, or unto the governors" (1 Pet. 2:13, 14). Hunt was particularly keen on the phrase, "every ordinance of man." He asserted that this was proof that men create their own governing bodies, or as he explained, "that men make them and give them their powers."[44] Ultimately, however, Hunt's arguments were not built on scriptural or historical arguments. History and Scripture only provided further evidence of what was obvious to man's reason: the natural and rational manner by which government was created and functioned.

Reason then—the way in which men understand God's natural law—was the basis upon which Hunt structured his political ideas. Reason proved that the principles of royalism were not only false, they were irrational, ungodly, and destructive. Rational analysis also showed that government was a secular institution, created by men; that its governors ruled by popular consent; and that should those governors abuse their powers, the people had the right to resist them. The foundation upon which Hunt's rationalist theory of government rested was the simple proposition that "men make governments." This concept that government was a secular creation, not divine, became the cornerstone of early Whig ideology, and Hunt was its most cogent exponent. While God "commands us in our nature to form ourselves into government," God does not (contra-Filmer) command what kind of govern-

---

44. *Mr. Hunt's Postscript*, 37. Naturally, Hunt does not quote the entire passage in his text, simply "the ordinance of man" part, since the command to "submit yourself" would justify passive obedience. It was not uncommon for both Whigs and royalists to omit parts of the sources they cited. The proponents of patriarchy would often cite the Fifth Commandment: "Honor thy father and thy mother," omitting the "mother" part.

ment men should choose.[45] Scripture does not dictate a universal model of government that all societies must follow. While the "Christian religion instituted no form of government," God "hath made governments necessary in the general order of things, but the specification thereof is from men."[46]

Royalists, following Filmer, argued that the monarchical government of the ancient Jews was a divinely conceived and hence a universal form of government to be imitated throughout the world. As the royalist critic of Hunt, Walter Williams claimed, "God's example of governing the particular people, the Jews," should be followed "all the world over."[47] But Hunt declared that the government of the Jews was of their own choosing, and that it was blatantly irrational to posit that the Jewish monarchical government was a universal model. "Nature [the will of God] hath made no laws about property, nor about governments." If it had, would not the governments of all nations be identical? Rather each nation constructs a government best suited to its particular needs: "what is greatly convenient and promotes the happiness of men therefore seems to be commanded and thereby a positive law of God in nature is declared." That "men make governments" is obvious to man's reason and is proven in nature. Hence it is God's will. Clerical dreams of divine-right monarchy misled kings, blindfolded the people, and would ultimately result in England's destruction. The fools from the pulpit, Hunt blasted, "obtrude upon the world their unnatural, monstrous, and incoherent conceptions. And if they chance mix their discourses with passages from Holy Scripture, and thereby entitle religion to their absurdities, they more powerfully amuse, distract and abuse the consciences of the people." The people will "perish by the deceit."[48]

The governments that men create are constructed with the end that they will provide for the people's safety and preservation. They are first formed by "pact and consent and not otherwise." The English people having set the king up in the first place, remain in control of the royal succession. "The succession to the crown is the people's right"; it is of a "civil nature and not established by any divine right." It "belongs to the people to make a new king, under what limitations they please, or to

45. *Great and Weighty*, 8.
46. *Mr. Hunt's Postscript*, 37, 38.
47. *An Answer to Sundry Matters*, 16.
48. *Great and Weighty*, 29, 8, 1.

make none for polity is not destroyed if there is no king created."[49] Hunt believed that the notion of unalterable government, as the court's defenders claimed for the royal succession, was patently absurd. What the people created, they could alter. Moreover, to allow the popish successor to ascend the throne was equivalent to the polity destroying itself and the community along with it. A government's first function was the people's preservation. "Can a government," Hunt asked, "be safe without a power to exclude a person inhabil [sic] in nature to support it, or of one principled to destroy it?" "No government made by men" would be so foolish as to leave their self-preservation "merely to chance and the contingency of birth."[50]

The power to alter the royal succession was invested in Parliament through its "unlimited power of legislative authority." Legislative authority, according to Hunt, was the concern of "three estates" that he defined as the "the Lords Spiritual, Lords Temporal, and the Commons."[51] This was a curious device. The three estates of the English polity were commonly identified after 1642, following Charles I in his "Answer to the Nineteen Propositions," as the king, Lords, and Commons. By this definition, Charles had unwittingly put himself into the arena with the two houses, where he was outnumbered. Parliamentarian theorists seized upon the king's words and made it part of their ideology. After all, Charles's "Answer" described the English constitution as a mixture of these three estates, representing and balancing monarchy, aristocracy, and democracy. When Hunt redefined the three estates as the Lords Temporal, Lords Spiritual, and the Commons, he was actually returning to a more traditional, pre–civil war, vision of the polity, which could be seen as empowering kingship, since the king was set outside and above the three estates, capable of directing or negating their functions. As a champion of the historic rights of the bishops, Hunt was sensitive to a definition that split and weighed evenly the Lords Spiritual and Temporal. He was certainly not interested in elevating kingly power. He placed the king outside the three estates in order to show that the constitution was perfectly capable of operating *without the monarchy.* His was a theory of a mixed government rather than

49. Preface to *Mr. Hunt's Postscript,* 43.
50. *Great and Weighty,* 5.
51. *Mr. Hunt's Postscript,* 43; *Apology,* 121.

a mixed monarchy.[52] Ultimately, insofar as Hunt was concerned, legislative power was located in Parliament alone. He did not deny that the "king in parliament" could make law, but he did deny that the king had any legislative power alone and implied instead that Parliament did. It was within Parliament "our government hath placed the making of laws."[53]

Hunt felt no special reverence for kingship and implied many times that it was quite possible for the people to govern themselves without it. He did believe that within the current English polity, the king had certain duties. The king should provide "a happy and wise administration" and "reduceth his prerogative to the measures of the common right and make the kingdom secure and safe." Hunt believed that Charles II was failing in his responsibility for the people's safety by his insisting upon his brother's right to the succession. And as the king was negligent in his duties, so Parliament must act in the peoples' interest. To this end, "the power of Parliament is unrestrained and unlimited."[54]

Hunt's "parliament unbound" could do anything necessary to preserve "the community and the polity itself." As every man has "a right in nature" to defend himself, so the government has a right to defend itself. "Can we imagine," asked Hunt, "a government of human contrivance to be without a power to preserve itself and an authority, in cases that threaten its ruin, to interpose with remedies for its preservation?"[55] Nor was popular resistance to a government that threatened the community's destruction illegal. "All the authority of all the legislation in the world cannot make unlawful any act that is done in self-preservation." The papists, Hunt wrote, mock us with their tears and prayers and visions of martyrdom, but "we are not bound to suffer."[56]

Hunt's argument that excluding the Catholic duke of York was a matter of survival was not new. Exclusion propaganda claimed again and again that a popish prince was unfit to govern a Protestant nation. Once he ascended the throne, Whigs claimed, James and his papist cronies would proceed to extirpate the reformed religion. But Hunt's power to persuade did not rely—like so much of the Whig literature of

52. Michael Mendle, *Dangerous Positions: Mixed Government, the Estates of the Realm, and the Making of the Answer to the xix Propositions* (University of Alabama Press, 1985), 171–83.

53. *Mr. Hunt's Postscript*, 28–29.

54. *Great and Weighty*, 21, 4.

55. *Great and Weighty*, 5.

56. Preface to *Mr. Hunt's Postscript*.

the Popish Plot and Exclusion era—on frightening images of Smithfield fires or St. Bartholomew-like massacres. Though Hunt often tongue-whipped his enemies, in his writings he neither sought to shock nor to arouse fear and anxiety. His rational analysis of government was forceful, thoughtful, and convincing. He made Whig positions sound logical, a matter of commonsense. Hunt's royalist foes admitted the appeal of his arguments. Walter Williams wrote that on his travels throughout England, he found that "several gentlemen" who "once had no great opinions . . . [about the Exclusion Bill] begin to entertain some favorable thoughts of it, and that which induced them to it, as I was informed, was the powerful arguments they met with in a very ingenious piece (as they termed it) called Mr. Hunt's *Postscript.*" Williams also noted that the *Postscript* was dispersed "in great plenty" "by some new true-Protestants and magnified by them equally with if not above the Scriptures."[57]

Moreover, Hunt's reputation as a defender of the Lords Spiritual and his aloof legalistic tone made his ideas all the more attractive and—to the opposition—dangerous. Not until 1681, when Hunt attached his infamous postscript to his *Argument for the Bishops Rights,* did royalists learn that the "Mr. T.H." who published the pro-exclusion tract, *Great and Weighty Considerations* in 1680, was the same Thomas Hunt of Gray's Inn who so strongly supported the bishops' rights in Parliament. With a sense of astonishment, the Tory divine Edward Pelling wrote, "But of all men living, I wonder at Mr. Hunt, a person whose name I cannot mention without due respect because of his *Argument for the Bishops Rights etc* where he hath shewed a great deal of good learning in the laws, and hath exprest his just zeal for the Church." Pelling could only believe that Hunt wrote his odious postscript as "penance and satisfaction (to a party) for the *Argument* [*for the Bishops Rights*] which he had before written."[58]

In Hunt, the Whigs had found a clever and sophisticated theoretician. His *Postscript* was one of the most influential pieces of exclusionist literature and statements of Whig principles in the early 1680s; other Whig writers acknowledged their debt to Hunt's ideas. It set out a secular understanding of the origins of government that became the basis for early Whig political thinking. Hunt's ideas about active resis-

57. *An Answer to Sundry Matters,* 5.
58. *The Apostate Protestant,* 21.

tance and the ends of government also became stock-in-trade Whig concepts. Certainly, other Whigs were writing feverishly in defense of the Exclusion Bill and, more important for the future of English liberalism, against Filmer's *Patriarcha*. Algernon Sidney and John Locke were both busily preparing detailed responses to Filmer, although neither was published until after the Glorious Revolution. Locke's young friend James Tyrrell did anonymously publish his reply to Filmerian principles, entitled *Patriarcha non Monarcha*. Long and rambling, it did not garner anywhere near the attention of Hunt's work and seems to have influenced only a handful of other Whig writers.[59]

It was Hunt, then, whom Whig politicians, future plotters, and other polemicists were reading; and it was Hunt to whom Anglican and Tory apologists responded; and it was Hunt's book the *Postscript* that scholars and clerics of Oxford threw into the flames in 1683. It was not without good reason that Locke was too timid to publish his ideas amid the heady days of the Exclusion Crisis. Hunt had narrowly escaped trial and most likely a long imprisonment. (His protégé Samuel Johnson was not as fortunate.) There is much about Hunt's political ideas that resembles Locke's. Both saw government as a product of the people's consent and both defended the right of revolution. But more striking is that both wrote predominantly in the language of natural law. Other Whig writers would also employ it; Robert Ferguson mixed natural law idioms with those from history and common law. But over the course of the 1680s, the dominant Whig discourse became ancient constitutionalism. Its proponents learned that this story of the old English past was far more familiar and communicable to a larger audience of readers. Hunt was a maverick. He held no such nostalgic views of English history, nor was he afraid of change and innovation. He had a far more progressive vision of the past and the possibilities of the future than most of his fellow Whig radicals.[60] In the end, they did not dare to fully incorporate Hunt's

---

59. Algernon Sidney, *Discourses Concerning Government*, ed. Thomas G. West (Indianapolis: Liberty Classics, 1990; pub.1698); John Locke, *Two Treatises of Government* (pub.1689); James Tyrrell, *Patriarcha non Monarcha, The Patriarch Unmonarched* (1681).

60. Of all the Whig ideologues of the Exclusion era, Algernon Sidney's vision of history was the closest to Hunt's. In the *Discourses*, Sidney asserted that "time can make nothing lawful or just, that is so of itself . . . therefore in matters of the greatest importance, wise and good men do not so much inquire *what has been*, as what is good and ought to be." Sidney, however, was by no means consistent and often resorted to a discourse based on English history and common law. *Discourses Concerning Government*, Chapter 3: 28.

rationalism into their thinking. Had Locke published his treatises in 1681, or thereabout, their reception and subsequent history might have been similar to the treatment and legacy of Hunt's work—influencing friends, outraging foes, certainly, but tellingly not becoming the predominant argument within early Whig ideology.

The Lawyer and the Divine

Hunt's brief career not only influenced the direction of early Whig thinking, it also had a direct impact on the early work of the Reverend Samuel Johnson. Like Hunt, the champion of the bishops' rights Samuel Johnson, an Anglican divine, was an unlikely proponent of the Whig cause. Overt support for the Whigs among the Anglican establishment was rare, and even more rare among the lower clergy, which radicals like Thomas Hunt, James Tyrrell, and John Locke saw as the most ardent propagators of Filmerian principles. Hence the Reverend Samuel Johnson, who became one of the Whig party's most talented theorists, and a notorious martyr, was truly an odd case.[61]

Johnson entered the political arena in 1679, the year he became the domestic chaplain of William, Lord Russell. Lord Russell was known to value Johnson for his knowledge of the "constitution and laws of this country and for speaking his mind freely." Russell urged Johnson to further studies of "the old English constitution" and introduced him into the Whig network. Johnson was not only acquainted with the aristocratic Whig leadership, such as Russell and the earl of Essex, but with prominent Whigs in the House of Commons, such as Sir William Jones and John Hampden, the younger. He was also friendly with the newest champion of the Exclusion Bill, Thomas Hunt.[62] Lord Russell's encouragement of Johnson's studies, along with Johnson's association

---

61. In his *First Treatise*, Locke attacked Filmer's *Patriarcha* and blamed the lower clergy for spreading its "false principles." Locke's attitude toward the lower clergy was identical to Hunt's. See Mark Goldie, "John Locke and Anglican Royalism," *Political Studies* 31 (1983), 64–66. Some of the material in this section draws on my article "Early Whig Ideology, Ancient Constitutionalism, and the Reverend Samuel Johnson," *JBS* 32 (1993): 139–65.

62. See "Some Memorials," which is prefixed to *The Works of the Late Reverend Samuel Johnson* (1713), iv–xvii, henceforth cited as *Works*. All of Johnson's tracts used in this study are cited from this volume of his writings. Also see Alexander Chalmers, ed., *The General Biographical Dictionary*, 32 vols. (1812), 19:40, and Samuel Knight, *The Life of John Colot, Dean of St. Paul's* (1724), 411.

with other Whig polemicists, paid off in the summer of 1682, when Johnson published his first political tract, *Julian the Apostate*. The tract was literally an overnight sensation. As the Reverend George Hickes observed, "The apostasy of Julian the emperor did not perhaps make a greater noise in the cities of the Roman Empire than did the short account of his life, called *Julian the Apostate*, did in the city of London at its first publication." On the very morning it was available at the bookstores, "two or three gentlemen" told Hickes, "it is an unanswerable piece, it hath undone all your pleas for succession, your passive obedience, and it is written by a Church divine and we thank God that there is one among them who is not enslaving the people."[63]

In *Julian the Apostate*, Johnson drew an elaborate and clever parallel between the fourth-century apostate emperor, Julian, and the popish successor, James, duke of York. The moral of the story was that, as the primitive Christians of the fourth century had openly resisted their pagan emperor, so Englishmen would be justified in opposing a popish prince. The tract aimed at, and for many quite effectively destroyed, stories told and retold by many Anglican priests to their parishioners of the passive suffering patiently endured by the ancient Christians. "Julian Johnson" was praised and celebrated by his fellow Whigs. After all, as one anonymous Whig writer put it, *Julian the Apostate* "had a very favorable entertainment among us, being only history and matter of fact." Johnson became the "oracle of the cause" and his tract was "the pocket-book of all the party, carried to coffee-houses in triumph."[64]

Naturally, such a strong and attractive assault on passive obedience did not go unanswered by the defenders of the church and the monarchy, many of whom found it difficult to accept that *Julian the Apostate* was the work of a cleric. Anglican divine Edward Pelling called it "a monstrous expression and from the pen of a Christian, of a Protestant, of a clergyman!"[65] Royalists also correctly assumed that Johnson had received some help. "The chaplain of the Prince of Whigland [Russell]," wrote one court sympathizer, was undoubtedly employed by "some more than ordinary persons and had somebody also to supervise it."[66] The assistance Johnson received, as he later admitted, came from Sir William Jones and Thomas Hunt—the latter having the strongest

---

63. George Hickes, *Jovian, or an Answer to Julian the Apostate* (1683), 1–2.
64. Preface to *The Account of the Life of Julian the Apostate Vindicated and the Truth of the Assertions therein* (1682); Hickes, *Jovian*, 3.
65. *The Apostate Protestant*, 42.
66. Edward Rawlins, *Heraclitus Ridens*, no. 76 (July 11, 1682), 2:212–16.

influence.[67] "The author of the life of Julian," wrote Thomas Long, a fellow Anglican cleric and critic of Johnson, has "taken his measures and chief materials from the late libels of Mr. Hunt." "These two," Long continued, "are worshipped by the rabble. . . . The one plays with the crown as if it were a tennis ball; the other derides the doctrine of the cross." They are, as another royalist put it, "doctor and student, both agreed on their divinity and law."[68]

The influence of Hunt on *Julian the Apostate* was evident throughout the tract, beginning with the parallel between popery and paganism that Hunt had already made in the *Postscript.* Johnson even quoted Hunt in a passage attacking passive obedience and justifying the right of resistance: "For as a worthy person has lately observed, 'one single arm unresisted, may go a great way in massacring a nation.'"[69] Like Hunt, Johnson maintained that government was a secular creation: "The Scripture does not meddle with the secular government of this world."[70] Nor does it provide a political blueprint or universal model upon which man is to form his governments; for if it did, Johnson asserted, would not all nations without Scripture be without government? A few years later, Johnson quoted the same passage from Scripture that Hunt had earlier used: "Whereas Scripture itself says," Johnson wrote, "that government is the ordinance of man and of human extraction."[71] In the course of Johnson's attack on basic royalist concepts (divine right, passive obedience, hereditary succession), he displayed a wider breadth of knowledge of Scripture and early church history than had Hunt, as might be expected from a clergyman. But what was most surprising from an Anglican divine was the contemptuous and sardonic manner with which Johnson assailed royalist ideology and its proponents. Johnson's irreverence, sarcasm, and biting wit became the hallmarks of his writing.

Mocking the believers of the divine right of kings, Johnson quipped in *Julian the Apostate*, "I know not what measure divine right will serve their turn unless they would have a crown drop from the clouds." The king is not a God, taunted Johnson in a later work, "has He a throne like

---

67. *CSPD*, 25:432. Hunt himself also let it be known that he had "perused it [*Julian the Apostate*] in manuscript." Hickes, *Jovian*, 2.

68. Long, *A Vindication of the Primitive Christians*, 291, preface; Northleigh, *Remarks*, 17.

69. Johnson, *Julian the Apostate*, 32; Hunt, *Mr. Hunt's Postscript*, 45.

70. *Julian the Apostate*, 83.

71. *Of Magistracy* (1689), 153. This tract was written between 1684 and 1688, during Johnson's imprisonment. It may have been printed earlier than 1688, but no copies exist before 1688.

God? Is He of Himself and for Himself?"[72] Johnson also satirized
Filmerian patriarchalism in a similar manner. If the king has "personal
patriarchal authority . . . then it must be proved that the king is the
eldest son of the eldest house of all the families of the earth." Or, if he
has the natural authority of a father to govern his children then it must
be proved that he has begotten his three kingdoms and all the people"
within them.[73] Johnson asserted that the role of God in human affairs
was extremely limited. God did not make or unmake princes. If God
were to interfere in human affairs, he would do so only in a "clear and
distinct" manner: "For I am not bound to what God would have me do,
till I can certainly know how he would have me do it."[74] Attacking
passive obedience, Johnson wrote, "oaths, vows, protestions, appeals to
heaven . . . come to nothing."[75]

Johnson agreed with Hunt that government was instituted through
popular consent, through the "just compacts and agreements which
have been made amongst men." Unlike Hunt, Johnson identified this
agreement with the coronation oath—an identification that would later
became a standard part of early Whig constitutionalism. Johnson's ideas
about the natural right of life and self-defense were similar to Hunt's,
and Johnson also asserted that "all men have both a natural and civil
right and property in their lives, till they have forfeited them by the laws
of their country." Resistance is both just and legal when exercised in the
name of self-defense. Again, in words very similar to those of Hunt,
Johnson claimed that all "illegal force maybe repelled by force."[76]

Yet Johnson was not nearly as clear about the locus of legislative power
and the authority to create law in *Julian the Apostate* as Hunt was in his
pro-exclusion tracts. Johnson backed away from Hunt's radical formu-
lation of the three estates as consisting of the peers, bishops, and
Commons. He seemed to retreat instead to the standard vision of law as
the creation of the "king in his parliament." On the other hand,

---

72. *Julian the Apostate*, 16; *Remarks upon Dr. Sherlock's Book intitled [sic] the Case of Resistance of the Supreme Powers Stated and Resolved* (1689), 241. Johnson later wrote that so much did Charles I insist "that he was accountable only to God, whereupon . . . they [Parliament] sent him to God to give an account" (*An Argument Proving that the Abrogation of King James by the People of England . . . was according to the English Constitution* [1692], 271).

73. *Remarks upon Dr. Sherlock's Book intitled [sic] the Case of Resistance*, 241.

74. *Julian the Apostate*, 83. The only example Johnson gave of a case in which God spoke "clearly and distinctly" is when he told Abraham not to sacrifice his son, Isaac (*An Argument Proving*, 263).

75. *Julian the Apostate*, 60.

76. *Julian the Apostate*, 83, 33, 31.

Johnson praised and celebrated "the law" in *Julian the Apostate*, in a laudatory manner that would become characteristic of his work. The law became for Johnson an immemorial and omnipotent entity. Whereas Hunt had placed his faith in Parliament, Johnson, who did not develop Hunt's sense of mutability and change, made common law the bulwark of English liberties.

Johnson openly boasted that his *Julian the Apostate* was "unanswerable" and challenged anyone to prove his thesis wrong.[77] His challenge was met. Anthony Wood reported that soon after the book's publication, it was "preached against from our pulpits" in Oxford.[78] In 1682, two responses were rushed to the press and in 1683, five more appeared.[79] Johnson himself was busy preparing a long and detailed reply to his critics in the summer of 1683. He was especially concerned to refute the powerful Filmerian arguments set forth by fellow clergyman George Hickes.[80] But once the Rye House Plot trials began, including that of Johnson's patron, Lord Russell, he prudently decided to suppress the already printed copies of his response. Nonetheless, word of Johnson's newest polemic circulated, and he was examined before the Privy Council three times in July 1683. Johnson consistently refused to tell the council the location of the hidden copies of his reply. At one point, he was fined and committed to Gatehouse Prison, though soon after, bail was posted.[81]

77. Hickes, *Jovian*, 2.

78. Anthony Wood noted four sermons in Oxford given against *Julian the Apostate*. *The Life and Times of Anthony Wood, Antiquary of Oxford, 1632–1695, Described by Himself*, 5 vols., ed. Andrew Clark (Oxford, 1891–1900), 3:18–19. Johnson was not completely without clerical supporters, however. James Parkinson, a fellow at Lincoln College, recommended *Julian the Apostate* to all who would listen, and when told that the book was "false as well as dangerous," Parkinson declared that, "If you write against him, I will write for him and answer all you say." He was later expelled from Lincoln College for his antimonarchial principles (*CSPD*, 25:320; *DNB*). Johnson found another friend in Edward Fowler, D. D. Fowler, known for his fiercely antipapist sermons, sent Johnson money during his imprisonment. See Mark Goldie and John Spurr, "Politics and the Restoration Parish: Edward Fowler and the Struggle for St. Giles Cripplegate," *EHR* 109 (1994): 572–96

79. *The Life of Boetius* (1683); *Some Remarques Upon a Late Piece of Nonsense called Julian the Apostate* (1682); John Bennet, *Constantius the Apostate* (1683); John Dowell, *The Triumph of Christianity* (1683); George Hickes, *Jovian* (1683); Thomas Long, *A Vindication of the Primitive Christians* (1683); and Edward Meredith, *Some Remarques upon . . . Julian the Apostate* (1682).

80. Johnson's countercritique, *Julian' Arts to Undermine and Extirpate Christianity*, was eventually published in 1689. George Hickes's *Jovian* is discussed in Chapter 3.

81. "Some Memorials," prefixed to *Works*, vii; *CSPD*, 25:432; *Observator*, no. 26 (March 6, 1683).

Then a second crisis arose for the Whig divine. On July 21, Lord Russell climbed the stairs of the scaffold. Within hours after his execution, his scaffold speech was widely distributed.[82] Russell's dying speech was highly offensive to the court. As I describe in Chapter 5, the Whig grandee portrayed himself as an innocent victim and martyr for the Protestant cause. Whig propaganda declared that his execution was a judicial murder. Many suspected that Johnson was the real penman behind Russell's scaffold sheet, and once again he was hauled before the Privy Council.[83]

The royalist press not only assumed Johnson was the author of Russell's speech, it also accused him of responsibility for the Rye House Plot itself. Did not, after all, his seditious doctrine exonerate the use of force against the supreme powers? In *An Antidote against Poison*, a critique of Russell's scaffold speech and a vigorous reaffirmation of Russell's guilt, Bartholomew Shower wrote that, in "his dying speech, Lord Russell writes that the paper says only what he thought fit to leave behind. No doubt he might have said, 'All that his faithful confessor [Johnson] advised him to leave behind.'" The "venomous book, *Julian*," Shower continued, "so much hugged and applauded by the conspirators" was seen as a "fit plaster" for their "violent designs."[84]

Under so much fire, Johnson probably considered escaping to the Continent while he still had the chance. Instead, he stayed and watched as one after another of his fellow partisans was charged, tried, imprisoned, fined, humiliated, and in a few cases, executed. Others in a steady stream made their way to Amsterdam, Utrecht, Cleve, and other Dutch and German cities. In November 1683, it was the Whig clergyman's turn to reap the effects of the royalist backlash. Johnson was charged with seditious libel for *Julian the Apostate*. At his trial, he came before the uncompromising and merciless defender of royal authority, Chief Justice George Jeffreys. He was fined five hundred marks, and *Julian the Apostate* was burned by the common hangman. Unable to pay his fine, Johnson spent the next four years in London jails, though he was

---

82. *The Speech of the Late Lord Russel [sic], To the Sheriffs: Together with the Paper delivered by him to them, at the Place of Execution, on July 21, 1683* (1683). Lois G. Schwoerer, "William Lord Russell," 52–53, discusses the speedy dissemination of Lord Russell's speech. Russell's dying speech is discussed in Chapter 5 of this book.

83. *Letters to Ellis*, 1:190; Roger L'Estrange, preface to *Considerations*.

84. Bartholomew Shower, *An Antidote Against Poison: composed of some remarks upon the Paper printed by the direction of the Lady Russell* (1683), 1.

not without company, since he was surrounded by other political prisoners. Furthermore, prison life did not silence him. His writings were smuggled out of his cell, published, and circulated. His tracts and his eccentric behavior kept him ever before the public consciousness. *Julian the Apostate* was but the beginning of a long polemical and public career.

Between Hunt's and Johnson's secular understanding of the origins of government, which destroyed the very heart of Filmerian ideology, and their promotion of the right of resistance, which threatened Charles II's government itself, it is little wonder that the dons and clerics of Oxford had ample reasons to consider their "pernicious books" dangerous in 1683. Elements of Hunt's influence were to remain constant in Johnson's propaganda. Johnson was the strongest Whig proponent of a thoroughly secularized political vision and the firmest opponent of passive obedience. Yet by 1688, he had abandoned the discourse of natural law for a far more popular idiom, the language of history and common law, upon which Whig propaganda built a radicalized version of the ancient constitution. Unlike Hunt, Johnson feared what he thought to be innovation, and he entertained only a poor sense of historical progression. He retreated from the rationalism he had learned from Hunt and moved toward an empiricist argument based on immutables—a place in which he undoubtedly felt more secure. Like his fellow Whig propagandist William Atwood, Johnson became a staunch promoter of a historicist vision of the English polity.

3

Refiguring the Past:
Constitutionalism and the
Debate over History

To Change Foundations, cast the Frame anew
Is work for Rebels who base Ends Pursue
—Dryden, *Absalom and Achitophel*

In the 1680s, radical Whigs attempted to refashion the English polity, both in its present form as well as in its historic past. Although the immediate moment was of utmost concern, they were convinced that a true and lasting settlement of the polity could be achieved only if the past were reconstructed to ensure the future of what they claimed to be England's "ancient constitution." The task of representing the old English government was eagerly taken up by several Whig barristers, who saw themselves as the keepers of this precious heritage. They styled themselves as the guardians of this inheritance from the newfangled doctrines of court flatterers, particularly churchmen.

To this end, the Whig constitutionalists were assisted in their task by the pronouncements of the radical Whig exclusionists Thomas Hunt and Samuel Johnson that "men make governments" and that "Scripture does not meddle with the secular government." If government was a man-made creation, scriptural interpretations, which were the foundation of Filmerian patriarchalism, were swept away, leaving room for the construction of alternative ideas and myths about its original formation. Secularizing the political discourse had another effect equally desired by radical propagandists; it diminished the authority of the Anglican establishment over the political debate. The Restoration Church, as Mark Goldie has pointed out, "was more vigorous, more adamantine, than is generally allowed." The church was not only vigorously trying to repress Dissent in the 1670s and 1680s, it was the Crown's most passionate defender and apologist. Furthermore, many of the church's most powerful spokesmen were eagerly adopting and asserting ever more extreme political positions. As we have seen, they were particularly enamored of the ideas of Sir Robert Filmer. Filmerian principles rested on Scripture and were rapidly being adopted by Anglican pundits and polemicists. As the Whig theorist James Tyrrell observed, "some modern churchmen" cried up *Patriarcha* as "their Diana," infecting the universities and deluding the young with its tenets.[1]

Whig politicians and theorists resented the clerical meddling in politics and political theory and their exceptional access and influence, through the pulpit, over the public. Many Whigs, particularly those among the leagues of young men trained at the Inns of Court, hoped that they themselves might replace the clergy's influence over the people and in government. After all, who could better instruct the people on their civic duties and the court on the constitution than those of the legal profession? Versed in the common law tradition, the Whig lawyer of the 1680s was interested in framing English politics in a secular, historicist discourse and in eliminating clerical influence over political matters.

An alternative to the Filmerian vision of government was readily available to Whig theorists in the form of the ancient constitution. As J.G. A. Pocock has shown in his classic study on the subject, the mythic ancient constitution was formed out of a preoccupation with immemorial custom, particularly by Elizabethan and Jacobean common lawyers. The "common law mind" became a pervasive mentality among the political nation and provided a "shared language" with which to discuss

---

1. Mark Goldie, "Priestcraft and the Birth of Whiggism," in Nicholas Phillipson and Quentin Skinner, eds., *Political Discourse in Early Modern Britain* (Cambridge University Press, 1993), 212; James Tyrrell, preface to *Patriarcha non Monarcha*.

England's political past and future on the eve of the civil wars.[2] For the Whig lawyer of the 1680s, the ancient constitution provided an alternative to the authority of Scripture. Set in the language of common law, it was a particularly English story that appealed to the educated person's empiricism and pride in his national heritage. The ancient constitution had an outwardly conservative appearance; it was supposedly based on age-old traditions that conveniently allowed Whig constitutionalists to represent themselves as restorers rather than innovators. As Conal Condren has pointed out, arguments from "tradition, conservation, and custom were so pervasive [throughout the seventeenth century] not because they furnished unequivocal arguments against alteration but because they could also accommodate and promote considerable change."[3] The ancient constitution was dependent upon historical constructions that were easily manipulated and were capable of diverse interpretation and of exhibiting a "radical face." The "venerated historical sources to which they [Whig ideologues] looked," as Janelle Greenberg has written, "allowed them to appeal to the past even as they molded the future."[4]

The process by which ancient constitutionalism came to play a dominant role in radical Whig thinking in the years before and after the Glorious Revolution was not a smooth or even one. Royalists were just as capable of using law and history for their own purposes and employing the same sources to counter Whig visions of the English past. Indeed, constitutionalism in the 1680s evolved as much in reaction to royalist historicism as out of a need to deny Filmerian positions. Whig dependence on historical argumentation was also challenged from within the radical network itself. Thomas Hunt strongly opposed the adoption of a historicist language by Whig ideologues and tried to warn his fellow partisans of the dangers and pitfalls of reliance on the past to fight the battles of the present. Hunt's opposition, as well as the challenges posed by royalists to Whig history, were both countered by the lawyer and pamphleteer William Atwood.

2. See Chapters 3 and 4 of J. G. A. Pocock, *The Ancient Constitution and the Feudal Law* (Cambridge University Press, reissue 1987). Glenn Burgess uses the term "shared language" (*The Politics of the Ancient Constitution,* 17).

3. *The Language of Politics,* 159.

4. Janelle Greenberg, "The Confessor's Laws and the Radical Face of the Ancient Constitution," *EHR* 104 (1989), 637.

William Atwood and the Debate over Parliament

William Atwood's early life remains a mystery.[5] He may have originally desired a career in the church. His first publication in 1678 was a versified treatment of Matthew's Gospel. He hoped, according to the preface, that his efforts would provoke some response, but none was forthcoming.[6] Throughout his life, Atwood remained keenly interested in church affairs and religious controversies. He was also highly critical of the Anglican priesthood, and a bitter anticlericalism became ever more present in his political writings of the 1680s and 1690s. Time and again, he asserted that politics was no place for churchmen, while arguing that laymen (like himself) were often just as qualified as the clergy to speak on topics of religious concern.

In the late 1670s, Atwood studied law at Gray's Inn. In those years he became acquainted with William Petyt, a "rising Whig barrister" from the Middle Temple, who had a powerful patron in Arthur Capel, the earl of Essex.[7] Petyt encouraged Atwood to study England's early charters, parliamentary and patent rolls, and the medieval chroniclers. He became highly proficient in early English law and administration and like his mentor, Petyt, used his knowledge of English history and law to promote a parliamentary historicist vision of England's government. But unlike Petyt, Atwood was a far more prolific and polemical writer, always willing to throw himself into the most volatile political and religious debates of the 1680s, the 1690s and the early eighteenth century. Armed with charters, writs, and declarations, Atwood sought to legitimize Whig politics based on what he saw as the immutable truths of the past.

Strung together, these "immutable truths" formed a familiar tale, propagated by common lawyers and antiquarians since the end of the sixteenth century. The stories of England's ancient heritage promoted by Petyt, Atwood, and other Whig constitutionalists in the last decades of the seventeenth century were certainly not new. They relied heavily on the same sources Elizabethan and Jacobean common law advocates had used before them, including Sir John Fortescue's *De laudibus legum*

---

5. There is little biographical information on Atwood. His birth date and birthplace are unknown. See the entries on him in the *DNB* and *BDBR.*
6. Preface to *A Poetical Essay towards an Epitome of the Gospel of the Blessed Jesus* (1678).
7. *The Ancient Constitution,* 186. Petyt's connection with Essex is discussed in Chapter 1.

Angliae, the legal treatises of Bracton and Fleta, the works of the medieval chroniclers, and Asser's *Life of King Alfred.* They also used those medieval texts, the *Leges Edwardi Confessoris,* the *Modus Tenendi Parliamentum,* and the *Mirror of Justices,* which supposedly described the laws and customs of Anglo-Saxon England. Moreover, Petyt and Atwood also depended on modern common law theorists, especially Sir Edward Coke (1552–1634).[8]

Whig constitutionalists in the 1680s strove to represent the English common law tradition. Common lawyers throughout the seventeenth century had elevated the common law over statute law.[9] Common law was valuable because it was customary; it had withstood the test of time and thus was obviously best suited to the needs of the people. It represented the most reasonable practices of the people since time immemorial. For Sir Edward Coke, following Fortescue, common law's roots were found in the traditions of the ancient Britons, but most common law advocates believed that common law reflected the practices of the Saxons.[10] Either way, the important fact was that the common law, in the words of J. P. Sommerville, was "exceedingly old," in a sense prehistoric, beyond the memory of man and accepted in turn by each invading nation. Common law embodied the wisdom of the ages, and any attempt to abrogate it was both supremely arrogant and dangerous.[11] After all, how could the rationales of a single moment compete with centuries of practice? This anxiety over innovation gave the common law tradition a distinctly conservative tone. Yet what seemed a very backward-looking discourse masked in reality a very pragmatic and malleable set of legal fictions, the cornerstone of which

8. The *Leges Edwardi Confessoris* like the *Modus Tenendi Parliamentum* and the *Mirror of Justices* were all written later then the time period they describe. The Laws of Edward the Confessor were probably written in the late eleventh, early twelfth centuries. Most seventeenth-century antiquarians, including John Selden, Henry Spelman, and William Dugdale, accepted them as the authentic work of King Edward. Greenberg, "The Confessor's Laws," 611, 617–21; Pocock, *The Ancient Constitution,* 42–43.

9. R.W. K. Hinton, "English Constitutional Theories from Sir John Fortescue to Sir John Eliot," *EHR* 75 (1969), 422.

10. Whig constitutionalists Edward Cooke and Henry Care, both discussed below, believed common law originated under the Saxons. For early Stuart constitutionalists on this point, see Sommerville, *Politics and Ideology in England,* 87–88, and Burgess, *The Politics of the Ancient Constitution,* 37–39.

11. Sommerville, *Politics and Ideology in England,* 90–91. Also see Burgess, *The Politics of the Ancient Constitution,* 24, on this point.

was that common law was the creation of the people and not that of royal will.

Out of the common law tradition came the historical fiction known as the ancient constitution. Simply stated, the ancient constitution represented England's peculiar form of government that originated as a consensual agreement between the people and the king, wherein the king swore to uphold the people's customary laws and liberties. Successive monarchs vowed at their coronations to maintain these ancient rights and liberties and respect the people's council, the Parliament. Over time, neither these ancient liberties nor Parliament had changed in any fundamental manner. As in the case of common law, the vital component of the story was that the ancient constitution originated through the customary habits of the people. An Englishman's rights and liberties were not bestowed upon him by a king, nor could they be wrested away by one.

The ancient status of both houses of Parliament was a fundamental component of this political mythology. In the 1670s and 1680s, royalists began attacking the notion of Parliament's antiquity, arguing that a medieval king's council consisted of merely the king's *tenants-in-capite*. No knights or commons were among them. The royalist antiquarian William Dugdale argued in 1675, that it was only during a baronial rebellion (1264–65) in the reign of Henry III that commoners were first summoned to meet and assist the king. Their very existence was an innovation born out of troubled times and could not, therefore, serve as a precedent.[12]

Whig antiquaries received a more forceful challenge to the notion of Parliament's antiquity in 1679, when Sir Robert Filmer's *Free-holders Grand Inquest* was republished.[13] Filmer asserted that both Houses derived their existence from the king. The function of the Lords was to aid and advise the king; the Commons to consent and execute the king's

12. *The Baronage of England* (1675); see Pocock's discussion of Dugdale in *The Ancient Constitution*, 182–87.

13. *The Free-holders Grand Inquest* was originally published anonymously in 1648. Corinne Weston questioned the attribution of the tract to Filmer. She argued that Sir Robert Holbourne was actually the author, noting among other things that Anthony Wood (*Athenae Oxonienses* 4:45) attributed *The Free-holders Grand Inquest* to Holbourne. James Daly countered Weston's arguments and demonstrated the many parallel passages between *Grand Inquest* and *Patriarcha*. I have accepted J. P. Sommerville's conclusion that "the weight of the evidence favors the authorship of Sir Robert Filmer, not Sir Robert Holbourne." See his introduction to *Patriarcha*, xxxiv–xxxvii.

wishes. Filmer's central thesis was that "the King himself ordains and makes law and is the supreme judge in Parliament."[14] Filmer also attacked the conception of customary or common law as the product of time immemorial. "For every custom," he wrote, "there was a time when it was no custom, and the first precedent we now have had no precedent when it began." The transformation of any custom to law has a definable beginning when "some superior power . . . did either command or consent unto their beginning."[15] For Filmer that "superior power resided" in one man in England, the king, the descendant of the first man, Adam.

The royalists' proposition that both the parliamentary Commons and the common law were but creations of the king's will, rather than the customary practices of the people, were devastating blows to the defenders of law and Parliament. In such a context, all discussion of the rights and privileges of trueborn Englishmen ceased to be meaningful. If the Commons were instituted by a king, then their powers and privileges were the gifts of a king and hence by implication, precarious. For what kings bestowed they could equally abrogate. So too the common law was set upon a weak and shaky foundation. If kings originally made the law, so they might at will unmake it. The potential for the assumption of arbitrary power was all too great.

Petyt and Atwood recognized the political implications of the debate over the Parliament's origins, and both published tracts in 1680 defending the notion of Parliament's antiquity.[16] As they saw it, the people's rights and privileges and their security from arbitrary government were at stake. Moreover, the debate over Parliament's origins was tightly interlocked with the great political controversy over the Exclusion Bill.[17] How could Parliament assert the right to alter the royal succession if Parliament itself was but the product of kingly will? Filmer's conception of the king as the sole legislator, echoed throughout the 1680s by courtiers and clerics, not only made the Exclusion Bill irrelevant but also called into question the law-making functions of Parliament.

---

14. *The Freeholder's Grand Inquest* in *Patriarcha and Other Writings*, 72.

15. Quoted in Pocock, *The Ancient Constitution*, 188–89.

16. Petyt, *Ancient Right of the Commons* (1680); William Atwood, *Jani Anglorum facies nova: or, Several Monuments of Antiquity touching the Great Councils of the Kingdom* (1680).

17. Pocock discusses this point in "The Ancient Constitution Revised, A Retrospect from 1986," in *The Ancient Constitution*, 345–47.

Both Petyt and Atwood constructed a history of Parliament, wherein it derived its mandate from the popular will of England's ancient peoples. Petyt approached the problem in the style of a pedagogue—as one who set out merely to correct a few modern misconceptions and innovations. At the same time, he warned of the dangerous implications of the novel opinions of men like "the author of *The Free-holders Grand Inquest.*" The opinions of these modern authors were "like a tempestuous whirlwind [which] not only rends off and dismembers an essential branch, but shakes the very root of the right and honour of our English Parliament and equally wounds both Lords and Commons." But these mistakes were correctable. "Out of the dark and neglected paths of antiquity," Petyt claimed that he "endeavoured to make publick and general . . . [as] I hope it will appear, that I have rescued from the force and power of a dangerous growing error, the just and ancient rights and privileges of our ancestors in a matter of the highest moment and concern."[18] The "dark and neglected paths of antiquity" were found in the Tower records, the medieval chroniclers, and the commentaries of the Elizabethan and Jacobean common lawyers.

William Atwood acknowledged his debt to Petyt for introducing him to the art of historical detection and confidently asserted that the "judicious Mr. Petyt . . . has laid the foundation and sure rule of understanding the ancient records and histories."[19] But apparently not everyone agreed with or followed Petyt's rule. Petyt's and Atwood's arguments met with strong opposition in Robert Brady's *Full and Clear Answer to a Book written by William Petit . . . together with some animadversions upon a Book, called Jani Anglorum facies nova* (1681).[20] Brady, a doctor of medicine, became the newest royalist combatant. He was an especially fearsome opponent, drawing his arguments from many of the very same sources as Petyt and Atwood. Brady not only reasserted Dugdale's argument that the Commons had arisen during a rebellion in 1265, his *Full and Clear Answer* also negated the entire common law tradition. What are so often called "our ancient English laws," he declared, "come from Normandy." They are, in fact, the feudal tenure

18. *Ancient Right of the Commons*, 125, 78; the preface, 74–75.
19. *Jani Anglorum*, 1.
20. For information on Brady, see J. G. A. Pocock, "Robert Brady, 1627–1700, A Cambridge Historian of the Restoration," *CHJ* 10 (1951): 186–204; and Weston and Greenberg, *Subjects and Sovereigns*, Chapter 7, passim.

established by William I after his complete and absolute conquest of the Saxons in 1066.[21]

For the Whig constitutionalists, the Norman Conquest was the great spoiler; admit the Conquest and England's cherished ancient constitution, her laws and liberties from time immemorial evaporated. Admit the Conquest and the law became a foreign imposition, inflicted upon the people by a conquering king. Petyt and Atwood were well aware of this historiographical trapdoor. Though neither Filmer nor Dugdale had argued in favor of the Conquest, Petyt and Atwood went to great lengths in 1680 to deny it. As Petyt asserted, William I "never made such an absolute conquest, nor did the kingdom receive so universal a change." In fact, Petyt posited, the only one William conquered in 1066 was King Harold.[22]

Brady's arguments destroyed the ancient constitution, attacked the common law tradition, and claimed the Commons were born out of rebellion—a rather ignoble pedigree. He further insulted the author of *Jani Anglorum*, calling Atwood a "new face-maker, new government-maker, and new parliament-maker [who] hath observed no order or method and his work being as wild, extravagant, and confused." Atwood was quick to defend Petyt and himself. In *Jus Anglorum ab antiquo* (1681), Atwood reasserted the antiquity of Parliament and replied to Brady, "There is a book lately published against Mr. Petyt and myself, which not only treats us with pedantic scorn . . . it seems to trample on the best constitution, our government itself, under the color of its being new in the 49th of Hen. 3. when it arose out of the indigested matter of tumults and rebellion [and] as not born in wedlock between the king and his people, it may be turned out of doors."[23] Atwood accused the doctor, not surprisingly, of being a bad historian, who mistranslated Latin words and phrases, gave them new meanings, and quoted sources out of context. He also accused Brady of playing politics, of seeking to ingratiate himself with the court with "his impertinent rhapsodies." He "glories much in taking all from the foundation head of original records," wrote Atwood, but his sole purpose is to "purge the body

21. *A Full and Clear Answer*, 31.

22. Preface to *Ancient Right of the Commons*, 17.

23. "Animadversions upon a Book called *Jani Anglorum*," attached to Brady, *A Full and Clear Answer*, 1; Atwood, preface to *Jus Anglorum ab antiquo: or, A Confutation of an important libel against the Government . . . under the Pretense of Answering Mr. Petyt and the Author of Jani Anglorum facies nova* (1681).

politick from the chronic disease of liberty and oppressing load of property."[24]

In fact, Atwood's own growing partisanship was becoming abundantly clear. Still, he was timid. He published his tracts anonymously and asserted his loyalty: "I know that it has been whisper'd about, as if I would have this government to be new modelled, which I utterly abhor." This did not prevent the court and its apologists from seeing Atwood as their foe, nor the Whig opposition from viewing him as one of their own. Nor did Atwood drop out of the partisan controversies of the 1680s as did Petyt.[25] He had only just begun. Despite Brady's use of his own weaponry, Atwood remained confident that his charters, writs, and patent rolls would not fail him. In the preface to *Jus Anglorum*, he warned his readers that his response to Brady might seem a bit "intemperate . . . [for] excess of truth has made me so." Nothing had moderated Atwood's enthusiasm for historical argumentation, and in 1682 and 1683, he went on the offensive. He published yet another reply to Brady and entered three more of the most controversial debates of the day.

24. Modern scholars are kinder to Brady. He is portrayed as the better historian in this debate. See Pocock, *The Ancient Constitution*, 197; and Weston and Greenberg, *Subjects and Sovereigns*, 193–94. While there is no doubt that Brady's portrayal of medieval history was superior to Petyt's and Atwood's, their histories were not void of a sense of historical method. They were concerned to retain the original sense of the documents they used and to place the text in its proper context. Mark Glat has argued that Locke had a more progressive, contextualist view of historical method than the Whig constitutionalists, because it was based on Bodin's regard for "returning facts to their context." See his "John Locke's Historical Sense," *Review of Politics* 43 (1981): 3–21. Glat's argument, however, ignores the standards by which Petyt and Atwood also tried to work. In the words of Petyt, "the sense [of the sources] is best understood by the practice of that time" (*Ancient Right of the Commons*, 34). Atwood, *Jani Anglorum*, 195, *Jus Anglorum*, 140, 2, for the quotations.

25. Preface to *Jus Anglorum*, for the quotation. Atwood was named and his ideas refuted in the royalist polemic *Antidotum Britannicum* (1681), as well as in other works. Fellow Whig lawyer and constitutionalist Edward Cooke praised Atwood and Petyt in his *Argumentun AntiNormannicum* (1682), lxix, as did the republican Henry Neville in *Plato Redivivus, or a Dialogue Concerning Government* [pub. c. 1681] in Caroline Robbins, ed., *Two English Republican Tracts* (Cambridge: Cambridge University Press, 1969). In addition to *The Ancient Right of the Commons*, Petyt published two other tracts in 1680: *Miscellanea Parliamentaria* (1680) (dedicated to William Williams, then speaker of the House of Commons) and *Britannia Languens, or a Discourse of Trade* (1680). Pocock notes that Petyt also wrote a reply to Brady in 1681, entitled *The Pillars of Parliament struck at by the Hands of a Cambridge Doctor* (1681), which he believes was "universally ignored" (*The Ancient Constitution*, 211). Indeed, I have not seen a single reference to it.

Atwood and the Church

In the summer of 1683, Atwood came to the defense of the Reverend Samuel Johnson. Johnson had been unable to publish a response to his many critics. Of the replies to *Julian the Apostate*, George Hickes's *Jovian, Or An Answer to Julian the Apostate* had made the biggest splash. The comment by Edward Petit, that *Julian the Apostate* was "so fully answered by the Reverend and learned Dr. Hickes that he [Johnson] may be glad of a prison to hide his face," was a typical statement of royalist glee at Hickes's triumph. Hickes was a rapidly ascending Anglican divine. In 1681, he had been appointed chaplain to the king; in August 1683, he was further promoted to the deanery of Worcester. Sometime in 1683, William Sancroft, the archbishop of Canterbury, asked Hickes to reply to Johnson's "unanswerable" *Julian the Apostate*.[26]

Hickes not only refuted the efficacy of Johnson's story of the apostasy of Julian, but also set forth an extreme Filmerian political statement. He was uncompromising on all of the basic points of royalism. The definition of true sovereignty, Hickes declared, was accountability to none but God. Placing any limitations on a prince, however minor, nullified his sovereignty. Moreover, kings were ordained by God and fully invested in their authority prior to taking the coronation oath. Naturally, Hickes proclaimed that the succession was divine and hence unalterable, and that the duty of the subject was to submit passively to the king's will regardless of the law. The king was the sole legislator, who "makes any form of words a law."[27]

In *A Letter of Remarks Upon Jovian*, Atwood accused Hickes of bad logic for misstating Johnson's parallel between popery and paganism; bad exposition, for undermining and contradicting himself throughout his text; and, above all, bad history, both English and Roman. According to Atwood, any examination of "the original custom and constitution of the English government" would prove that the succession was always alterable, and that lawmaking always required the consent of the people. He defended Johnson's tale of the resistance made by the early

26. Petit, *The Visions of Government, wherein the Antimonarchical Principles and Practices of all Fanatical and Commonwealthsmen . . . are discovered, confuted and exposed* (1684), 198. Hickes's *Jovian* went into two editions in 1683; I am unsure when the first edition was published, but the second was licensed in December. On Hickes, see the entry in the *DNB*. Sancroft was also responsible for the republication of Filmer's works and had also supported Brady's endeavors.

27. *Jovian*, 202.

Christians to the apostate Roman emperor and concluded by declaring that Hickes's response to Johnson was in fact a very poor performance that Hickes's friends (meaning the clergy) could only find embarrassing. He has done "no service to any interest or his own reputation. But thus it often happens when clergymen will be hooking civil rights in *ordine ad Spiritualia.*"[28]

Atwood's attack on the Anglican clergy did not end with George Hickes. In 1683, he stood up as a defender of Dissent and launched an assault on the prominent divine Dr. William Sherlock, lecturer at St. Dunstan's-in-the-West. Atwood attended several of Sherlock's sermons and engaged him in a public debate, ostensibly over Sherlock's definition of the visible church. In his *Letters Concerning Church Communion,* published anonymously in 1683, he asked Sherlock numerous questions meant to confound his logic. Much to Atwood's delight, no doubt, Sherlock responded to his letters. In *A Letter to Anonymous in Answer to His Three Letters,* Sherlock asserted that he was amazed that "anonymous" claimed to be "a hearty lover of the Church of England" and yet made "such a zealous defense of the Dissenter."[29]

Indeed, Atwood proclaimed himself a loyal son of the church again in his second tract to Sherlock, *A Seasonable Vindication of the Truly Catholic Doctrine of the Church of England.* But he also further defended nonconformity in the tradition of the good Samaritan. The Anglican Church, on the other hand, was like the Pharisee who left the beaten and bruised traveler unattended by the roadside. Atwood went on to attack the church hierarchy. In particular, like Thomas Hunt, he targeted the lower clergy for their incessant preaching of passive obedience and divine kingship. The only reason for having an "episcopal government," Atwood sneered, was so "the extravagance of many of the inferior clergy" could be restrained and disciplined. He further asserted that it was foolish to allow a few rituals and different procedures to keep Protestants apart. These "things indifferent" were not worth the price of disunity. This was a familiar Whig argument. Hunt made it in his *Postscript;* Johnson would make it from his jail cell.[30]

Not surprisingly, Atwood also entered the bishops' rights controversy,

---

28. *A Letter of Remarks upon Jovian, or An Answer to Julian the Apostate* (1683), 4, 13, 15.

29. *A Letter to Anonymous in Answer to His Three Letters to Dr. Sherlock* (1683), 56.

30. Atwood, *A Seasonable Vindication of the Truly Catholic Doctrine of the Church of England in a Reply to Dr. Sherlock's Answer to Anonymous* (1683), 8, for the direct quotation and passim; Hunt, *Mr. Hunt's Postscript,* 89, 90–93; Johnson, *The Way to Peace amongst all Protestants* (1688), passim.

which was the perfect forum for the Whig lawyer. It offered him an opportunity to strike a blow at the power of the prelacy while showing off his skills as a historian. Once again, the historical records were at the heart of the matter, for only they could answer whether the Lords Spiritual had throughout Parliament's history the right to judge in capital cases. One of the first to attack the rights of the bishops at the outset of the debate had been Lord Holles, the great parliamentarian and political leader of Presbyterians.[31] Holles was busy composing a second diatribe against the bishops in 1680, when he died. Atwood saw to it that this second assault was published and added his own contentions against the bishops and their defenders. He also mounted a further attack on Robert Brady in his *Lord Hollis, [sic] His Remains* (1682) and, once again, defended his and Petyt's histories of Parliament.

Atwood also felt compelled to answer the work of a fellow lawyer and Whig partisan, Thomas Hunt. In his last tract on the bishops' rights controversy, *An Apology for the Government of England and the Reason and Structure thereof declared* (1682), Hunt heaped scorn and ridicule on those investing time and energy dredging through the Tower records, with the intention of searching out and establishing England's ancient constitution with all its age-old rights and liberties. They were wasting their time, warned Hunt, for all of the efforts of Petyt and Atwood could not possibly secure the rights and privileges of the freeborn English against the powers mounted against them. Atwood was furious.

The Debate over History

Thomas Hunt's *Apology* is a peculiar piece of Whig polemic, remarkable on many accounts. It is at once a defense of the English government and the bishops' rights and an apology for both; it argues from historical evidence and at the same time chastises the use of historical research in the service of politics. It contains contradictions within itself and with statements Hunt had published elsewhere. Nor does one have to look far to find Hunt's other works, since he conveniently attached his two pro-exclusion pieces, *Great and Weighty* and the *Postscript* to the *Apology*.

---

31. Denzil Holles, *Letter of a Gentleman to His Friend shewing that the Bishops are not to be Judges in Parliament in Capital Cases* (1679).

The *Apology* must have struck both Whigs and Tories as a puzzling text; it contains positions with which both parties would heartily agree and to which both would stridently object. It marked Hunt as a truly maverick polemicist: dialoguing, agreeing, disagreeing with both friends and foes as well as with earlier stages of his own thought.

Hunt devoted the first hundred pages to reasserting the bishops' right of judicature in Parliament, using historical evidence to prove his arguments and concluding that the bishops may withdraw if they chose from capital cases, but they certainly had the right to sit and judge them. This was a right guaranteed them and "nothing can alter civil rights or civil constitutions but law."[32] Hunt's claim that rights and constitutions can be amended by law was, in part, the motif of the second half of his polemic, which was devoted to what he saw as misapplication of history to political issues.

Hunt found the controversy between Whig and royalist antiquarians over the origins of the parliamentary Commons both a troublesome waste of time and attention and an abusive use of the nation's past for political purposes. "It is a thing to be wished," he wrote, "that the gentlemen that apply themselves to the study of antiquities that relate to our law and government would design to adorn and cultivate the present laws and to make out their reasonableness rather than to innovate upon us by bringing back what is obsolete." Why, asked Hunt, should any man believe that "nothing is stable in our government but what hath been ever so and in the same form?" Why should any man "be so affrighted with the objection which some slight antiquaries make (for little learning in antiquity will serve the purpose) that our Parliament was at all time such as it is this day."[33]

Naturally, those who objected to the assertion that Parliament had changed over the centuries were Petyt and Atwood. Hunt believed that "little learning" was enough to prove Robert Brady's point. He agreed with the doctor that the Commons were established in 1265 and had already said so in the *Postscript*. Still, Hunt wondered why it took Brady "great labour" to demonstrate what was "hard for any man acquainted with our English history to be ignorant of," namely, "that our Parliaments were not always such as now constituted."[34] Hunt also agreed with

32. *Apology,* 91.
33. *Apology,* 151, 165.
34. *Mr. Hunt's Postscript,* 56.

Brady about 1066, maintaining that there was indeed a Norman Conquest.[35] Yet, Hunt was hardly Brady's friend or supporter. He refuted
Brady's notion that the Commons were a product of a rebellion. They
might have been established in 1265, but "this change was promoted by
universal consent," not "by rebellion as some bad men, enemies to our
religion and government designfully and maliciously in this age suggest."[36] Hunt realized, as much as Atwood or any of the Whigs, that
Brady's ideas about the English past could be used to support the most
absolutist pretensions of the Stuarts. "The nation," Hunt proclaimed,"
will never be persuaded by any thing that he [Brady] hath found out in
his diligent research."[37]

Hunt was equally critical, if not more so, of Whig historians. While he
never identified the targets of his derision, it was fairly obvious that he
had Petyt and Atwood in mind. Atwood certainly thought so. Hunt had
two main concerns with their dredging through the past. First, he
believed that in their efforts to prove that Parliament in its present form
was always the same throughout the ages, these historians were introducing a portrait of English government as unchanging and timeless.
They were creating an *ahistorical* vision of government: one that denied
or failed to incorporate progression, change, mutability, and imperfec-
tion. Hunt was not protesting the ever more prevalent Whig representation of the English polity as the ancient constitution, so long as that
depiction allowed for growth, change, and refinement. The English, he
wrote, were born to "so excellent a government . . . which was arrived
at by several slow steps and beaten out by the long experience of former
ages." It was not always a government without "great faults or inconve-
niences." Sometimes its various component parts became "ill-sized" or
not "well-joined or united." But it was always possible to "alter, amend,
improve."[38]

Yet it was just such talk of altering the government that many Whigs
feared. They were afraid that the court wished to alter the government
until it resembled French-style tyranny. Hunt, on the other hand,
believed that absolutism was exactly where the government was heading
if it was not altered—especially with a popish prince next in line to the

35. *Apology*, 128–29.
36. *Apology*, 183.
37. *Mr. Hunt's Postscript*, 56.
38. *Apology*, 255, 243, 247, 261.

throne. With the Exclusion Bill in mind, he asserted that the government "was never intended unalterable, or at least, inflexible, but was intended and made under reservations, reasonable exceptions of unforeseen accidents, and rare contingencies in human affairs."[39]

In the debate over Exclusion, Hunt, like many Whig propagandists, asserted that the nation had historically held the right to determine the royal succession, and hence the Exclusion Bill was no innovation. But he was also convinced that historiography alone was a far too unstable place to allow such issues to stand or fall. If change were necessary for the nation's preservation, then it was simply irrelevant whether there was a precedent for such an alteration or not. Moreover, the past was too easily manipulated and too often used for ill purposes: "For I am sure there is nothing so absurd and irregular that rude antiquity and the miscarriages of human affairs in length of time will not furnish a precedent for."[40] On the other hand, innovation, novelty, and change did not frighten Hunt.

Hunt's second concern with the Whigs' new obsession with historical argumentation was that their rummaging through the records might delude them into a false sense of security. "Let them not think," he wrote in 1681, "that our government as it lies in history and our laws in books and Parliament rolls . . . can defend us and it against the instruments and engines designed for its subversion." To prove that the English government was from time immemorial essentially the same would not halt the forces of popery and arbitrary government. "If our government must take its fate upon such issues as these," Hunt warned his fellow partisans, "I am sure we shall not long hold it."[41]

Did Hunt mean to offend his political allies? He probably did not care. He was twenty years older than most of the Whig propagandists and conspirators of the early 1680s. He sought, it seems, to alarm his younger colleagues. But clearly Atwood was offended. He was not convinced by Hunt's argument nor did he comprehend the meaning of Hunt's foreboding predictions. Rather he accused Hunt of being confused and contradictory—a bad tactician who simply did not understand the consequences of his statements. Hence armed with his writs and charters, Atwood entered the tournament. "Mr. Hunt," wrote Atwood, is a man "of much longer standing and greater natural and

---

39. *Great and Weighty*, 13.
40. *Apology*, 6.
41. *Great and Weighty*, 15; *Apology*, 154, for the quotations.

acquired parts than I can pretend to; yet if I have the good fortune to fall into the paths of ancient truth, no modern authorities ought to beat me out of them." Once again, Atwood was confident that antiquity would not fail him. Hunt, wrote Atwood, states "that this dispute over Parliament is not worth the cost and pains spent about it." He "might have spared his censures upon them who apply themselves to the study of antiquities." For the ideas Hunt himself expresses in his *Postscript*—government by popular consent, the royal succession determined by the people, and the right of resistance to that which threatens the nation's preservation—have no foundation without recourse to the nation's past. How else can such rights and liberties as Hunt grants the people be justified if not through the nation's ancient laws? If Saxon rights and liberties were cast aside by the Normans, as Hunt suggests when he owned the Conquest, then they certainly cannot be claimed now. Admit a Conquest in 1066, admit the Commons arose from rebellion in 1265, and the floodgates to kingly absolutism were opened. Hunt "grants many of Dr. Brady's hypotheses, but denies his consequences and so allows him to be a good antiquary, but an ill logician."[42]

Naturally, Atwood was attracted to Hunt's depiction of the English government as a secular institution based on popular consent. Yet Atwood felt that Hunt's ideas were but muddied abstractions if they were not grounded in English law and history. He recognized Hunt's use of the rhetoric of natural law and spoke disdainfully of Hunt's talk of the laws of nature, calling them "metaphysical existences." Few men can judge a controversy framed in such obscurest terms. Few can understand or evaluate "naked rights," "metaphysical notions," and such a "scheme of probabilities." On the other hand, many can understand the "meaning of writers and records carefully compared together."[43] "I have shown," boasted Atwood, "(which Mr. Hunt does not) that our government exactly answers his rule or idea of a lawful government, which he says, 'Is the representative of the people.'"[44] The records of England's ancient history can settle all disputes, Atwood confidently proclaimed. They are the true foundation of the politics expressed in Hunt's *Postscript*.

Clearly Atwood recognized that he and Hunt fought the same en-

---

42. Atwood, *Reflections on Antidotum Britannicum and Mr. Hunt's Late Book and Postscript as far as concerns the controversy between Dr. Brady and the author of Jani Anglorum facies nova,* which is attached to *The Lord Hollis[sic]: His Remains* (1682), 203.

43. *Reflections on Antidotum Britannicum,* 297, 293, 294, 298.

44. *Reflections on Antidotum Britannicum,* 290. Atwood is quoting Hunt, *Apology,* 155.

emies. But he was as anxious about Hunt's faith in philosophical reasoning as Hunt was about the growing Whig preoccupation with history. Although Atwood believed that natural law was far too open to interpretation and manipulation, he failed to appreciate that the artifacts of history were no less so. Hunt's dire predictions about the use of history as an argumentative device were in part on target. The language of natural law, as Locke's *Two Treatises* proves, was indeed translatable over oceans and centuries. But he was flatly wrong in the short run, insofar as his contemporaries were concerned. Locke's work received a less than spectacular reception when it was published in 1689.[45] Little wonder that radical propagandists time and again chose to argue their case through the particularism of English history. Both the rationalism of natural law and the more empirical rhetoric of ancient constitutionalism were exploited within the Whig literature of the 1680s and 1690s. But the discourse of law and history, which told and retold the stories of England's ancient heritage, became the most prevalent political language of Whig polemic by 1689. Atwood was certainly right about one thing: ancient constitutionalism was far more easily transmittable and digestible to the reading public. It became one of the Whigs' most powerful propaganda tools in their war against popery and arbitrary government. It became the story at the very heart of their revolution culture.

The Triumph of History and the Radical Face

Atwood and Petyt were by no means the only Whigs promoting the antiquity of Parliament, denying the Conquest, and glorifying the common law tradition. Others also struck out against the aspersions launched against Parliament's ancient heritage by the likes of Filmer, Dugdale, and Brady. In addition to the republication of a series of pro-parliamentary and constitutionalist tracts from the era of the civil wars and Interregnum,[46] various new defenses of the ancient constitution's narrative also appeared in bookstores. Two of the most influential

45. Martyn Thompson, "The Reception of Locke's *Two Treatises of Government, 1690–1705*," *Political Studies* 24 (1976): 184–91. A debate between Thompson and J. M. Nelson is in *Political Studies* 26 (1978): 101–18, and 28 (1980): 100–108.
46. For example, [Sir John Doddridge] *The Antiquity and Power of Parliaments in England* (1658, repr. 1679), and Thomas May, *A Breviary of the History of Parliament* (1650, repr. 1680).

were Henry Care's *English Liberties* and Edward Cooke's *Argumentum Anti-Normannicum.*

Care was a Whig scribbler who had been dragged before the law on numerous occasions for his virulent antipapist weeklies and pamphlets. He had a wonderful sense of public opinion and tastes, and in 1682, he decided that Whig constitutionalism was a fashion worthy of supporting and exploiting. He composed an anthology of pivotal documents in English history selected, introduced, and arranged to tell the story of England's ancient liberties and "the original happy frame of government." In the preface to *English Liberties,* Care reminded his countrymen that each was created with "a fixed fundamental right born with him as to [the] freedom of his person and property in this estate which he cannot be deprived of." "All our kings take a solemn oath at their coronation to observe and cause the law to be kept."[47]

Care's notes to each of the documents published in *English Liberties* contain the standard ancient constitutionalist rhetoric, replete with quotations from Bracton and Fortescue, about the antiquity of the law, its supremacy over the king, and the king's ultimate accountability to the law. Among the documents that Care published was the Magna Carta. The Great Charter played a central role within the political narrative of the ancient constitution. Whigs argued that the Magna Carta was composed from many of the liberties of ancient customary practice. Indeed, the charter was simply declarative of every Englishmen's rights and liberties from time immemorial. Nothing new had been enacted in 1215. The Magna Carta's declarative nature became a trope of Whig constitutionalism. The idea was not new; the Leveller cum Whig John Wildman had asserted such in 1651. In the 1680s, the constitutionalists Petyt, Atwood, Edward Cooke, and Shaftesbury's propagandist, Robert Ferguson, reiterated it. After the revolution, Samuel Johnson and the gentleman Whig James Tyrrell would do the same.[48]

Care also described the Norman Conquest of 1066 as no conquest at

---

47. *English Liberties: or The Freeborn Subject's Inheritance* (1682), 4 and 2, for the direct quotations. Two editions were published in 1682; an enlarged edition came out in 1700; fourth and fifth editions were published in 1719 and 1721. Care was most infamous for his antipapist *Weekly Pacquet of Advice from Rome* (1678–83).

48. Care, *English Liberties,* 17; John Wildman, *London Liberties: or, A Learned Argument of Law and Reason* (1651, repr. 1682), 8–9; Petyt, *Ancient Right of the Commons,* 104; Atwood, *Jani Anglorum,* 236; Edward Cooke, *Argumentum Anti-Normannicum* (1682), xvii; Robert Ferguson, *The Second Part of No Protestant Plot* (1682), 21, and *A Brief Justification of the Prince of Orange's Descent into England* (1689), 12–13; Samuel Johnson, *The Second Part of the Confutation of the Ballancing Letter: Containing an Occasional Discourse in Vindication of Magna Carta* (1700),

all. William I, "commonly called the Conqueror, yet in truth he was not so," was "admitted by compact and did take an [coronation] oath to observe the laws and customs of Saxon times."[49] The submission of William I was an essential component to the ancient constitution. The Saxons' laws and liberties, which he swore to uphold at his coronation, were embodied in the so-called Laws of Edward the Confessor. St. Edward's laws were not only accepted by William I, but King Stephen, Henry II, and, after 1307, when the coronation oath was rewritten, every sovereign of England at their coronation.

This was the theme of Edward Cooke's *Argumentum AntiNormannicum*, which was published anonymously in 1682. *Argumentum* was not, as J. G. A. Pocock has described it, "a minor Whig tract."[50] Rather, it was one of the most important statements on ancient constitutionalism in the late Stuart era. *Argumentum* was cited by other Whigs throughout the 1680s and 1690s, although the "ingenious author" was as yet unknown. It was invariably attributed to either Petyt or Atwood, and Robert Brady probably thought he was responding to one or the other when he devoted part of his *Introduction to Old English History* (1684) to refuting *Argumentum*. During the Glorious Revolution, *Argumentum* was rushed to the press to remind the Conventioneers, who were charged with settling the government, of the limits of kingship and the sovereignty of the law. In the 1690s, Whig theorist James Tyrrell often cited *Argumentum* but not until 1704 did he attribute it to "Mr. Cooke."[51]

We know very little about Edward Cooke. He studied law at the Middle Temple and became an ardent Whig during the Exclusion Crisis. His polemical career began with an antipapist diatribe entitled, *A True Narrative of the Inhumane Positions and Practices . . . of the Jesuits and Papists, toward all good Protestants* (1680), the most notable feature of which is its extremely laudatory dedication to the earl of Shaftesbury, to whom Cooke appealed "for [His] Lordship's patronage and protec-

340–41; James Tyrrell, *Bibliotheca Politica: An Enquiry into the Ancient Constitution . . . in Thirteen Dialogues* (1694), Dialogue 3, 187–88.

49. *English Liberties*, 20.

50. *The Ancient Constitution*, 212.

51. Edward Cooke, *Argumentum Anti-Normannicum*, reprinted as *A Seasonable Treatise: wherein it is proved that King William, commonly called the Conqueror did not get the Imperial Crown of England by Sword* (1689). James Tyrrell referred to the "ingenious author" of *Argumentum* in his preface to *The General History of England . . . to the reign of William III*, vol. 1 (1696). Then in the appendix of volume 3, published in 1704, he identified Cooke as the author.

tion." Cooke hailed Shaftesbury as the "champion of truth," claiming that the "advancement of the Protestant religion [and] the welfare of this kingdom doth chiefly depend" on Shaftesbury's efforts. *A True and Perfect Narrative* was followed by a translation of the Magna Carta and a history of the royal succession in 1682.[52] Cooke had joined the leagues of Whig lawyers determined to use history to legitimize exclusion politics.

Argumentum was written in defense of Petyt's *Ancient Right* and against Brady's objections to Petyt in *A Full and Clear Answer.* Cooke focused most of his attention on the conquest controversy rather than on the debate over the antiquity of Parliament, though the two issues were not unrelated. The frontispiece to *Argumentum,* which also serves as the frontispiece to this book, illustrates the cornerstone of ancient constitutionalism by depicting King William I accepting Holy Edward's Laws from Britannia at his coronation. The text to the frontispiece explains that a "noble prelate" administers the coronation oath to duke William only after the English people have consented to have him as their king. In the introduction, Cooke asserted that William I "came to the crown by election and consent of the clergy and the people" and that he swore to preserve England's *antiquae leges regni.* In fact, "the mighty conqueror" was "himself conquered" in 1066, "and solemnly renouncing all arbitrary will and power, submit[ed] his will to be regulated and governed by justice and the ancient rights of the Englishmen."[53]

With its various component parts promoted and defended in the work of Petyt, Atwood, Care, Cooke, and others, the ancient constitution continued to be a powerful and convincing narrative fiction in the pre-Revolution era. But why was its affirmation so important? What did it have to do with the pressing concerns of the Exclusion debate? The answer was, as both Whig and Tory knew, everything. The issue of the succession, and the foreboding future that loomed ahead should the Catholic duke of York ascend the throne, was at the very heart of Whig constitutionalist propaganda. Were the succession to be altered, it was up to Parliament to do so; for Parliament to do so, it had to be shown throughout history that Parliament had this right. The efforts of Petyt,

52. Edward Cooke, *Magna Carta made in the ninth year of King Henry the Third . . . faithfully translated for the benefit of those that do not understant the Latin* (1680); *The History of the Successions of the Kings of England* (1682).

53. Cooke, "An Explanation of the Frontispiece," pages unnumbered, and introduction, xxii, xxx, both in *Argumentum Anti-Normannicum.*

Atwood, and others were aimed at legitimizing the power of Parliament and proving that it was by no means an innovation for Parliament to enthrone the next successor. Their refutation of the Norman Conquest paved the way for the future succession to be altered, for another round of kings to be exchanged, and the ancient constitution to continue unharmed. The Catholic James could be replaced by either the duke of Monmouth, hailed by Whigs as the "Protestant Duke," or by James's elder daughter, Mary, princess of Orange, who had been raised Protestant. They too, like William I in 1066, would take the coronation oath upholding English laws and liberties. The royal line would break a bit, but the law would remain unbroken.

What was truly innovative, the Whigs blasted, was to suggest that the succession was hereditary and divinely ordained, or that the once enthroned kings had no superior on earth and that their powers were limitless. Yet this was exactly what was being preached and published by the defenders of the duke of York's succession. Some historians have recently argued that during the crisis over the succession, many Whigs and Tories actually spoke the same languages and shared similar ideas about powers and limitations of kingship and Parliament. There was more consensus, they tell us, than conflict.[54] But this was not how contemporaries would have viewed the times that they described over and over again as tumultuous and combative. Nor do we find much in the way of shared opinion or political theories. Tories opposed the exclusion of the duke of York, defended hereditary succession, and resisted any attempts to alleviate the plight of the nonconformists.[55] But more troubling still, insofar as the Whigs were concerned, were the "ecclesiastical courtiers" with their notions of divine right and passive obedience.[56] Sermons such as *The Power of Kings from God* (1683) and *Of Patience and Submission to Authority* (1684) and the hundreds of others

---

54. Jonathan Scott has been the most ardent proclaimer of this view (*Algernon Sidney and the Restoration Crisis*, 46–49), but also see Susan Staves, *Players' Scepters: Fictions of Authority in the Restoration* (Lincoln: University of Nebraska Press, 1977), 77.

55. Tim Harris, "Tories and the Rule of Law in the Reign of Charles II," *The Seventeenth Century* 8 (1993), 12. Harris also points out that all Tories, cleric and lay alike, "would have agreed that monarchs ruled by divine right" (14).

56. *A Brief Discourse Between A Sober Tory and a Moderate Whig* (1682). In this dialogue, the "moderate Whig" asks that the "ecclesiastical courtiers might be a little better regulated and the Dissenters . . . a little more mildly dealt with" (2).

just like them left little room for compromise.[57] Consensus was out of the question.

Making the succession susceptible to human intervention meant secularizing the government's origins. The ancient constitution did just that. It was not only compatible with Hunt's and Johnson's arguments that "men make governments," but through its survey of medieval English history it proved as much. The various peoples of England had over time constructed their own particular form of government. Ancient constitutionalism was attractive for other reasons as well. It had an aura of legitimacy. It was documented in the great charters and petitions of the past and hence not based on any airy metaphysical claims of right. It offered a rival secular conception of the English polity with which to challenge Filmerian patriarchalism and divine right daydreams. Best of all, it took the language of politics out of the hands of the churchmen and placed it into those of the lawyers.

Did ancient constitutionalism have a "radical face" in the early 1680s? Unlike Hunt and Johnson, who had both asserted the people's right to resist tyranny, Petyt and Atwood had avoided the question of popular resistance. Yet they certainly understood the potentially radical nature of their polemics. By positing an image of government first formed by the people in whom sovereignty had originally resided, they suggested that power could be returned to the people. By glorifying the wisdom of the people's common law, wherein their rights and privileges were protected, they suggested that no one but the people could or should alter those laws. Should they be altered without the people's consent, recourse to resistance was the obvious solution.

Indeed, resistance to the king for his continuing opposition to the Exclusion Bill was already being boldly proposed by radical Whigs in Parliament. At the Exclusion Parliament of 1680, the Green Ribbon brother and future Rye House plotter John Trenchard described the dilemma posed by the succession, "When a popish king comes to the crown, either we must submit and change religion or resist." City Whig Sir Thomas Player made his position clear: "As for that one argument, of a Civil War that may come upon this Exclusion, I would let the world

---

57. Paul Lanthom, *The Power of Kings from God* (1683); John Moore, *Of Patience and Submission to Authority* (1684). There are numerous others such as Thomas Pomfret, *Passive Obedience stated and asserted* (1683), and James Ellesby, *The Doctrine of Passive Obedience Stated in a Sermon* (1685).

know, that we are not afraid of war upon that occasion."[58] With the death of the Exclusion Bill at the abortive Oxford Parliament, a peaceful solution to Whig demands died too. Radicals began drawing war plans. They were justified by the arsenal of ideas stockpiled for them by the propagandists of the Exclusion Crisis.

58. Grey, *Debates*, 7:413, 406.

4

Creating Revolution:
Robert Ferguson and the Rye House Plot

On August 5, 1682, the sexton's maid at St. Giles, Cripplegate, came across a paper left on a pew. Addressed to all "Dissenters and Persecuted Sincere Christians," it was highly seditious: "The Gospel preaching prohibited, papistical perjured rogues plunder, the law prevented, justice abolished, our charter in contest, our privileges taken away, arbitrary policy prevails . . . no parliaments suffered to rectify our injustices, widows weep, orphans cry, murderers pardoned, debauchery in fashion, bastards, whores, and enemies to the nation promoted to honour, Tories drive all before them. . . . Confounded be such laws and lawmakers." The libel, "Now or Never, or When Shall it be Mended," was a five-page catalogue of Whig and Dissenter grievances.[1] Their complaints were many, from the persecution of nonconformist preachers and gatherings and the court's quo warranto proceedings

1. *CSPD*, 23:562.

against the London City charter, to disgust over the king's libertine court and the grim future that loomed ahead with a Catholic next in line to the throne. The libel was not unique. Numerous newsletters, songs, and satires poured forth similar lists of complaints, anxieties, and fears. "We yet live and are in peace," Nathaniel Mather wrote to his brother in America, "on which account we are a wonder to ourselves. The interest of the papist is potent and I fear increasing."[2] This was the tincture of the times. Whig hopes for a peaceful solution to the succession crisis dimmed.

Efforts to exclude the duke of York from the throne had galvanized Whigs into action in 1678 and 1679, unifying their numbers and motivating their cultural initiates. But by 1682, amid the ferocity of a royalist backlash, their demands had multiplied. They may have also begun experiencing a broader and more responsive popular reception, particularly within London and the west country. The court's efforts to stifle the opposition press, prosecute libelers, assert the penal laws against Dissent, and dominate civic politics in London and elsewhere deepened disaffection and augmented Whig causes. In 1682 and 1683, the actions of Whigs and Dissenters became more desperate; the tone of their demands more agitated; their political positions more radical. The use of force was becoming an ever more realistic option in the struggle against what they believed to be the growing oppression of the government.

Royalist Backlash

> Why what's become of all your vindicating Patriots,
> Your Packed Juries, your National Saviors, your
> Unforgettable Charters, are they all vanished?
> —*The Whigs Lamentation* (1683)

The royalist backlash, beginning with force in 1681, was an all out effort by the court and its allies to fight the Whig exclusion movement in the courts, in Parliament, in the counties, in the corporations of London, in the press, and in the streets and coffeehouses. The considerable re-

---

2. *Collections of the Massachusetts Historical Society: The Mather Papers*, 4th ser., vol. 3 (Boston, 1866), 23–24.

sources of the Crown, particularly the power of patronage, were mobilized to put an end to Whig politicking and propaganda. Among Charles II's targets were the press and the judicial system. His efforts were in many respects highly successful. But they also left deep wounds, creating fresh injuries and martyrs for the Protestant cause.

The case of Stephen Colledge was, in many ways, the opening shot of the backlash. Known as the "Protestant joiner," his was a familiar sight around Whig coffeehouses and taverns. He was infamous for his anti-papist outbursts and his numerous libels attacking Chief Justice Sir William Scroggs, Roger L'Estrange, the duke of York, the king's mistresses, and the king himself. In one little ditty that circulated in manuscript, Colledge had Charles II singing, "I'll damn their Old Cause / Their Religion and Laws / For I will never sway / After any English way."[3] Colledge had powerful friends, among them William, Lord Russell, who probably encouraged the joiner's antics.[4] The Green Ribbon Club employed Colledge's skills as a carpenter; he built seven of the popes they immolated at their effigy-burning processions.[5] In March 1681, Charles II moved Parliament to Oxford, a royalist enclave where the king could expect a considerably more sedate and loyal atmosphere. Colledge traveled to the Oxford Parliament on horseback, armed, making bold threats against the king should he prevent the Exclusion Bill from further progress. He played the "part of dispersing libelous pictures and libels, together with prating against popery and slavery."[6]

The following July, Colledge was tried in London for seditious words and actions, but the Whig jury, empanelled by sheriffs Henry Cornish and Slingsby Bethel, came back predictably with an *ignoramus* verdict. The court was not deterred and had Colledge retried in Oxford. He was charged with plotting to seize the king during the previous March meeting of Parliament. In Oxford, the government could expect a far

---

3. BL, Harley 7,319, fol.35. Among the other libels attributed to Colledge were *Truth Brought to Life, or Murder Will Out* (1679), concerning the murder of Sir Edmundbury Godfrey, and *A Raree Show* (1681), a broadside ballad mocking Charles II and accusing him of governing arbitrarily. On Colledge's propaganda, see B. J. Rahn, "*A Ra-Ree Show*—A Rare Cartoon: Revolutionary Propaganda in the Treason Trial of Stephen College," in Paul J. Korshin, ed., *Studies in Change and Revolution*, (Menston: Scolar Press, 1972), 78–97.

4. *DNB*; [Tutchin] *The Western Martyrology*, 17.

5. Harris, *London Crowds*, 101.

6. North, *Lives of the Norths*, 3:159.

more compliant jury, and this time Colledge was found guilty and sentenced to be hanged, drawn, and quartered. He maintained his innocence throughout his trial and on the scaffold. In his dying speech, he declared that he knew of no plot but the Popish Plot.[7]

Colledge's case left a vivid impression on contemporaries. He became an emblem of the times, exploited by both sides. Royalists hoped that his execution might serve as a lesson to the Whig opposition by demonstrating just what kind of end "Protestant plotters" could expect. They brought out numerous satiric songs and ballads on Colledge.[8] The Tory playwright Aphra Behn invoked his memory at the outset of her play, *The Roundheads*, to remind her audience what befalls plebeian types like Colledge who spout Whig slogans and meddle in politics instead of minding their trades.[9] Whig propagandists, on the other hand, were given one of their first Protestant martyrs. They portrayed Colledge as a victim of venomous popish malice, injustice, and arbitrary government. They even sold a commemorative picture of their new hero with verses beneath that read:

> By *Irish* Oaths, and wrested Laws I fell,
> A Prey to *Rome*, a sacrifice to Hell
> My guilty Blood for speedy Vengeance cries;
> Heaven, hear and help, for Earth my Suit denies.[10]

Both sides also learned important lessons about the power of the dying speech, which was to become one the Whigs' most potent weapons in their propaganda arsenal.[11] Colledge's speech not only asserted his innocence, it also predicted that the enemies of Protestant-

---

7. *The Arraignment, Tryal, and Condemnation of Stephen Colledge for High-Treason, in Conspiring the Death of the King, the Levying of War, and the Subversion of Government* (1681); *The Speech and Carriage of Stephen Colledge at Oxford* (1681), 2.

8. For example, *The Whigs Lamentation for the Death of their Dear Brother Colledge, the Protestant Joiner* (1681); *A Poem by way of Elegie upon Mr. Stephen Colledge* (1681); *A New Song on the Death of Colledge* (1681); and *Stephen Colledge's Ghost to the Fanatical Cabal* (1681).

9. *The Roundheads* (1681), 1.i

10. *A Modest Reply to the too hasty and malicious Libel entitled An Elegy upon Mr. Stephen College* (1682); *The Duke of Monmouth's Case* (1682); [John Tutchin] *A New Martyrology, or the Bloody Assizes* (1693), 22.

11. Along with the speeches of several other Whig martyrs, Colledge's was reprinted during the Glorious Revolution in *The Dying Speeches of Several Excellent Persons who suffered for their Zeal against Popery and Arbitrary Government* (1689).

ism would not be sated with his blood alone. His death was but "a prelude" to a far greater popish assault yet to come upon Protestant lives and liberties.[12] The Reverend Samuel Johnson later thought the effects of Colledge's speech upon the public counteracted all of the passive obedience sermons of the Anglican clergy put together.[13] Royalists, naturally, did not allow the speech to go unanswered. Not only did L'Estrange rush a defense of Colledge's guilty verdict to print, a royalist publisher put out a fallacious dying speech by Colledge wherein the "Protestant joiner" confessed his guilt.[14]

Further efforts by the court to prosecute notorious Whigs did not always go as planned. Following Colledge's execution, the court decided to pursue bigger fish and had the earl of Shaftesbury charged with treason in July. But as he was tried in London the following November, he was protected by the Whig shrievalty who handpicked his jurors, including City Whigs Thomas Pilkington and Sir Samuel Barnardiston. The jury's verdict was once again *ignoramus*. For the court it became increasingly apparent that London had to be subdued. As they were reminded by loyalists of the city of Exeter, "'Tis come to a civil war, not with the sword, but law, and if the king cannot make the judges speak for him, he will be beaten out of the field."[15] Royalists turned their energies to taking control of civic politics and curbing the opposition press.

Insofar as the press was concerned, the court had a tireless champion in Roger L'Estrange, who had been appointed surveyor of the printing presses in 1663. As "judge, licenser, and rifler of the press," as one Whig writer called him, L'Estrange doggedly supervised and harassed London booksellers.[16] He brought several Whig publishers successfully to trial in 1680 and 1681, secured the inventories of others, and hunted down the authors of sedition.[17] He also kept up a running correspondence with Secretary Jenkins, recording the deeds and movements of disaffected publishers, printers, and scribblers. Equally important, he

---

12. *A True Copy of the Dying Speech of Mr. Stephen College* (1681).

13. Johnson is quoted in Nathaniel Salmon, *Lives of the English Bishops from the Restauration [sic] to the Revolution* (1733), 90.

14. Roger L'Estrange, *Notes upon Stephen College* (1681); *The Last Speech and Confession of Mr. Stephen Colledge, Who was Executed at Oxford* (1681, 2 eds.).

15. Address of the City of Exeter to Secretary Jenkins, *CSPD*, 22:660.

16. Roger Coke, *A Detection of the Court and State of England during the Last Four Reigns and Interregnum*, 2 vols. (1694), 2:291.

17. Crist, "Government Control of the Press," 56–65; Fraser, "The Intelligences of the Secretaries of State," 122–23; Walker, "Censorship and the Press," 224–31.

countered the arguments of Whig propaganda in his weekly, the *Observator*. More than anyone, L'Estrange kept the loyal voice ever before the public. From the perspective of radicals like Thomas Hunt, L'Estrange's *Observator* did nothing less than "put out the eyes of the people and leave them without understanding."[18]

Controlling the press, however, could never be completely effective without control of the judiciary. This was also the case insofar as the enforcement of the penal laws against nonconformity were concerned. The court's quo warranto proceedings against the charters of cities and boroughs, between 1682 and 1685, were aimed at seizing control of municipal office from the Whigs and their supporters, and hence dominating local and civic governments. As John Miller has pointed out, Tory control of the boroughs was "important for military, electoral, and judicial reasons." The towns, of strategic importance should civil war erupt, would be held in loyal hands; local sheriffs, justices of the peace, and juries would prosecute and convict Dissenters; and men loyal to the Crown would be sent to Westminster.[19] The court would create an acquiescent judiciary and, in the future, more compliant Parliaments. Of the thirty boroughs and other corporations that surrendered their charters under Charles II, only London contested the quo warranto proceedings that sought to dispense with the City's charter and hence its independence.[20]

The contest over London's charter was a long and drawn out process. Though the writ of quo warranto was served in December 1681, hearings did not begin until February 1683. A furious propaganda war ensued wherein radical papers and broadsides demanded "Charles Steward" to answer "*quo warranto*, art thou king of England?"[21] At Walbrook, a London ward, "the Whigs read a paper published by Francis Smith about the loss of the charter which startled a great many

---

18. *Defense of the Charter,* 28.

19. Miller, "The Crown and the Borough Charters in the Reign of Charles II," 70–71.

20. Most boroughs were too poor to contest quo warranto proceedings and often surrendered their charters when the court merely threatened to contest them. Jennifer Levin, *The Charter Controversy in the City of London, 1660–1688, and its Consequences* (London: The Anthlone Press, 1969), 1–16; Sharpe, *London and the Kingdom,* 2:476–77, 494–95.

21. Verses enclosed in a letter from the mayor of Bristol, *CSPD,* 23:72. Also see *The Last Will and Testament of the City Charter of London* (1683) and *The Citizens Loss, when the Charter of London is forfeited, or given up* (1683), both of which were reprinted in *Somers Tracts,* 8:385–95. Tory propaganda mocking the Whigs' beloved charter includes *The Charter: A Comical Satyr* (1682), which concludes with "Damn the old Charter and God save the King!"

of the indifferent sort of voters." In the Common Council, Whig councilmen accused their Tory rivals of being so "mad-blind as to run out of freedom into slavery which will bring in popery." Though the court ultimately won the battle and London's charter was surrendered in June 1683, the price was high. Charles II's administration was increasingly seen as arbitrary and justice as unobtainable through peaceful means. As a simple parish laborer at St. Giles without Cripplegate asserted, "If the City loose the charter, the King would loose his head."[22]

Revolution Culture and The Plotter

While radical Whigs remained a small network of committed propagandists and conspirators, their aims and aspirations were finding a wider audience within the climate of discontent created by the royalist backlash. This was true not only in London but also in western England, particularly in cities with large populations of Dissenters like Bristol and Taunton. In these cities, Whig propaganda was finding a more ready reception and influencing people's beliefs. It was fashioning political opinion and helping to create an atmosphere wherein violence was increasingly seen as a justifiable preventive to the establishment of popery and arbitrary government.

Whig slogans, rhetoric, ideology, pictures, verse, and ballads together created a revolution culture, a culture that was highly accessible, promoted dramatic change, and provided the political principles behind the Rye House plotting in 1682–83 and Monmouth's Rebellion in 1685. Moreover, it was a culture that ultimately made the events of the Glorious Revolution more readily understandable, acceptable, and justifiable to a large number of English. Revolution culture was the work of many Whig scribblers and appealed to many audiences. The ideas of Whig theorists like Thomas Hunt, the Reverend Samuel Johnson, and the Whig constitutionalists were echoed by disaffected London artisans and country gentlemen, as were the fears, lies, and fables disseminated by the leagues of anonymous Whig hacks. Many such propagandists

---

22. T. Deane to Thomas Atterbury, *CSPD*, 26:161; Meeting of the Common Council, May 22, 1683, *CSPD*, 24:259; *Middlesex County Records*, 4:227, for the quotations.

were paid for their work by Whig elites. The earl of Shaftesbury supposedly kept a stable of such writers.[23] The most prolific and clever of these was Robert Ferguson, the Independent preacher and the infamous "Plotter."

Ferguson's work in particular met with a wide reception. His propaganda was a skillful combination of Whig political principles, communicated through various tropes and Whig myths, an assortment of lies and exaggerations that played on popular fears and bigotry. Yet despite Ferguson's willingness to exploit his audience's anxieties, his propaganda was by no means unsophisticated or void of important political concepts, something scholars of Restoration political thought have ignored. In 1981, historians Corinne Weston and Janelle Greenberg recognized that Ferguson was "a daring and clever pamphleteer, [who] . . . wrote tracts of high quality that at least in one case exerted a great deal of influence." But their analysis of his work went little further. Five years later, Richard Ashcraft concluded that Ferguson's "political views . . . were identical to those of Locke."[24] Ashcraft's verdict betrays a common tendency in much of the scholarship on late Stuart political thought that weighs all early Whig thinking in terms of Locke's *Two Treatises*. The Whig polemicist whose thinking bears any similarity to that of Locke's is described as "Lockian." Further analysis of their work is apparently not worth the bother, yet Whig thinking in the 1680s was as diverse as the individuals who created it. Robert Ferguson's particular genius lay in his ability to represent and synthesize various strains within radical Whig ideology.

Ferguson was one of the most notorious characters of his times. He was both Shaftesbury's scribbler and Monmouth's advisor; he was both a Rye House conspirator and a Monmouth rebel. He marched onto the battlefield at Sedgemoor, and he accompanied the prince of Orange's invading army to Torbay. He was a far more active participant and propagator of radical politics in the 1680s than John Locke, and Ferguson's escapades as well as his pamphlets made him far better known to his contemporaries. Ferguson was a prolific and ingenious

23. Roger North, *Examen: or an Enquiry into the Credit and Veracity of a Pretended Complete History* (London, 1740), 88; *Memoirs of the Life of the Earl of Shaftesbury* (1683), 6; William Smith, *Intrigues of the Popish Plot Laid Open* (1685), 31.

24. The influential tract to which Weston and Greenberg (*Subjects and Sovereigns*, 218) refer is Ferguson's *Brief Justification of the Prince of Orange's Descent*, discussed in Chapter 6. Ashcraft, *Revolutionary Politics*, 55.

propagandist—a collector and collator of various Whig positions. In service to the Whig cause, he authored, revised, and collaborated in the production of at least fifteen Whig tracts between 1679 and 1689. Many went into multiple editions, were plagiarized by others, and translated into foreign languages.[25] Readers of Locke's *Two Treatises* in the post-Revolution era would undoubtedly have noticed how virtually identical many of Locke's ideas were to Ferguson's.

In the London coffeehouses, Ferguson was known to have one of the "glibbest tongues in town upon all subjects."[26] He also seems to have been a great listener, reader, and absorber of ideas from the pulpits, the press, and coffeehouse and tavern gossip. Ferguson knew everyone: important Dissenting and Anglican divines; old-time Cromwellian soldiers, Levellers, and republicans; Whig publishers, parliamentarians, and Green Ribbonites; London City Whigs as well as nonconformist teachers and preachers in Holland, Scotland, and New England. He even claimed to have informants within the ranks of the royalists themselves.[27] During the Rye House interrogations, nearly everyone

25. The question of exactly how many tracts Ferguson published throughout his career is slippery. In a list drawn up in 1712, by Ferguson himself, he claimed to have written twenty-nine tracts. After 1712, he began another book entitled, *The History of all Mobs, Tumults, and Insurrections in Great Britain,* which was continued in "another hand" and published posthumously in 1715, bringing the total to thirty. But Ferguson's list is problematic. He forgot some of the tracts he wrote and took full credit for others that were probably collaborative efforts. He did not list Monmouth's *Declaration* or *An Impartial Enquiry into the Administration of the Affairs of England* (1684). The latter was attributed to Ferguson by English spies in Holland (BL, Add. 41,811, fol. 268), and Richard Ashcraft has made a strong case for its being Ferguson's work (*Revolutionary Politics,* 337, note 207). Further, many of the Jacobite tracts he listed were probably written in collaboration with or were by James Montgomery of Skelmorlie. Further, six other tracts have been attributed to Ferguson that he did not list. His 1712 list is published in James Ferguson, *Robert Ferguson, the Plotter* (Edinburgh, 1887), 385–86. Ferguson's *Enquiry into and Detection of the Barbarous Murther of the late Earl of Essex* (1685), to give just one example of the dissemination of his writings, was translated into Dutch, Flemish, and French in 1684 and 1685.

26. Robert Wodrow, *Analecta, or Materials for a History of Remarkable Providences,* 4 vols., ed. M. Leishman (Edinburgh, 1842–43), 2:270–71.

27. Through his association with Shaftesbury, Ferguson was acquainted with old soldiers like Colonel John Rumsey and former Levellers like Major John Wildman. He was also known as Shaftesbury's paymaster of Whig scribblers. James Ralph asserted that Ferguson "was personally known to every minister" in Britain (*The History of England during the Reigns of King William, Queen Anne, and King George I,* 2 vols. [1744–46], 2:524). Ferguson claimed to have informants among the Tories at home (*State Trials,* 9:412), and Lord Grey believed Ferguson knew several Dutch lords at the Hague (Grey's Confession, 170–208). Ferguson also had connections with American Puritan divines such as Increase Mather and Dutch ministers like Reverend William Gouge and Abraham Kick. See Francis Bremer, "Increase Mather's Friends:

examined was asked, "Do you know Mr. Ferguson?" Almost all answered "yes."

Ferguson was educated in Scotland and began his career as a Presbyterian vicar of Godmersham in Kent. He was ejected in 1662, and made his living teaching "university learning" at Islington.[28] In 1668, he published a religious tract that caught the attention of the Independent theologian John Owen. Sometime in the 1670s, Ferguson converted to Independency and became Owen's assistant at a gathered church on Bury-Street in London. Owen, the former vice-chancellor of Oxford and chaplain to Cromwell during the Protectorate, was still an active and influential divine in the 1670s.[29] Under his tutelage, Ferguson wrote two more religious tracts concerning the value of reason in religious thought and defending Owen's ideas from his harsher critics, especially the Anglican divine William Sherlock.[30] But Ferguson was not satisfied with religious controversy alone, and by the late 1670s he was active in London Whig politics. He was initially attached to the household of the City Whig Thomas Papillon, and had a chapel in Moorfields, where he apparently preached to "great multitudes."[31] By 1679, Ferguson was a "constant consulter and advisor with the earl of Shaftesbury," and his first pieces of propaganda were written in collaboration with Shaftesbury and the earl's circle of friends, supporters, hacks, and henchmen.[32]

Ferguson's early forays into political polemic were Exclusion-era

---

The Trans-Atlantic Congregational Network of the Seventeenth Century," *Proceedings of the American Antiquarian Society* 94 (1984): 59–96.

28. Anthony Wood, *Athenae Oxonienses,* 4:97–114; James Ferguson, *Robert Ferguson,* 8–15; Matthews, *Calamy Revised,* 193–94.

29. The tract that caught Owen's attention was Ferguson's *Justification onely [sic] upon a satisfaction* (1668). On Owen, see Matthews, *Calamy Revised,* 376–77; and Walter Wilson, *The History and Antiquities of Dissenting Churches,* 5 vols. (London, 1808), 3:260–82. On Owen and Ferguson, see William Orme, *Memoirs of the Life, Writing, and Religious Connexions of John Owen, D.D.* (London, 1826), 301; and Peter Toon, *God's Statesman: The Life and Work of John Owen* (Exeter: The Paternoster Press, 1971), 156.

30. Robert Ferguson, *A Sober Enquiry into the Nature, Measure, and Principle of Moral Virtue* (1673), and *The Interest of Reason in Religion* (1675).

31. Robert Ferguson, dedication to *The Interest of Reason in Religion*; Sir Walter Scott, *Somers Tracts,* headnote, 9:315; Roberts, 309.

32. John Bramston, *Autobiography,* ed. Lord Braybrooke (London, 1845), 182. Shaftesbury had a large and fluid circle of friends of high and low birth, and it is impossible to identify everyone who had a hand in the propaganda generated under his influence. Among his more infamous associates were Algernon Sidney, Sir William Jones, John Hampden, the younger,

pieces that championed Shaftesbury, supported Monmouth's ambitions for the throne, and demonized the duke of York. The central premise of Ferguson's two "black box" tracts (a black box supposedly contained evidence of Charles II's marriage to Monmouth's mother), published in 1680, was that the "Protestant duke," Monmouth, was the true heir to the royal succession.[33] Most of Ferguson's efforts in these tracts, however, were directed toward impeaching the life and character of the "popish successor." The king's brother was guilty of approving "the burning of London, endeavoring to alter the limited monarchy into a despotic rule, and combining with papists in all the part of the late [popish] plot." These crimes "make him liable to the ax, while his is aspiring to a spectre."[34] Both Shaftesbury and Monmouth paid Ferguson for his "black box" tracts; their political goals in 1681 seem to have been in relative harmony.[35]

Ferguson was probably also paid for his three *No Protestant Plot* tracts. This series (published in 1681 and 1682) was written in defense and praise of Shaftesbury, who "by his courage, wisdom, and intelligence hath both withstood and defeated so many of their [papists] designs against our religion and the safety of the nation." It also recounted a long history of popish conspiracy and treason, and warned Charles II that he was losing his subjects' fidelity by allowing his brother "to rival him in his authority." These tracts also contained some not so subtle hints that force might be the only option against the mounting popish threat to their Protestant lives and liberties. The Dissenters, in particular, being daily harassed by the execution of the penal laws, may become "exasperated and incensed"; "no man can undertake what a rich and courageous people may do."[36]

Though his "black box" and "protestant plot" tracts were published anonymously, Ferguson's authorship or at least co-authorship was

John Locke, Henry Care, and Elkanah Settle. Haley, *Shaftesbury*, 670–71; Knights, *Politics and Opinion*, 162–63.

33. *A Letter to a Person of Honour, Concerning the Black Box* (1680); *A Letter to a Person of Honour, Concerning the King's own Disavowing the having been Married to the Duke of Monmouth's mother* (1680).

34. *A Letter to a Person of Honour concerning the King's disavowing*, repr. *Somers Tracts*, 8:191.

35. The Information of Robert West, *CSPD*, 25:439; Greaves, *Secrets of the Kingdom*, 19.

36. *No Protestant Plot, or the Pretended Conspiracy of Protestants against the King and Government discovered to be a Conspiracy of the Papists against the King and his Protestant Subjects* (1681), 8, for the first two quotations; *The Third Part of No Protestant Plot* (1682), 35, for the last quotation.

widely suspected. Many other antipapist tracts were attributed to him as well. Ferguson was vigorously attacked in the royalist press. In ballads, pamphlets, weeklies, and poems, he was portrayed as a dangerous incendiary. The royalist playwright and poet John Dryden immortalized him in the *Second Part of Absalom and Achitophel* as "Judas," Shaftesbury's paymaster of Whig hacks:

> Judas that keeps the Rebels Pension-purse;
> Judas that pays the Treason-writers fee,
> Judas that well deserves his Namesake's tree.[37]

Ferguson's most persistent critic was Roger L'Estrange, who used the pages of his weekly, the *Observator*, to report every bit of gossip concerning Ferguson's comings and goings. L'Estrange created a larger-than-life image of Ferguson as the man at the bottom of every seditious libel and every plot, consorting with rebels and fugitives, at once everywhere and yet nowhere to be found. He can turn a "lawful congregation into a common sanctuary for renegades and fugitives"; his nature as well as his principles are "fierce, bloody and rebellious"; he is the "son of thunder," a "Lucifer," the "mouth of the Party." L'Estrange linked all seditious activities and treasonable books to the Plotter, calling any conspirator "a Ferguson."[38]

L'Estrange's obsession with Ferguson attests to the power and appeal of his early propaganda. L'Estrange believed Ferguson's ideas had the ability to "mislead the weak and confirm the wavering." They could even influence the Anglican faithful: "one Ferguson, let me tell ye, in a parish church . . . does more hurt than forty Fergusons in as many conventicles."[39] Indeed, as Shaftesbury undoubtedly recognized, Ferguson was an extraordinarily able and artful propagandist, one who understood the power of language, the power of half lies, the power of grand allegations, and the power of emotion. Ferguson provoked his audience. He lavishly employed harsh and violent words: "by force and fraud," "force and violence," the popish successor seeks to "destroy," "violate," "pervert," "invade" England's privileges and liberties and

---

37. *The Second Part of Absalom and Achitophel* (1682), lines 321–23.
38. *Observator*, no. 398 (September 5, 1683), no. 396 (September 1, 1683), no. 179, (January 19, 1685).
39. *Observator*, no. 398 (September 5, 1683).

impose on her "thraldom and bondage." Ferguson's verbal violence and impassioned tone played on the reader's fear and anxiety. Yet his tracts were not merely populist diatribes meant for common consumption alone. They contained multiple argumentative devices and worked at several levels. Each, in fact, was a collection of various radical political positions, replete with Whig lore, myth, and history.

Central to Whig propaganda in the late 1670s and early 1680s was the image of fire. Like many a Whig scribbler, Ferguson blamed the London fire of 1666 on papist incendiaries who were ready once again at a moment's notice to set the city ablaze. This accusation was particularly believable following Titus Oates's revelations concerning the so-called Popish Plot in 1678.[40] It reminded Londoners both of the horrific Smithfield fires during the reign of Mary I and their recent terrible trauma in 1666. But Ferguson was even bolder than Oates. He specifically accused the duke of York of ordering the 1666 fire of London. It was the king's "dearly beloved brother" who "authorized the burning of London," an allegation Ferguson repeated in five of his early tracts.[41]

This outrageous charge was part of a whole catalog of lies, half-truths, and distortions that Ferguson regularly employed and which together made up a grand mythic Whig history of an on-going, world-wide Catholic conspiracy. The papists were not only responsible for the Smithfield fires, the Armada, and the Gun-Powder Plot, they also had started the civil war, had massacred thousands of Protestants in Ireland in 1641, and were behind the execution of Charles I. Since the Restoration, and in league with Louis XIV and the "popish successor," the papists had started the trade wars with Holland, plotted to assassinate the king, murdered Sir Edmundbury Godfrey, advised the dissolving of Parliaments, and robbed the City of its charter. After the discovery of the Rye House Plot, Ferguson added that the papists were responsible for the "murders" of Lord Russell and Algernon Sidney and had slit the throat of the earl of Essex in the Tower. Bold lies, oft repeated: presumably for popular consumption. Portions of Ferguson's mythic Whig history appeared in all of his tracts between 1679 and 1685.

---

40. Oates published his narratives in 1679. See his *Discovery of the Popish Plot* (1679), and *A True Narrative of the Horrid Plot and Conspiracy of the Popish Plot and Conspiracy against the Life of His Sacred Majesty* (1679). Other tracts that blamed the London fire of 1666 on Catholics include Thomas Hunt, *Great and Weighty* and *A Defense of the Charter*, and [Charles Blount] *An Appeal to the Country from the City* (1679).

41. *A Letter to a Person of Honour Concerning the Black Box* (1680), 15.

John Dryden accused Ferguson of plagiarizing his history of popish plotting, as recounted in the third part of *No Protestant Plot*, from Andrew Marvell's *Account of the Growth of Popery and Arbitrary Government* (1677).[42] Indeed John Kenyon has described Marvell's elaborate history of popish conspiracy as "one of the most influential pamphlets" of the Exclusion era, and it is very likely Ferguson used portions of it as a basis to construct his popish history.[43] He was probably further aided by Henry Care's stridently anti-Catholic *Weekly Pacquet of Advice from Rome* (1678–83). Ferguson simplified and synthesized the antipapist material of writers like Marvell and Care. He did not need to provide much in the way of evidence for his history of popish plotting, murder, and massacre. Oates's narrative had already found "eager acceptance" among all levels of society.[44] But more important, Fox's *Acts and Monuments* had made Protestant suffering and martyrdom at the hands of papists part of the English national consciousness.[45] Images engraved in the English memory, from the Smithfield fires and crescent-shaped Spanish flotilla to Guy Fawkes and his powder kegs, made any further demonization of Catholics believable enough.

Ferguson's early tracts were great reservoirs of Whig slogans, rhetoric, and ideology. They fused together arguments from history and law, reason and commonsense. From the Whig constitutionalists, Ferguson gathered notions of the people's "ancient rights and privileges"; the importance of the coronation oath, by which the king agrees to "always govern his subjects according to the law"; and the significance of Magna Carta, which Ferguson maintained contained "no new privileges, wrested from our kings, but only the ancient rights of the people."[46] Ferguson employed the language of natural law as well. The existence of natural rights, Ferguson maintained, was consistent with the "true principles of reason." He asserted that the king's duty was to uphold the laws of nature, including the "fundamental right" to life. The violation of one subject's rights by the government placed all

---

42. Preface to *Satire Against Sedition* (1682).

43. J. P. Kenyon, *The Popish Plot* (Harmondsworth: Pelican Books, 1974), 21.

44. Jonathan Scott, "England's Troubles: Exhuming the Popish Plot," in Tim Harris, Paul Seaward, and Mark Goldie, eds., *The Politics of Religion in Restoration England* (Oxford: Basil Blackwood, 1990),103–31.

45. On Fox's influence on the English psyche, see John Knott, *Discourses of Martyrdom in English Literature* (Cambridge: Cambridge University Press, 1993), passim.

46. *The Second Part of No Protestant Plot* (1682), 2

subjects' lives at risk and demonstrated that "those whose duty it is to defend our lives invaded them."[47] The abjuration of the people's natural rights by the king cancels "all bounds [by] which subjects are tied to their princes" and casts the kingdom into a "state of war."[48]

Ferguson's propaganda reached and influenced a wide and diverse audience. The simplicity and force with which he expounded his basic themes—antipopery, the coming of arbitrary government, the need to resist the succession of the duke of York—probably made his propaganda the most successful of all the Whig writers. Hunt, Johnson, and the Whig constitutionalists provided Whig conspirators with the ideological underpinnings of their subsequent manifestos and declarations. Ferguson took those ideas, mixed them with antipapist rhetoric and lies, and popularized them. Little wonder his work was most often cited, his language most often echoed. On the eve of the Rye House Plot, men and women from London to Lyme Regis, and Canterbury to Cornwall, whose "seditious words" were recorded by worried authorities, asserted the truth of a Whig vision of the times.

Part of that "truth" was the imminent coming of arbitrary government with the ascension of the duke of York, and the consequent extirpation of the Protestant religion and Protestant lives at the hands of the papists. In February 1683, the yeoman Robert Humes boldly told his neighbor's wife that "Popery is coming into this kingdom and if the duke of York should succeed his brother, he would be a worse popish tyrant then ever Queen Mary was." As the Presbyterian Timothy Eastwood of London declared in July 1682, "there never would be any good times till the King and the duke of York were put by and the duke of Monmouth made king. . . . for if the duke of York should be king, they should have their throats cut."[49] Yet there was an alternative to the "popish successor." In Lyme, "one Lucey" was prosecuted in 1682, for saying that "it could and should be proved that the King was married to the duke of Monmouth's mother and that nought but knaves, rascals, and fools signed the Dorsetshire address to the King."[50] In 1683, William Leeke of Wellington showed his neighbors a "pamphlet on the

---

47. *An Enquiry into the Barbarous Murther of the Earl of Essex* (1689), 1.

48. *The Second Part of No Protestant Part*, 2.

49. *Middlesex County Records*, 4:201; the Information on oath of John Posser, *CSPD*, 25:31, for the quotations.

50. Captain Gregory Alford to Marmaduke Alford (*CSPD*, 23:60). The Dorsetshire Address pledged support against the king's enemies, particularly Whigs. Numerous addresses by

Black Box," which he asserted proved the legitimacy of the duke of Monmouth.[51]

Since the very existence of "old English government" was threatened, as one Protestant from Dublin put it, active resistance was becoming a credible option. "Times looked very black and therefore to keep arms in our houses is better than food, to defend us, if there should be occasion," so one Mr. Cittle of London advised his friends in 1682. In March 1683, an attorney and a minister overheard in Dunsborne (Gloucestershire) echoed the arguments of Thomas Hunt and other Whig polemicists by declaring that, "There was a statute made in Queen Elizabeth's reign that no person popishly affected should enjoy the crown of England and that it was lawful to take up arms against any such person." A London tailor said the king was a papist and wondered "why Parliament doth not chop off his head." "Rather [than] the duke of York should come to the crown," the mayor of Derby asserted that, "he would be the first man that would draw a sword against him."[52]

The Rye House plotters decided to do just that in the winter of 1682–83. In the depositions and confessions gathered by the government following the plot's discovery, conspirators used the ideas propagated by radicals like Ferguson to justify and vindicate their actions. As Ferguson himself had patiently explained to fellow partisan Zachary Bourne, there exists "a mutual covenant between the king and the people [and] that his majesty had broke it on his side so the people were again at liberty." The lawyer and conspirator Robert West understood that as a result of the "attempts" by the Stuart kings to "introduce popery and arbitrary government . . . the government was dissolved and the people at liberty to settle another."[53]

---

corporations, common councils, and other bodies of citizens were draw up in reaction to the Whig petition movement in 1681 (see Harth, *Pen for a Party*, 80–84).

51. The Information on oath of Andrew Sockett of Wellington, mercer; and the Information on oath of William Leeke, *CSPD*, 25:167–68. Two years earlier, Leeke had tried to persuade a local minister that the duke of York was a papist by showing him Titus Oates's *True Narrative of the Horrid Plot* (*CSPD*, 25:301).

52. An Examination on oath of Owen Duffy, *CSPD*, 23:201; Statement by Constant Oates, *CSPD*, 23:227; the Information of Oliver Dowle of Dunsborne, Gloucestershire, *CSPD*, 24:118; *Middlesex County Records*, 4:153; the deposition on oath of John Adderley, July 26, 1683, *CSPD*, 25:209, for the quotations.

53. Information of Zachary Bourne, *State Trials*, 9:413; Robert West's Confession, BL, Add. 38,847, fol. 91, for the quotations.

The Plot

The Rye House Plot has been draped in myths and exploited for political purposes since it was first reported to Secretary Jenkins in June 1683.[54] Its reality and its importance remain controversial today. My interest lies in the very ideas that propelled radicals to justify their intended actions. Examining the aspirations and aims of the plotters, both high and low, reveals that the conspirators were motivated by the ideas set forth in radical Whig polemic, and that their designs were far more extreme and violent than is commonly recognized.

Ferguson was privy to the plans for a general insurrection in London and several western counties from the outset. He and Colonel Rumsey acted as the earl of Shaftesbury's envoys to an inferior cabal of conspirators and to other Whig lords. Ferguson was also supposedly Shaftesbury's "aid-de-camp" within London as well as his paymaster and purchaser of arms.[55] Shaftesbury had first begun discussing a rebellion against Charles II's government after the dissolution of Parliament in 1681, but not until the summer of 1682 were plans for a general insurrection seriously considered by other prominent Whigs. They included William, Lord Russell; the duke of Monmouth and his supporters, Lord Grey of Werk and Sir Thomas Armstrong; and the parliamentary leader and former chair of the Green Ribbon Club, John Trenchard of Somerset.[56] A lower circle of conspirators included the lawyers John Ayloffe, Robert West, Aaron Smith, Edward Norton, John Wildman, Nathaniel Wade, and the Goodenough brothers, Richard and Francis; and the soldiers Richard Rumbold, Thomas Walcot, and John Rumsey.

---

54. The secondary literature on the Rye House Plot is unsatisfactory. A narrative of events is found in Richard Greaves, *Secrets of the Kingdom*, chapters 4 and 5. Greaves offers little interpretation and does not concern himself with the conspirator's demands and grievances. D. J. Milne discusses the plot in her article, "The Results of the Rye House Plot and Their Influence on the Revolution of 1688," *TRHS*, 5th Ser., 1 (1951): 91–108. Neither Haley, *Shaftesbury*, 707–24, nor Ashcraft, *Revolutionary Politics*, Chapters 7 and 8, are centrally concerned with the plot. Shaftesbury, Haley's focus, left England in November 1682, and thus had nothing to do with the plotting in 1683. The extent to which Locke, Ashcraft's concern, was brought into the plans or even knew of the plot is still debatable. His participation, if any, was certainly far more peripheral than Ferguson's.

55. The Examination of Zachary Bourne before the King and Council, July 5, 1683, *CSPD*, 25:41; West's Confession, BL, Add. 38,847, fols. 100–101.

56. Grey's Confession, 3–18.

Throughout the autumn of 1682, Shaftesbury urged his fellow conspirators to act. He told Lord Howard of Escrick that he had "several thousands of men that were all in readiness to rise when he did but hold up his hand."[57] But, in fact, there was little evidence that this was the case. The other Whig lords hesitated. Lord Russell advocated patience, pointing out that there were no provisions for arms and ammunition, nor had they drawn up a declaration of their intentions and grievances. "Patience," Shaftesbury angrily responded, "will be our destruction."[58] Aware that the government was preparing new charges against him, Shaftesbury went into hiding in October 1682, and finally, in frustration and fear, left England for the last time the following month, seeking refuge in Amsterdam. He took Colonel Rumsey, Captain Walcot, and Robert Ferguson with him. Before he parted, Shaftesbury reportedly said of his fellow conspirators that "they were too few to do the work, and too many to conceal it."[59] His words proved prophetic.

At first the departure of Shaftesbury and Ferguson, the two firebrands of the conspiracy, was greeted with relief by the other Whig conspirators. But according to Lord Grey, it soon became apparent that it was "impossible for us to act, they [Shaftesbury and Ferguson] having managed the greater part of our City affairs, knew all those considerable gentlemen." Ferguson was sent for in order to "explain Shaftesbury's connections with the City."[60] He returned shortly after Shaftesbury's death at the end of January 1683, and the meeting and planning of the higher and lower conspirators resumed.

In the winter and spring months of 1683, both circles of conspirators often spoke of the need to compose a declaration of their reasons for overturning the government. According to the testimony and confessions of those who later turned king's evidence, Robert Ferguson, John Wildman, Algernon Sidney, the earl of Essex, and Nathaniel Wade (the latter in collaboration with several other lower level conspirators) all

---

57. Howard's testimony at the trial of John Hampden, junior, (*State Trials*, 9:1066). Nathaniel Wade also reported that Shaftesbury "imagined to himself that he had thousands at his devotion in an hour's warning" (BL, Harl. 6,845, fol. 266).

58. Grey's Confession, 20, 26.

59. Haley, *Shaftesbury*, 708–12; *State Trials*, 9:364.

60. Grey's Confession, 41; Dalrymple, 1:25. It is not certain who exactly sent for Ferguson. Grey made it sound like the higher cabal of conspirators did so in his confession, but Robert West reported that a group of the lower level of conspirators agreed that Ferguson should be sent for and claims he wrote, "a canting letter to Mr. Ferguson, inviting him over for his health" (West's Confession, BL, Add. 38,847, fols. 95, 96).

drew up or planned to draw up declarations.[61] None of these declarations survives today, and only the briefest description remains of some of them. This is especially true of those declarations merely discussed or supposedly written by the higher cabal of conspirators, the so-called Council of Six. It is very likely that they were so divided among themselves that they were never able to compose a declaration. The Scottish conspirator William Carstares wrote that the "schemes" of the English lords "were crude and undigested and they were all of different minds."[62]

Lord Grey's confession describes an important meeting of the higher circle of Rye House conspirators in April 1683. Present, in addition to himself, were Sidney, Essex, Hampden, Russell, and Monmouth. Sidney proposed that their declaration "tell all the world how the king had broken the laws and his own oath." But Grey, coached ahead of time by Ferguson, interrupted Sidney to say that while there had been a failure of justice on the king's part, "that was not the defect of the constitution." Nor, asserted Grey, would he draw his sword with the intention of destroying either the king or the government. Monmouth, Russell, and Hampden declared that they were of the same mind as Grey. Lord Grey was concerned that their declaration stay within the bounds of the old English constitution. Their goal was to redress the nation's grievances and reverse the government's progress toward "absoluteness."[63] Yet only weeks later the two cabals agreed to assassinate the royal brothers at Rumbold's Rye House Mill as the king and duke of York returned by coach from Newmarket. Not surprisingly, by that time, Robert West learned that the lords were not going to draw up a declaration, but were resolved simply to "leave all things to a parliament."[64]

There is more information about those declarations discussed and written by the lower level of conspirators. They too presented their grievances and demands in a conservative language, the rhetoric of

61. On the declarations by Ferguson, see Grey's Confession, 39–40; Zachery Bourne's Information to the Privy Council, CSPD, 25:40; and Rumsey's Information, State Trials, 9:379. On Wildman's declarations, see State Trials, 9:399, and West's Confession, BL, Add. 38,847, fol. 122. On Sidney and Essex, see Grey's Confession, 59, and State Trials, 9:381. On the collaborative efforts of Nathaniel Wade and others, see State Trials, 9:405, and West's Confession, fol. 102.
62. Carstares Papers, 13.
63. Grey's Confession, 54, 39–40.
64. West's Confession, BL, Add. 38,847, fol. 97.

restoring lost liberties. Yet what they proposed would have fundamentally altered the church and state in England. Taken together, they comprised a Whig program for revolutionary government. Their most frequent demand was for liberty of conscience for nonconformists.[65] As Thomas Walcot stated shortly before his execution in July 1683, he entered the plot to "stand for liberty of conscience and to assert and preserve the people's liberties now in hazard." The desire for religious toleration for Protestants, so often asserted in Whig propaganda, was in reaction to the sufferings caused by the enforcement of the penal laws against Dissent and what the Whigs believed to be the coming of popery. "The King had a visible enough design to introduce popery and arbitrary government and overwhelm the light of the Scripture," John Ayloffe told his fellow plotters. Aaron Smith agreed. He told his clerk that, "The King and his cursed Council were papists in their hearts, that they were resolved to destroy all old English liberty and totally extirpate the Gospel and that it was high time to arm themselves against such horrid designs and regain their lost rights and privileges."[66]

Frustrated by the frequent dissolution of Parliament, the lower cabal of plotters also demanded the establishment of annual Parliaments, which could only be dissolved after all petitions and other business were addressed. They were also nervous about the threat posed by standing armies, which were created and maintained by the Crown. Hence several of their declarations called for the militias to be placed in the hands of the Parliament. Other declarations demanded that all bills that passed both houses of Parliament twice be made law without the king's consent and that all sheriffs be popularly elected.[67]

Members of the lower cabal also discussed how they would secure London and reform English society. After the assassination of the royal brothers at Rye House Mill, they hoped to terrorize the opposition into submission and appease the populace into compliance. These plans included murdering the former Tory lord mayor, Sir John Moore, "if the people did not pull him to pieces, his skin should be fleeced off and

65. West's Confession, BL, Add. 38,847, fols. 96, 102; Colonel Rumsey's Information, *State Trials*, 9:379; Zachary Bourne's Information, *State Trials*, 9:416.

66. Certificate by Samuel Smith, ordinary of Newgate, *CSPD*, 25:154; the Information of Nathaniel Hartshorne, *CSPD*, 25:12; the Information of Samuel Starkey on oath, *CSPD*, 25:42, for the quotations.

67. West's Confession, BL, Add. 38,847, fol. 96; Bourne's Information, *State Trials*, 9:416; West's Information, *State Trials*, 9:405; Rumsey's Information, *State Trials*, 9:379.

stuft and hung up in Guild-hall as one who betrayed the rights and privileges of the City." The same fate was designated for the present royalist lord mayor and Tory sheriffs of London. The wealthy City Whig Thomas Papillon was to be declared one of the new sheriffs and the Whig alderman and former sheriff, Henry Cornish, the new lord mayor. If they refused these new offices, they too would be executed.[68]

Most of the judges "should be killed or brought to trial for their arbitrary judgements and their skins stuft and hung up at Westminster hall." The Oxford judge who had sentenced the Protestant joiner Stephen Colledge to death was to be hanged from the same post as had Colledge. Several of the king's chief ministers of state should be "taken off," including lords Halifax, Hyde, and Rochester.[69] Ferguson wanted his archenemy Roger L'Estrange seized as well as the presses at Whitehall. He also believed that "nothing was to be expected from the rich old citizens [of London] and therefore a half dozen of them must be taken out of their houses and hanged on sign-posts and their houses given as plunder to the mobile." This, Ferguson argued, would certainly frighten the rest.[70]

Still further, it was decided that the people should be "eased of the chimney money" and that no taxes be imposed in the future except a moderate excise and land tax. The lower echelon of conspirators also discussed the general "uselessness" of the bishops and deans and decided they should be "wholly laid aside." Some of the revenues allocated for the universities were to be confiscated and used to relieve the people's burden from taxation. Several colleges were to be converted into schools for the teaching of mechanical arts.[71] The conspirators also discussed making England a free port and naturalizing all aliens as a "means to engage foreigners on our side." Finally, they resolved that Princess Anne, the duke of York's second daughter, should be "preserved" and married to "an honest country gentleman to raise a breed for keeping out foreign princes to the crown."[72]

---

68. The Further Examination of Robert West, *State Trials*, 9:420.

69. *State Trials*, 9:394, 422; West's Confession, BL, Add. 38,847, fols. 103–4.

70. *State Trials*, 9:419, 417. Also see Robert Ferguson, *The History of All Mobs, Tumults, and Insurrections in Great Britain* (1715), 43, wherein Ferguson reiterated these plans.

71. *State Trials*, 9:420–21; West's Confession, fol. 104. On popular resentment to the chimney tax, see Lydia Marshall, "The Levying of the Hearth Tax, 1662–1688," *EHR* 51 (1936): 628–46.

72. West's Confession, BL, Add. 38,847, fol. 104; *State Trials*, 9:421–22.

Though their plans were wild and extravagant and motivated by a fair amount of revenge, they nonetheless resonated with certain consistent themes. These lawyers, soldiers, and tradesmen wanted to retake control of London, place their candidates back into positions of power, and punish the opposition. They even wanted their own partisans, City Whigs Sir Patience Ward and Sir Robert Clayton, both of whom had served as lord mayor, to publicly apologize for not doing enough during their terms of office to prevent the ascension of royalist candidates. If Ward and Clayton refused to do so, they were to be "knocked on the head." In addition to retaking London, the conspirator's designs also displayed a degree of populism, pragmatism, and anticlericalism. A large part of their populism was probably motivated by their need to secure the support of the "meaner people." Their plans to keep the excise and the land tax, but remove the chimney tax—which was especially unpopular with the lower orders—suggests a desire to please the common people without offering any compensation to the wealthy. In fact, the lower echelon of conspirators never once discussed measures to ensure the support of the landed and merchant classes. They may have felt some degree of support within these groups from the beginning; they may also have simply been willing to terrorize any opposition into submission.

Their feelings that the bishops were useless and that the colleges would better serve the "public use" if they taught vocational skills, or if their revenues were used to "ease the people from taxes," betrayed a strong anticlericalism and a sort of hard-boiled utilitarianism. Their attitudes toward the universities were not surprising; civil war radicals had attacked them as well. Oxford remained a royalist stronghold. Charles II had moved Parliament there in 1681, because he could count on the loyalty of the scholars and students. Likewise the clergy had ardently supported the court and preached against the tenets of the Whigs and Dissenters. Confiscating church lands and transforming the universities would not only avenge past wrongs but would forever cripple two royalist centers of strength.

These plans discussed by the lower circle of Rye House conspirators amounted to a revolution complete with the kinds of atrocities modern historians usually associate with the French Revolution. How much the Whig lords who met regularly with Ferguson and Rumsey were told of these plans is impossible to know. They may have passively approved or they may have found them absolutely abhorrent. Yet they themselves were not unwilling to use violence to obtain the exclusion of the "popish successor." Only their endless delays, as Shaftesbury had predicted, made for their destruction.

The plans of the Whig plotters became public in June 1683. They were betrayed by one of their own, a salter with great debts and a bad conscience named Josiah Keeling. He exposed the plot to Secretary Jenkins on June 12, including the plan to assassinate the king and his brother at Rye House. The exposure of the Rye House Plot, as it was soon known, became public knowledge around June 19, 1683. As diarist Narcissus Luttrell faithfully recorded, "About the 19th was discovered a dangerous and treasonable conspiracy against the person of his Majestie and the duke of York by some of those called Whiggs."[73]

Aware that their designs had been exposed, several of the lower echelon of conspirators met one last time. Nathaniel Wade proposed that they immediately muster what men they could and lead a rising "here or in the west to die like men than be hanged like dogs." But Colonel Rumsey declared that their situation was hopeless: "The hearts of the people are down and our great men are good for nothing."[74] Feeling confused and dejected, they finally decided that each man should "shift for himself." But Robert Ferguson did not share their fears and somber mood. He "laughed at us all and gave us his parting complement, Gentlemen, you are all strangers to this kind of exercise; I have been used to flight and I will never be out of a plot so long as I live, and yet I hope to meet some of you at Dunbar before Michael-mas."[75]

Rye House, Myth and Reality

Did Whig radicals really hatch a conspiracy in the winter and spring of 1682 and 1683? Or was the so-called Rye House Plot merely another phase of the royalist backlash? Had Whigs designed to lead a popular insurrection or assassinate the royal brothers, or had it been designed for them? Both contemporaries of the plot and modern scholars have

73. Luttrell, 1:262.
74. The Further Examination of Robert West, State Trials, 9:409.
75. BL, Add. 38,847, fol. 119; State Trials, 9:409.

wondered if the entire conspiracy was somehow manufactured by court supporters with the intent of either destroying or discrediting the Whig movement, thereby preventing any further efforts on its part to bar the duke of York from the throne. If this was the case, royalists were extraordinarily successful.

Quite naturally, it was the Whigs themselves who first denied the reality of the plot. In November 1683, Sir Samuel Barnardiston referred to the Rye House Plot as "the late sham Protestant plot" for which he was charged with libel and imprisoned for the next four years. Over forty-eight years later, Whig historian John Oldmixon confidently declared that "Rye house" was but "a sham plot."[76] Others—some contemporaries as well as later historians—found it conceivable that a plot existed, but without the active involvement of the Whig elites.[77] Either the Whig lords knew nothing of the assassination plans against the lives of the royal brothers, or they were manipulated and misled by "lewd and beggarly fellows of no religion and morals, particularly, Sir Thomas Armstrong, Julian [Samuel] Johnson, Robert Ferguson, West, the lawyer." Thomas Bruce, earl of Ailesbury, believed that the earl of Essex, the duke of Monmouth, and Lord Russell "were guided and gulled by a lewd bully and gamester [Armstrong], by a profligate parson [Johnson], by a fanatick teacher [Ferguson] and a hot-headed paltry barrister" [West]. Diarist John Evelyn believed that Essex and Russell had been "drawn in" "some bloody design" manufactured by "Ferguson and his gang." The Whig lords' only intention had been to "rescue the king from his present counselors and secure religion from popery and the nation from arbitrary power."[78]

The notion that the "noble-minded Russell," the "generous Monmouth," the "illustrious" Essex, and the "courageous" Sidney were somehow deceived by the devious and vulgar Robert Ferguson and men of like ilk was an oft-repeated interpretation, especially in the Whig

---

76. *The Tryal and Conviction of Sir Samuel Barnardiston, bt. for High Misdemeanor* (1684); John Oldmixon, *The History of England, during the reigns of King William and Queen Mary* (London, 1735), 679.

77. Jonathan Scott is the newest champion of this idea, arguing that Sidney and the other Whig leaders were simply concerned with "the self-defense of Protestants," not to be confused with the Rye House Plot with its "pub talks" and "cutlasses at dawn" (*Algernon Sidney and the Restoration Crisis*, 267).

78. Ailesbury, *Memoirs of Thomas Bruce, Earl of Ailesbury written by himself*, ed. W. E. Buckley (Roxburghe Club, 1890), 2 vols. 1:72; Evelyn, *The Diary*, 4:329.

histories of the eighteenth and nineteenth centuries.[79] Yet other contemporaries and historians have wondered how it was possible for the Whig leaders to be ignorant of the plots and machinations of those within their party, men whom they protected and patronized and within whose company they dined, drank, traveled, and lodged. The duke of Ormonde, who was present at the examinations and trials of the conspirators, found it difficult to believe that Russell, Grey, and Essex had no part in the assassination plan: "Either they had no intelligence within the party or they were ill-befriended, how otherwise did they not know?" More recently, historian J. H. M. Salmon also asserted that it was highly unlikely that Robert Ferguson, Colonel Rumsey, Major Wildman, and the others acted without the consent of their leaders.[80]

The evidence weighs heavily in favor of the conspiracy's existence and the Whig lords' knowledge of and consent to the activities of the lower circle of conspirators, including the assassination plan. The examinations, the testimony, and the confessions of the major and minor plotters, English and Scottish, taken in the months and years following the plot's exposure, all tell the same basic story. But it is highly unlikely that it was one simply fed to the informants. Details (dates, names, decisions taken, who said what) varied from one confessor to the next—to be expected as time lapsed and memories faded—but the contours of the narrative remained the same. Not only did those who turned king's evidence admit the plot, those who suffered for it did as well. Two of the lower-level conspirators, Captain Walcot and William Hone, admitted their guilt upon the scaffold. Shortly before his suicide, the earl of Essex sent his wife a "very melancholy message; that what he was charged with was true."[81] Even if one rejects the evidence given by the confessors and sufferers, it is difficult to dismiss the letters and memoirs of those who remained at large and owned up to the conspiracy.[82]

79. Sir Walter Scott, headnote, *Somers Tracts*, 13 vols. (1813), 9:526–27. Charles James Fox, for example, asserted that the lords had nothing to do with the assassination component of the plot (*A History of the Early Part of the Reign of James II* [1808], 46).

80. Bodleian Library, Carte 219, fol. 560; J. H. M. Salmon, "Algernon Sidney and the Rye House Plot," *History Today* 4 (1954): 704–5.

81. *The Examination and Confession with the Behavior and Speeches of Captain Walcot, William Hone, and John Rouse* (1683); Burnet quoted in *State Trials*, 9:504.

82. The ciphered letters, between the Scottish conspirator, the earl of Argyle, and his wife and other Scottish and English conspirators, speak of the plot. See *Carstares Papers*, 106–21. Ferguson's own manuscript, "Concerning the Rye House Business," while dubious in many

Yet the best proof of the Rye House conspiracy, in all its facets, is that it was never proven to be a royalist concoction even after the Whigs had the power to do so. Whig fortunes did eventually change. Following the Glorious Revolution, when Whig conspirators and rebels were transformed into saints and martyrs, the Rye House Plot remained a Whig endeavor, not a royalist fraud meted out upon innocent victims. Those still living after 1689–among them, John Hampden, the younger, John Trenchard, and John Wildman—never denied the existence of the plot or accused the royalists of manufacturing it. In November 1689, John Hampden affirmed the existence of the Council of Six and his membership.[83] The majority of the historians, Whig and otherwise, writing in the 1690s and early eighteenth century, also believed in the plot.[84] In fact, it is difficult to find a single contemporary in the last decades of the Stuart era who doubted the reality of the Whig conspiracy of 1682–83.

It might be argued that the post-Revolution Whigs were not interested in revenge but reconciliation; that they were not guilty of an assassination plot, though they had certainly resorted to some sleazy politics in the early 1680s, including clubbing and caballing with men like Robert Ferguson and Titus Oates. Perhaps they simply wished to forget the past. Yet this would be to deny what had happened to them in 1683. The exposure of the plot cost the exclusion movement dearly, nearly destroying it. The price in blood alone was enormous. The deaths of Russell, Essex, and Sidney and the flight of Monmouth, Grey, and others left Whig radicals demoralized and leaderless. Almost all active Whig politics had to be carried out abroad between 1683 and 1688. If the plot was a royalist invention, considering all that it had cost the Whigs, the truth (never mind retribution) would have been clarified after the Glorious Revolution. Nerves were still raw in 1688 and 1689, memories still vivid. Popular vengeance was wrecked upon the hapless Judge Jeffreys for his orchestration of the "bloody assizes" in the west. In a debate in the House of Commons in June 1689, over a bill of indemnity for the Rye House prosecutors, John Hampden, the younger, gave a moving speech in opposition to the bill: "Blood," he charged, "no

---

respects, certainly owned up to the conspiracy. He was in exile, when he wrote the manuscript, and under no compulsion to admit its existence.

83. *Journals of the House of Lords*, 14:379.

84. Laurence Echard, *The History of England*, 3 vols. (1707–18), 3:1028–31; White Kennett, *A Complete History of England*, 3 vols. (1706), 3:408–12; Ralph, *The History of England*, 1:723.

mortal man can forgive."[85] If the Rye House conspiracy were a royalist fabrication, the Glorious Revolution would surely not have been the bloodless event we know it today. Vengeance against the plot's informants and the Crown's prosecutors would doubtlessly have soiled the Revolution's otherwise nearly unspotted reputation.

The plot was not a fraud, but it was yet another Whig failure. This time the experience of defeat did not just thwart Whig goals, it took Whig lives, and not simply one obnoxious joiner, but those of the Whig leadership. Russell, Essex, and Sidney were lost. Important members of the Whig gentry were imprisoned. With the exposure of the plot also came a radical diaspora as Whig plotters and propagandists fled to Dutch cities, particularly Amsterdam and Utrecht. Among them, the indomitable Robert Ferguson and the ambitious and gullible Monmouth, the center of the Protestant cause after 1683. The exclusion movement continued, and so too the vicious cycle of violence.

85. Grey, *Debates*, 8:306.

5

Making Martyrs:
Rye House Legacies and
Monmouth's Manifesto

Russell's Head for Common House votes Elevated,
And Essex's Razor at Rome Consecrated.
    —"A New Protestant Litany" (1689)

The discovery of the Rye House Plot, with the trials and executions that
followed, prompted a new phase in the radical Whig exclusion movement. On the one hand, the plot's discovery was devastating, effectively
removing all radical activity to the Continent. The network's leadership
was decimated. Lord Shaftesbury died in exile in January 1683; the earl
of Essex committed suicide in July 1683; a few days, later Lord Russell
was beheaded. Algernon Sidney followed him to the scaffold in December. A second tier of potential Whig leaders—John Trenchard, Lord
Delamere and his son, Henry Booth, John Hampden, the younger, and
others—were imprisoned, tried, fined or otherwise humiliated. All that
remained of the leadership were the Lord Grey of Werk, who managed
to escape to Holland shortly after his arrest, taking his mistress with him,
and, of course, "Absalom," the duke of Monmouth, who lost his father's
favor and soon roamed about the Continent as well.

Yet the effects of the plot's disclosure were not all destructive. After all, the radical network's great patrons and its one republican ideologue, Sidney, had done little for the movement in practical terms. They had not dared to print their own political principles; others had done so for them and could continue to do so. Though Colonel Rumsey had flatly declared that the lords "were good for nothing," in many ways they turned out to be more useful to the cause without their heads than with them. The deaths of Essex, Russell, and Sidney gave the Protestant cause its most powerful martyrs. Whig scribblers now accused the government of an actual murder cover-up, in the case of Essex, and of judicial murder in the deaths of Russell and Sidney.

The Whig Grandees

It is not entirely surprising, then, that reports from around the country in the months following the first Rye House trials describe local Whigs and Dissenters as ever "bold and venomous," "insolent and proud," and "bold and presumptuous." A new round of propaganda wars had begun, and Whig scribblers were hard at work declaring the plot a royalist fraud and canonizing the new martyrs for the cause. A London newsletter from July 1683 reported that, though proof of the plot was clear, "yet the factious party have the face to make a sham of almost every branch of it. They have this day published a sly Relation of Rouse's Case and wild stories of Lords Russell and Essex insomuch that the King has ordered a Declaration of the conspiracy to be forthwith published."[1]

The "wild stories" concerning the earl of Essex proved to be the most damaging. Essex had been arrested and charged with high treason shortly after the Rye House Plot's discovery. He was imprisoned in the Tower, and on the morning of July 13, 1683, his servant found him lying in a pool of blood with a razor beside him. Essex's throat was cut from ear to ear; the gash had severed his windpipe, nearly decapitating him. A coroner's inquest was held the next day. Twenty-three wealthy citizens

---

1. *CSPD*, 25:307 (London, August 19, 1683); 26:89 (Kingston, November 14, 1683); 25:330 (Windsor, August [?], 1683); 25:215–16, for the quotations. The latter writer is referring to a Whig polemic defending John Rouse who was convicted of treason for the Rye House Plot and executed on July 20, 1683.

were chosen by the government to hear and examine the evidence in the case. They returned a verdict of self-murder.[2]

Even before the results of the inquest were known, many royalists assumed that Lord Essex, out of guilt over his role in the plot against the royal brothers, had taken his own life. News of Essex's death reached Lord Russell's treason trial and helped convict him. The solicitor general instructed the jury that Essex's suicide was still more proof of the plot's existence and of the guilt of the Whig lords.[3] Yet despite royalist assumptions and the verdict given in the coroner's inquest, there were others who adamantly asserted that a dark deed had ended the Whig grandee's life, that lies were being perpetuated in order to cover it up and ensure guilty verdicts in the remaining Rye House trials. Whig newsletters, ballads, and handwritten papers positing a murder theory circulated almost immediately. George Speke of White Lackington in Ilminster had such a paper in September 1683. He offered it to a neighbor in order to convince him that "the earl's throat was not cut by himself but by some other." When his neighbor refused it, Speke "called him a cursed Tory and struck him in the face with a stick."[4] George Speke's son, Hugh, and his friend and fellow Green Ribbon brother Laurence Braddon were the first to bring the murder charge to the national stage. Braddon, a Whig lawyer, began his own investigation into Essex's death, aimed at proving his murder. He was interviewing witnesses and collecting evidence when the government moved to arrest him. Letters of introduction by Hugh Speke were found in Braddon's possession at the time of his arrest, and Speke was jailed and tried with Braddon for high misdemeanor.[5] At their trial, Braddon sought to prove his case, questioning a thirteen-year-old schoolboy who supposedly saw a razor tossed from Essex's Tower window. The boy later retracted his story, and Braddon's other witnesses seemed nervous and confused.

2. *An Account of How the Earl of Essex Killed Himself in the Tower of London* (1683); Michael MacDonald, "The Strange Death of the Earl of Essex, 1683," *History Today* 41 (1991): 13–18; Greaves, *Secrets of the Kingdom,* 219–29; Michael MacDonald and Terence R. Murphy, *Sleepless Souls: Suicide in Early Modern England* (Oxford: Clarendon Press, 1993), 70–57.

3. *State Trials,* 9:633.

4. The Information on Oath of Henry Warr of Ilminster, *CSPD,* 25:430.

5. In August 1683, Speke wrote Braddon letters of introduction to persons of quality, including Sir Richard Atkyns. Speke claimed he was drinking at the time he wrote the letters and "knew not well what I writ." The letters were plainly incriminating, informing Atkyns that, "we hope we can bring the earl of Essex's murder on the stage, before they can any of those [Rye House plotters] in the Tower to a trial" (*State Trials,* 9:1196, 1162).

Braddon and Speke were found guilty, and both remained in prison until the Glorious Revolution.[6]

Their trial made a lot of noise. A transcript was published that only increased doubts and suspicions over Essex's death.[7] Colonel Henry Danvers believed Braddon's witnesses, and he too began asserting the murder theory. Danvers had a long history of radicalism. A Baptist, he had fought for Parliament during the civil wars and adopted Fifth Monarchist views in the Interregnum. He was rarely out of plot during the Restoration, consorting with Dissenters, republicans, and Green Ribbon radicals. In the late 1670s, he was attached to Algernon Sidney, managing Sidney's bid for Parliament in 1679.[8] He was certainly aware of the Rye House Plot, if not an active participant. In December 1684, he published *Muther Will Out*, in which he charged that Essex had been murdered by royalist conspirators in order to "confirm a Protestant Plot," "stifle the Popish Plot," and "destroy the Lord Russell."[9] The government moved quickly to arrest Danvers, but he successfully evaded their grasp and eventually escaped to Holland shortly after Monmouth's failure in 1685.[10]

By far the most sophisticated polemic asserting the murder theory was, not surprisingly, penned by Robert Ferguson. His elaborate *Enquiry into and Detection of the Barbarous Murther of the late Earl of Essex* was first published in Holland in 1684. It was far more radical than Danvers's piece and played on popular fears and suspicions. Ferguson ascribed Essex's murder to part of the ongoing worldwide Catholic conspiracy movement. Those who had fired London in 1666, and murdered Sir Edmundbury Godfrey in 1678, and Stephen Colledge in 1681, could now add to their list the slaughter of the "virtuous and religious,"

---

6. Braddon was fined two thousand pounds and was only liberated after the prince of Orange's invasion in 1688. He wrote two tracts asserting Essex's murder in the post-Revolution era: *Essex Innocency and Honour Vindicated* (1690), and *Bishop Burnet's late History charged with great Partiality and Misrepresentations to make the present and future Ages believe that Arthur, Earl of Essex, in 1683, killed himself* (1725). He may have also penned *A True and Impartial Narrative of the Murder of Arthur, Earl of Essex* (1729).

7. *The Tryal of Laurence Braddon and Hugh Speke, gent. upon an information of high misdemeanor* (1684).

8. Richard Greaves, "The Tangled Careers of Two Stuart Radicals: Henry and Robert Danvers," *The Baptist Quarterly* 29 (1981): 32–43; *BDBR*.

9. *Murder Will Out; or a Clear and Full Discovery that the Earl of Essex did not Murder Himself, but was murdered by others* (1684; repr. in *Somers Tracts*, 10:65–71).

10. *CSPD*, 27:268, 292; Luttrell, 1:324.

"heroic and generous" Essex. The "Vatican, Louvre, and St. James [the duke of York's residence]" conspired to ruin Essex because he had sought to expose the Popish Plot, defend the Protestant religion, and fight against the introduction of popery and slavery.[11]

Ferguson's *Enquiry* painstakingly reviewed the Braddon and Speke trial, asserting the credibility of Braddon's witnesses. But more important, Ferguson used Essex's murder as more proof that violence had first been perpetrated by a popishly infected government and that radicals like the Rye House plotters were merely defending themselves and the nation's liberties: "If we hear of our neighbor's throat getting cut, should not we look to our own?" Ferguson concluded his tract by laying the murder of Essex at the feet of the duke of York, and by calling on all "English peers and gentlemen" to awaken and avenge Essex's death.[12]

The charge of murder against the duke of York, crowned James II in February 1685, had tremendous propaganda value, as Ferguson well understood. It was a charge not easily answered or forgotten. It haunted James II's reign. Yeomen farmers and London gentlemen echoed the charge. Papers lying on country roads blamed the murder of "Justis Godfrey and Grate Essex" on the new king.[13] Dissenters in New England grieved to hear "how barbarously the Earl of Essex was murdered in the Tower."[14] The *Declaration* accompanying Monmouth's invasion, in June 1685, accused James of Essex's murder. In 1687, writing from Amsterdam, Ferguson reminded his readers once again of the barbarous murder of Essex and claimed he had "convincing proofs of it" that he would gladly present if he could return home with immunity. When asked by a fellow Whig what those proofs could be, the wily Plotter replied, "take no thought of that, it doth not concern you or me whether it be true or false. The report is spread and will have all the effects as true and so serve our end."[15]

Whig aims were also served by the trial and execution of William, Lord Russell. In the post-Revolution era, the much remembered Russell

---

11. *An Enquiry into the Barbarous Murther of the Earl of Essex*, 5–12.
12. *An Enquiry into the Barbarous Murther of the Earl of Essex*, 1, 75.
13. *Middlesex County Records*, 4:268, 292; *CSPD, James II*, 1:61.
14. *Collections of the Massachusetts Historical Society: The Mather Papers*, 4th ser. (Boston, 1846), 3:105.
15. The tract in which Ferguson repeated the murder charge was *A Representation of the Threatening Dangers, impending over Protestants in Great Britain* (1687). Ferguson is quoted in Salmon, *The Lives of the English Bishops*, 212.

became the ultimate martyr-patriot of the Whig version of English history. While Shaftesbury, the crafty schemer whose long political career had taken numerous shifts and turns, was quietly forgotten by the Whigs, the images of Russell and Sidney, the fallen liberators, loomed large.[16] Russell, "the most virtuous, noble, and innocent person," appeared a victim of royalist wrath; his only crime had been his steadfast defense of the nation's religion and liberties.[17] Whig propaganda asserted time and again that Russell's trial had been a "travesty of justice and his execution judicial 'murder.'"[18] As Russell himself put it in his dying speech, "For to kill with forms and subtleties of law is the worst sort of murder."[19]

Russell's fiery antipapist speeches in Parliament during the Popish Plot and Exclusion Crisis had already made him something of a popular hero among London Whigs and Dissenters in the early 1680s. In November 1680, he declared before Parliament that should the nation ever be so transformed "that I should not have the liberty to live a Protestant, I am resolved to die one." Russell was well on his way to martyrdom. His theatrical trial on July 13, 1683, helped to promote his image as a sacrificial lamb. Not only did the news of Essex's death stun the courtroom, but Russell dramatically placed his much esteemed wife, Lady Rachel Russell, beside him to take notes. He defended himself by declaring that though he had been in the company of the other alleged conspirators, he had never taken part in any discussions about rebellion. At one of the key conspiratorial meetings at a wealthy London merchant's house, wherein an insurrection in Taunton was supposedly plotted, Russell claimed that he was simply there to taste the merchant's wines.[20]

At his grisly execution in Lincoln's Inns Fields, during which the executor wielded three strokes to severe Russell's head, spectators

---

16. So Charles James Fox would write many years later, "thus fell Russell and Sidney, two names that will, it is hoped, be forever dear to every English heart. When their memory shall cease to be an object of respect and veneration, it requires no spirit of prophecy to foretell that English liberty will be fast approaching its final consumption" (*A History of the Early Part of the Reign of James the Second*, 50).

17. *An Account of the Pretended Prince of Wales* . . . *[and] A Short Account of the murther of the earl of Essex* (1688).

18. Schwoerer, "William, Lord Russell," 50. Also see Schwoerer, "The Trial of Lord William Russell (1683): Judicial Murder?" *The Journal of Legal History* 9 (1988): 142–68.

19. "The Paper delivered to the Sheriff by my Lord Russell," in *State Trials*, 9:694.

20. *History of Parliament*, 3:1,219, for the direct quotation; *State Trials*, 9:578–636.

dipped handkerchiefs in his blood.[21] After the Revolution, the Whig martyrologies described Russell's execution as curiously reminiscent of that of the greatest seventeenth-century martyr, King Charles I of Blessed Memory. On the day of Russell's martyrdom, the sky grew dark and great claps of thunder were heard as the axe fell. And when his head was held up, a "considerable groan" arose from the crowd.[22]

Russell said little on the scaffold, but instead assured his martyrdom with the paper he handed to the sheriff. Russell's dying speech magically transformed the Whig lord from a political agitator and conspirator to a Protestant hero and patriotic liberator. He probably had some help crafting his speech. Russell was far from eloquent during his trial, but his dying speech was a masterpiece of propaganda, blending together both the tropes of Protestant martyrdom and those of radical Whig polemic. It may well have been the work of several hands, including the divines Gilbert Burnet and Samuel Johnson, who were both suspected by the government as the true authors of Russell's speech.[23]

It began in the formulaic discourse of the martyr, wherein he declared that he had "found the assurances of the love and mercy of God" and did not question but that he would "partake of that fullness of joy which is in His presence." He went on to plead with all Protestants to give up their "unhappy differences" and consider "the common enemy," popery. This was standard Whig rhetoric, to which Russell added, in typical martyr fashion, his prophecy that the worst was yet to come. "Popery is breaking in upon this nation"; the Smithfield fires lurk but around the corner. "Blessed be God," Russell declared, "I fall by the axe and not by the fiery trial." Naturally, Russell asserted that he died wholly innocent of the charges brought against him, which he saw as the court's revenge for his zealous promotion of the Exclusion Bill. True, he had had some discourses with like-minded men "about making some stirs"; true too, he knew of the "ill designs" discussed by "my Lord Shaftesbury and some hot men." But this was at most misprision. He had

21. Schwoerer, "William, Lord Russell," 50; David Ogg, *England in the Reign of Charles II*, 2 vols. (Oxford: Clarendon Press, 1955), 2:649.

22. [Tutchin] *The Western Martyrology*, 47. See William Dugdale's description of Charles I's execution in his *Short View of the Late Troubles in England* (Oxford, 1681), 371–75.

23. *The Ellis Correspondence, 1686–1688*, 2 vols., ed. G. A., Ellis (London, 1831), 1:190–91; Dalrymple, 1:49.

never plotted against the king's life. His blood was innocent, a sacrifice to "satiate some people's revenge."[24]

Russell's speech was published by radical printer John Darby, who made it available, according to John Evelyn, "within an hour." Three different editions were published in 1683 alone.[25] As with Stephen Colledge's speech, Tory propagandists produced their own fraudulent edition of Russell's speech, wherein he properly confessed his crimes.[26] Still this was not enough; the speech had to be answered point by point. L'Estrange rushed into print his *Considerations upon a Printed Sheet entitled the Speech of the late Lord Russell* (1683), which blamed Russell's misguided principles on his chaplain, the Reverend Samuel Johnson. Russell, L'Estrange asserted, could not possibly have been responsible for "this poison." His dying sheet was "undoubtedly the strokes of another pen, that took more care to advance and support the credit of a faction" than prepare Russell for the afterlife.[27]

But neither L'Estrange's tract nor that of Bartholmew Shower, discussed in Chapter 2, could squash Russell's growing legacy.[28] Whigs countered Tory polemics with their own broadsides and pamphlets, vindicating Russell's speech and fashioning his martyrdom.[29] His dying sheet was reprinted in Edinburgh and Dublin, sent in cartons to the countryside, and reprinted during the Glorious Revolution.[30] For his part, L'Estrange received a death threat following the publication of his response, "first for reviling that martyr for the people's privileges good Stephen Colledge . . . secondly for performing the same piece of villainy on Lord Russell's speech." By the time of the Revolution, Russell

24. "The Paper Delivered to the Sheriffs by my Lord Russell," *State Trials*, 9:689–91, 692–94.

25. Evelyn, *The Diary*, 4:332. The three 1683 editions of Russell's speech are *The Last Speech and Behavior of William, Lord Russell, upon the Scaffold in Lincoln's-Inn Fields* (repr. in Edinburgh, 1683); *The Last Speech and Carriage of Lord Russell upon the Scaffold* (repr. in Edinburgh, 1683); *The Speech of the Late Lord Russel [sic], To the Sheriffs* (printed for J. Darby by direction of Lady Russell).

26. *The Speech and Confession of William, Lord Russell, Who was Executed for High Treason against His Majesty* (1683). The fraud, of course, did not go undetected or unanswered; see *Animadversions on the Last Speech and Confession of the late William, Lord Russell* (1683); and *Animadversions upon a Paper entitled, The Speech of the late Lord Russell* (1683).

27. *Considerations*, 10–15.

28. Shower, *An Antidote against Poison* (1683).

29. *A Vindication of the Lord Russell's Speech and Innocence* (1683); *A Vindication of the Lord Russell's Speech and Paper . . . from the foul imputations of falsehood* (1683); *The Last Legacy or Affectionate and Pious Exhortations of the late W. Lord Russell to his Lady and Children* (1683).

30. Schwoerer, "William, Lord Russell," 55.

had become a powerful and evocative symbol for the Whig cause. In the Whig martyrologies published and republished in the post-Revolution era, their author, John Tutchin, reserved his highest praise for Lord Russell. He was simply "the finest gentleman England ever bred."[31] Death had glamorized Russell and made him useful to the cause.

Colonel Algernon Sidney's trial in November, and execution on December 7, 1683, was the last truly dramatic episode of the Rye House conspiracy investigation and trials that had begun some six months earlier.[32] Whereas Russell had appeared cowed and inarticulate during his trial, Sidney gave a strong and eloquent defense of himself. The case against him was weak. Lord Howard was the only witness to Sidney's treason. Lacking a second witness, the government resorted to introducing the colonel's own unpublished papers, found in his study, which they argued proved that Sidney sought to "persuade the people of England that it was lawful to raise rebellion." Those papers were published posthumously in 1698, as Sidney's *Discourses Concerning Government*.[33]

Sidney's "papers," extracts of which were read during his trial and summarized in his dying speech, were his most significant contribution to the radical Whig cause after his martyrdom. Although Sidney denied his authorship of the manuscript, arguing that the ink on the pages was over twenty years old, and that the handwriting was never proved to be his, "the papers" were obviously his answer to Filmer's *Patriarcha*, which had been published only three years earlier. The portions of his "papers" pulled out by the attorney general, Sir Robert Sawyer, to prove

---

31. *CSPD*, 25:309; [Tutchin] *The Western Martyrology*, 31–35, for the direct quotations.

32. Since there was only one witness against John Hampden, the younger, one of the members of the so-called Council of Six, he was indicted on a misdemeanor in February 1684, and fined forty thousand pounds, an enormous sum. Unable to pay, he was imprisoned until 1686. A more minor conspirator, James Holloway, a Bristol linen merchant, had escaped to Barbados, where he was betrayed and sent back to London in chains. He confessed his part in the plot, hoping for a pardon. But as he was attainted for outlawry upon an indictment of high treason, no trial was necessary, and Chief Justice Jeffreys simply ordered his execution. He was hanged and quartered on April 30, 1684. *The Tryal and Conviction of John Hampden upon an indictment of high misdemeanor* (1684); *The Free and Voluntary Confession and Narrative of James Holloway* (1684).

33. *State Trials*, 9:838, for the direct quotation. The *Discourses* were published in London in 1698, 1704, 1705, 1730, 1751, 1763, and 1772, and in Edinburgh in 1750. French translations appeared in 1702 and 1794, and German in 1705 and 1793. Alan Craig Houston, *Algernon Sidney and the Republican Heritage in England and America* (Princeton: Princeton University Press, 1991), 285–86.

Sidney's treason, asserted three propositions: that "the power of the king was derived from the people upon trust"; that "the king has no authority to dissolve parliament"; and that since the king had dissolved Parliaments and thus "invaded" the peoples' rights, "he hath broken his trust." Therefore the people "might assume that original power they had conferred" upon him.[34]

Sidney argued that the passages read by the prosecution were taken out of context and asked for the whole manuscript to be read. But in fact Sidney's long, point-by-point refutation of Filmer did posit these principles and much more. Sidney also found himself condemned as much for his past politics as for his present. His former adherence to the "good old cause" was well known. When Sawyer instructed the jury to "show your abhorrence of these republican principles," he raised the bogey of the civil wars and Protectorate.[35] It was "forty-one all over again." This was a powerful talisman, and Sidney recognized the tactic. He denied his "papers" and labeled Cromwell "a tyrant."[36] But the jury, all well chosen by the new Tory sheriffs, predictably came back with a guilty verdict.

After all appeals for a pardon to the king, including one by Sidney himself, had failed, the colonel prepared a powerful dying speech, wherein he fully embraced his republican principles and his past.[37] He used his dying speech "freely" and "publicly" to declare his political thinking. Sidney glossed four main points from his "papers": first, that governments were man-made; second, that "magistrates were set up for the good of nation"; third, that magistrates derived their "right and power" from the laws of the nation and were bound by those laws; and fourth, that each nation's laws "have the force of a contract between the magistrate and people." Should that contract be violated, the "whole fabric" of government would be dissolved. Only in the final paragraph of his dying speech did Sidney sound anything like a martyr. But Sidney was not the patient sufferer; instead he was the angry prophet in the desert, calling upon God to "suffer not idolatry [popery] to be established in this land. . . . Defend thy cause and defend those that defend

---

34. *State Trials*, 9:866, 840.

35. *State Trials*, 9:854, 840.

36. "Cromwell . . . was a tyrant and a violent one (you need not wonder I call him tyrant, I did so every day of his life and acted against him too)" (*State Trials*, 9:866).

37. "To the King's most Excellent Majesty, The Humble Petition of Algernon Sidney, esq.," printed in *State Trials*, 9:904–6.

it. Stir up such as are faint; direct those that are willing; confirm those that waver." Defiant to the end, Sidney sneered in the face of his enemies with his final sentence in which he thanked God that he died "for that OLD CAUSE in which I was from my youth engaged."[38]

Unfortunately for the radical network, Sidney's trial and dying speech, both of which were published, were not nearly so useful as propaganda tools as Russell's had been.[39] They were far too blackened by the dark strokes of republicanism and its association with the chaos of the civil wars. Though the same principles had been espoused by numerous radical Whigs, most stridently by Thomas Hunt and Samuel Johnson, the taint of republicanism, so willingly embraced by Sidney in his dying speech, made it hard for Whigs to defend their hero's final moments. The civil wars, commonly believed to have been the product of such thinking, were still too vivid and painful a memory. L'Estrange even entitled his response to the dying sheet, *Mr. Sidney His Self Conviction.*[40] Whigs did come to Sidney's defense, but their responses to Tory attacks on his dying speech were tempered and lukewarm. Even a sympathetic account of Sidney's execution and burial for Dissenters in New England reported that his speech was "stufft with expressions savoring of Republican principles."[41]

Whig glorification of Algernon Sidney began in earnest only after the Glorious Revolution. He was most certainly a "posthumous hero." He

38. Sidney's dying speech was published in George Meadly, *Memoirs of Algernon Sidney* (London, 1813), 390–98. The dying speeches of Protestant martyrs, following Foxe, were often prophetic, and there were certainly those among the Whig faithful who believed Russell's and Sidney's speeches predicted a grim future. A letter to the major of Bridgewater in February 1685, describing papist gains under James II, commends the major to read the dying speeches of Russell and Sidney, for they "foretold [that] which is now most demonstrable" (*CSPD, James II,* 1:41).

39. Two editions of both the trial and the dying speech were published: *An Exact Account of the Trial of Algernon Sidney, esq., who was tryed at the King's Bench-Bar* (1683), and *The Arraignment, Trial, and Condemnation of Algernon Sidney, Esq., for High-Treason* (1684); *A Very Copy of a Paper Delivered to the Sheriffs upon the Scaffold on Tower Hill* (1683), and *Colonel Algernon Sidney's Speech, delivered to the Sheriff on the Scaffold* (1684).

40. Roger L'Estrange, *Mr Sidney His Self Conviction: Or His Dying Paper Condemned to Live* (1684). Other Tory attacks on Sidney's speech included *Some Animadversions on the Paper Delivered to the Sheriffs . . . by Algernon Sidney* (1683); [Elkanah Settle] *Remarks upon Algernon Sidney's Paper Delivered to the Sheriffs* (1683); and [John Nalson] *Reflections on Coll. Sidney's Arcadia, the Old Cause, Being Some Observations Upon his Last Paper* (1684).

41. For an example of a half-hearted defense of Sidney, see S. Ward, *The Animadversions and Reflections upon Col. Sydney's Paper Answered* (1684). "Account of Transactions in Europe, 1683," probably written for Increase Mather, in *The Mather Papers,* 3:636, for the direct quotation.

had published nothing in his lifetime except for a co-authored, anonymous tract that was "singularly uninfluential."[42] Sidney's *Discourses* were not published until 1698. He was to be the hero-liberator of the eighteenth century far more than the seventeenth, a development attributable in greater measure to his martyrdom rather than to his ideas. The radical Whig martyrologies of the post-Revolution era, produced by veterans of the 1680s, would praise and vindicate Sidney's principles. Yet though the "brave old man" was great, Russell was greater still.[43]

The Monmouth Episode

By 1684, the radical network was dispersed and, for the most part, leaderless. Radical Whig activity reached a low ebb. Though many in England had already placed "all hope" in the duke of Monmouth following the deaths of Shaftesbury, Essex, Russell, and Sidney, Monmouth himself was at first slow to take on the mantle of radical leadership.[44] Though continually in touch with Whigs both in Europe and at home, Monmouth spent much of 1684 skating, dancing, and dining with the prince and princess of Orange at the Hague. He did not become serious about returning home and championing the Protestant cause, as well as his own, until after Charles II's death in February 1685, and the ascension to the throne of his uncle and enemy, the duke of York.

At home, many ordinary folk not only placed "all hope" in Monmouth, they were dragged before their local magistrates for declaring so. Their offenses included drinking healths to Monmouth, often followed by wishing confusion and damnation to the king and the duke of York, or singing a ballad with the refrain, "Let Monmouth Reign, Let Monmouth Reign," as happened in Chester during Monmouth's

---

42. James Conniff, "Reason and History in Early Whig Thought: The Case of Algernon Sidney," *Journal of the History of Ideas* 43 (1982), 404; Houston, *Algernon Sidney and the Republican Heritage*, 10.

43. [Tutchin] *The Western Martyrology*, 67.

44. A conversation among Dissenters overheard at a coffeehouse in Wiltshire (The Information of William Warde, *CSPD*, 25:13) for quotation.

progress in 1682.[45] To the Whig advantage, Monmouth enjoyed a popularity among many English that the politicians like Shaftesbury or even Russell could never galvanize. Monmouth, after all, had royal blood coursing through his veins. He had even touched for the "king's evil" (scrofula) during his west country progress in 1680.[46] He was a captivating young man: "His motions all accompanied with grace, / And paradise was painted in his face," as Dryden himself wrote. Monmouth was the embodiment of the beautiful cavalier, adorned with the most romantic physical features of the Stuarts as well as their tragic flaws, including their usual myopia. Even Aphra Behn, the royalist playwright and poet, found Monmouth

> a Lad,
> Of Royal Birth and Breeding,
> With ev'ry Beauty Clad;
> And ev'ry Grace Exceeding;
> A face and shape so wondrous fine,
> So Charming ev'ry part;
> That every Lass upon the Green:
> For *Jemmy* had a Heart.[47]

But whereas Behn was partly mocking the romantic Protestant duke, many in the streets and coffeehouses of London and elsewhere took Monmouth very seriously. John Self of London was reported to have "leaped with joy" in July 1683, when he heard it rumored that Monmouth was raising an army in Scotland. Self declared that "it was no [Rye House] plot concerning the Majesty's life" and that "if the duke of Monmouth came into England, he would raise men to assist him." The yeoman Phillip Wallis told neighbors that the "duke of Monmouth would be king," asserting that "he would lose his right hand if he would not fight to make the duke of Monmouth king of this kingdom." Deborah Hawkins of St. Andrew's Holborn, discussing the death of

---

45. There were numerous reports of healths being drank to Monmouth between 1683 and 1685; see, for example, The Information of Elizabeth Wicker, in *CSPD*, 24:3, which describes a group in Chichester drinking healths to Monmouth. The song with the refrain, "Let Monmouth reign," is described in *CSPD*, 23:406.

46. Roberts, 89; Clifton, *The Last Popular Rebellion*, 127.

47. "Song. To a new Scotch Tune," in *Aphra Behn Poems: A Selection*, ed. Janet Todd (New York: Pickering, 1994), 17.

Charles II, asserted that she would "put on breeches myself to fight for the duke of Monmouth." At a coffeehouse in Devizes, Wiltshire, one Dissenter assured a table of others that "if he [Monmouth] appeared in the field many thousands out of those countries would soon be with him."[48]

Numerous reports of seditious words such as these were copied down by worried officials throughout England in 1684 and 1685. In Europe, restless Whig radicals, many of whom were former Rye House plotters, gathered not around Monmouth but yet another possible savior of Protestantism, Archibald Campbell, the ninth earl of Argyle. Argyle, a powerful Highland chief, was outlawed for high treason in 1681, at the direction of the duke of York, who was royal commissioner of Scotland at the time. He had escaped to London, plotting to return to Scotland at the head of an armed invasion. His plans had received only mild encouragement from the higher cabal of Rye House plotters in 1682 and 1683. Regardless, Argyle was resolved to lead a rebellion in Scotland with or without English assistance.[49]

Between 1682 and the spring of 1685, Argyle traveled from his estate in Friesland to the various Scottish and English refugee communities in German and Dutch cities, gathering support, money, arms, and enlistees to his cause. The arms and ammunition of the fanatical Cameronians, whose leaders had all been hunted down and killed by 1683, had come into his hands.[50] Argyle's resolution attracted many of the English refugees of the Rye House conspiracy to his cause, including Nathaniel Wade and the Goodenough brothers. The Scottish dissident Sir Patrick Hume of Polwarth, observed that the earl was often surrounded by "English friends," who "carr[ied] him a great respect and esteemed him highly." Nathaniel Wade reported that some of the English were suspicious of Monmouth's commitment to their cause and against informing him of Argyle's plans.[51] Some believed that Monmouth was in daily contact with his father, the king, and would betray their plans. Even after Monmouth was brought into the Argyle design, in the spring of

48. The Information on oath of Benjamin Gosmere, *CSPD*, 25:165; *Middlesex County Records*, 4:255, 285; the Information of William Warde, *CSPD*, 25:13, for the direct quotations.
49. Melinda Zook, "Propagators of Revolution: Conspiratorial Politics and Radical Whig Culture in Late Stuart England" (PhD diss., Georgetown University, 1993), Chapter 5, "The Argyle Rebellion and the Scottish Whigs," 229–86.
50. The Information of Robert Smith, *State Trials*, 9:481.
51. Hume, 17; Wade's Confession, BL, Harl. 6,845, fol. 270.

1685, and it was decided that he would lead a joint rising in England, two English, John Ayloffe and Richard Rumbold, remained with Argyle. Argyle's confidence, courage, and resolve stood in stark contrast to the hesitance and apprehension of Monmouth and the other Whig lords during the months of plotting in 1682 and 1683. Small wonder an old soldier like Rumbold opted to stay with the Highland earl.

Argyle's English friends were also encouraged by the prophecies of English astrologer and almanac maker, John Partridge. He had fled London upon the disclosure of the Rye House Plot and was living in Amsterdam. In December 1684, he was engaged by several English radicals to produce an almanac for the year 1686.[52] Argyle's English companions had already seen part of Partridge's new book and claimed that his "hieroglyphics" "represented many events," including the duke of York's coming to the throne and "a little Highland man . . . brandishing a sword over a field of dead bodies." "None," Sir Patrick Hume of Polwarth reported, "was so vain as to apply to the Earl plainly, but it was clear enough by their way of talking and insisting on these idle trifles . . . that they did desire the hearers might apply them."[53]

The prophecies of Partridge were not convincing to several of the Scottish dissidents who wanted Monmouth brought into the plans. The Plotter, Robert Ferguson, pleaded for Anglo-Scottish unity. He met Lord Grey of Werk in Amsterdam in the winter of 1685, and informed him of Argyle's plans, urging him to arrange a meeting between Argyle and Monmouth. The time had come, Ferguson told Lord Grey, in which "perfect unity amongst us" is essential.[54] Patrick Hume also insisted on bringing Monmouth into the plans, hoping to gain assurances of a joint English invasion.

In the spring of 1685, a series of meetings took place between Monmouth, his closest advisers, namely Lord Grey and Robert Ferguson, and Argyle and his advisors.[55] As the English envoy Bevil Skelton

---

52. *BDBR*, s.v. "Partridge, John"; Partridge is discussed in Paul Hoftijzer, " 'Such only as are very Honest, Loyall, and Active': English Spies in the Low Countries, 1660–1688," in P. Hoftijzer and C. C. Barfoot, eds., *Fabric and Fabrications: The Myth and Making of William and Mary* (Amsterdam: DQR Studies in Literature 6, 1990), 86–90.

53. Hume, 18–19. Partridge's almanac was entitled *Merlinus Liberatus, Being an Almanack for the Year of our Redemption, 1686* (1686); there is a copy in BL, Add. 41,813, fols. 28–44.

54. Grey's Confession, 85.

55. Grey's Confession, 92–93; Wade's Confession, BL, Add. 38,847, fol. 270; Hume, 12, 17, 18, 25, 37.

reported home, "the gang are all in continual consultations. . . . There is something now hatching amongst them."[56] Argyle had reservations about "meddling with" Monmouth, but they were smoothed over when Monmouth made the Scots two promises: that he would launch his invasion of England by the sixth day after the Scots' departure, and that he would not take the title of king but rather let a free Parliament decide the issue. He would break both promises.[57]

During these meetings, Monmouth's and Argyle's respective declarations were drawn up and discussed. James Stewart of Coltness drafted Argyle's *Declaration*, which, according to Hume, after "much pain and after many alterations and amendments was concluded and agreed upon." The eighteenth-century historian Sir John Dalrymple summarized Argyle's *Declaration* as a document concerned with the Protestant religion, in contrast to Monmouth's *Declaration*, which he saw as interested in "civil liberty."[58] But, in fact, both Argyle's and Monmouth's ventures were animated by a combination of religious and political motivations, as reflected in their respective declarations. Their basic messages were the same. The "great trust" that existed between subject and sovereign had been "perverted," resulting in a "total dissolution of all the bonds of subjection." The subjects were thus free to liberate themselves and recover "our just rights and liberties."[59]

Monmouth's *Declaration* has received little scholarly attention. Partly this is a result of the rebellion's dismal failure, but it is also because of the manifesto's own black legacy. The earl of Rochester described it to the prince of Orange immediately after Monmouth's landing as the "most villainous and abominable in its language as well as traitorous that was ever put forth certainly." Monmouth himself disowned the *Declaration*, swearing Ferguson made him sign it without reading it.[60] Bishop

56. BL, Add. 41,812, fol. 9.

57. BL, Lansdowne Collection, 11,52A, fol. 234; Hume, 12, 37. Monmouth did not intend to break his promises. He was unable to set sail until May 24, due to lack of supplies and ill winds. He took the title of king on June 20, hoping to attract the aid and support of the gentry to his flagging cause. See his Proclamation, BL, Harl. 7,006, fol. 186.

58. Hume, 36; Dalrymple, 1:59.

59. *The Declaration of the Earl of Argyle with Noblemen, Gentlemen, etc* (1685), in *State Trials*, 10:1032–40.

60. *CSPD, James II*, 1:201, for the direct quotation; Bramston, *Autobiography*, 188. Monmouth was undoubtedly lying, hoping to save his life. Even Aphra Behn promoted the idea that Monmouth was victimized by Ferguson and had nothing to do with the *Declaration*. In *Love Letters Between a Nobleman and His Sister* (New York: Viking Penguin, 1987), her character

Burnet later characterized the *Declaration* as "tedious and fulsome," "full of much black and chill malice." In the nineteenth century, Macaulay found that "for insolence, malignity, and mendacity," it "stands unrivalled even among the libels of those stormy times." For the most part, historians of the past twenty years have let these descriptions of the *Declaration* stand. Even those solely interested in Monmouth's Rebellion have never investigated the *Declaration*'s origins, intentions, or reception.[61] Yet Monmouth's *Declaration* is the only surviving manifesto of radical Whig proposals from the early 1680s. Robert Ferguson, who was responsible for its initial drafting, had not forgotten the various discussions and plans of the Rye House plotters to compose a manifesto. His declaration, approved by Monmouth and other former Rye House conspirators, was as much a reflection of the Whig politics in 1682 and 1683 as it was an expression of their desires in 1685.

Quite naturally, the *Declaration* reiterates many of the demands discussed by the lower cabal of Rye House plotters. Ferguson drafted the document and brought it to Thomas Dare's house "to be approved" by Monmouth, Lord Grey, and others, including Richard Nelthorpe, Nathaniel Wade, Joseph Tily, and Richard Goodenough.[62] The version agreed upon was printed in English, Flemish, and French and distributed in Holland and England.[63] An early version of Ferguson's declaration also exists. The British Library holds a manuscript draft, possibly in his own hand.[64] It is lengthier than the printed version and filled with

---

"Cesario," who is based on Monmouth, "would have no hand in this gross piece of villainous scandal" (428).

61. Burnet is quoted in Sir Walter Scott's headnote to Monmouth's *Declaration*, in *Somers Tracts*, 9:253; Thomas Babington Macaulay, *History of England from the Accession of James II*, 6 vols., ed. C. H. Firth (London: Macmillan & Co., 1913–15), 2:650. The best recent studies of the Rebellion are Clifton, *The Last Popular Rebellion*, and Peter Earle, *Monmouth's Rebels: The Road to Sedgemoor, 1685* (New York: St. Martin's Press, 1977), though neither examines Monmouth's *Declaration*.

62. Richard Goodenough's Testimony, BL, Lansdowne Collection, 11,52A, fol. 242. George Roberts believed this meeting took place on April 3, 1685 (Roberts, 232).

63. *The Declaration of James Duke of Monmouth, and the Noblemen, Gentlemen, and others, now in Arms for the Defense and Vindication of the Protestant Religion and the Laws, Rights, and Privileges of England from the Invasion made upon them and for delivering the Kingdom from the Usurpation and Tyranny of James Duke of York* (1685).

64. BL, Harl. 6,845, fols. 256–59. Scholars have known that this copy exists but have incorrectly assumed that it was the same version as the printed one. It has the same title as the printed version, but the first several pages are very different. Both George Roberts and Richard Ashcraft examined one of the original printed versions in the Lansdowne Collection (1152A,

revisions: lines are scratched out, additions are scribbled in. It may well be the draft that Ferguson read at Dare's house. It is undoubtedly Ferguson's work, filled with his phraseology and the same sort of violent and unsparing language he so often employed.

A comparison of the two versions of the declaration is revealing. We find that Ferguson's draft is a more brutal and uncompromising invective against the government. We also find that its language and ideas are reminiscent of those of Thomas Hunt. In the draft, Ferguson makes no mention of God, instead asserting that government is a purely secular creation "instituted only to the end [that] people under it might find safety and refuge from violence and oppression." The draft continues in the discourse of natural law: "it cannot be imagined that mankind would part with their natural freedoms and liberty and submit themselves to government to the end they might more certainly and effectively be destroyed by their governors, than they could have been had they continued in the state of nature."[65]

The printed version, on the other hand, is actually a moderated, tempered version of the draft—far less wordy, violent, and radical. It begins by stating that government "was originally instituted by God," though its "form" was the decision of men. There is no use of the discourse of natural law in the printed version, which instead launches into a discussion of the "primitive frame" of England's government wherein the king is "limited and restrained by the fundamental terms of the constitution." The king's prerogative powers are to be used solely for the defense of the people and for the promotion of their happiness. Not without "violation of his oath" can the king do the people any "hurt." Thus the "prerogatives of the crown" and "privileges of the people" stand in balanced harmony. Yet "all human things being liable to perversion as well as decay," so "the boundaries of the government have late been broken," which has resulted in "turning our limited monarchy

---

fols. 558–62), also in the British Library, which is the same version printed in modern collections; see State Trials, 11:1,032–40, and the Somers Tracts, 254–58.

65. BL, Harl. 6,845, fol. 256. Richard Ashcraft suggests that John Locke, who was also in Amsterdam in the spring of 1685, and known to associate with many of the Whigs around Monmouth, "had a hand" in the composition of the Declaration. However, there is no evidence that Locke had anything to do with the production of the Declaration, and more important, those positions in it that might be styled "Lockean" can all be found in Ferguson's earlier tracts as well as in the work of other Whig propagandists. Much of the language in Ferguson's draft of the Declaration is closer to that of Thomas Hunt than John Locke.

into an absolute tyranny." The printed version of the declaration also assures readers that those in arms now have no desire to lay "aside any essential part of the old English government."[66]

Both versions state that Monmouth's mission is to preserve the "reformed Protestant religion," vindicate "the laws of the land and the rights of the people," and promote "the passing of the articles above mentioned into laws."[67] Those "articles" or rather proposals for change are, with a few exceptions, the same in both declarations. Not surprisingly, they include many of the same demands made by the Rye House plotters, including liberty of conscience, annual Parliaments, removal of the king's right to dissolve Parliaments, and placement of the militias under the control of the people's elected representatives. While both versions also proclaim that standing armies will not be permitted without the consent of Parliament, Ferguson's draft renders Parliament still more authority by giving it the right to approve all the king's judges and to "regulate" the king's Privy Council.[68] Both versions urge that all of the judges, the sheriffs, and the lord mayor of London be replaced; new elections be held; habeas corpus be reaffirmed; and the practice of demanding exorbitant fines as punishment be forbidden. Further, all "worthy and zealous assertors of the Protestant interest now in jail will be released."[69]

Both Ferguson's draft and the final version of the declaration indulge in the same fabricated history of Protestant suffering and popish conspiracy that Ferguson employed in all his earlier tracts, and to which long list of accusations he now added that "James, duke of York" "poisoned the late King."[70] The great martyrs of the cause, Sidney and "that loyal and excellent person" Lord Russell, were not forgotten; and the charge against James for the murder of the earl of Essex in the Tower was renewed. The draft version, however, contained a much longer and more violent diatribe against the "duke of York" and his

---

66. Monmouth, *Declaration*, in *Somers Tracts*, 9:254, for the first two quotations, and 256, for the last.

67. BL, Harl. 6,845, fol. 259. The printed version asserts that Monmouth will "promote the passing into laws all the methods aforesaid" (*Somers Tracts*, 9:258).

68. BL, Harl. 6,845, fol. 258.

69. Monmouth's *Declaration*, in *Somers Tracts*, 9:256–57.

70. Monmouth's *Declaration*, in *Somers Tracts*, 9:257; BL, Harl. 6,845, fol. 257. Both versions asserted that the duke of York assassinated Charles II "to prevent the discovery and punishment of the murder of the earl of Essex."

papist supporters. Papists had "murdered" Stephen Colledge "under pleasure of law" and "forged plots against patriots of the country and the Protestant religion."[71]

Monmouth and his supporters either altered or encouraged Ferguson to alter his draft. In the final version, the language is toned down, much of Ferguson's antipapist diatribe and furious attack on the present government are expunged, and a paragraph has been added describing the "primitive frame of the government." The Monmouth conspirators at Dare's house that day apparently decided that the language of ancient constitutionalism was ultimately more communicable than that of natural law. Ferguson, who was equally skilled in both arguments, probably wrote the new paragraph. He was at heart a pragmatist, and he probably had no qualms about altering his text. Moreover, whether cast in a constitutionalist or rationalist framework, the basic message of the manifesto remains the same. The essential and sacred bond between prince and people has been encroached upon and destroyed. The people are at liberty to defend themselves and erect a new political settlement.

Although it is a less brutal assault on the Stuart government than originally designed, many still felt the Declaration to be simply a vulgar libel. Sir John Dalrymple believed Monmouth's manifesto contained serious flaws, including the many "outrageous invectives" against James II. But more important, Dalrymple felt it alienated far too many important groups. The court's supporters would feel that it "impaired the crown too much"; republicans would find the assertion of Monmouth's right to the Crown upsetting; and the Anglican clergy would be worried by its grant of toleration to Dissenters.[72] But Dalrymple failed to understand that Monmouth and his band were not trying to reach out to Anglican clerics, royalists, or republicans. They had placed their hope in the west county gentry. No doubt, Monmouth recalled his famous western progress in 1680, when many powerful and wealthy gentry families had greeted and entertained him with enthusiasm. Families such as the Spekes of White Lackington, the Strodes of Barrington, and the Yonges of Colyton were to have been his base of support. The Declaration was meant to appeal to their sense of honor and devotion to Protestantism. Their ancient rights were invaded; the Protestant reli-

71. BL, Harl. 6,845, fol. 257.
72. Dalrymple, 1:59.

gion was in peril. As Monmouth's banner summed it up, his mission was "For God and Privileges."[73] For these reasons, it was hoped that these old and honorable families would come to the duke's aid and lend his cause, among other things, legitimacy.

Yet it was not the gentry that Monmouth's cause attracted. The risks that he was asking them to take were far too great, and they may have been cowed by the arrests, trials, and scaffold dramas that had followed the discovery of the Rye House Plot. Moreover, many were swept up and imprisoned by an official dragnet prior to Monmouth's landing.[74] Those who did come out for Monmouth were the artisans, tradesmen, shopkeepers, cloth workers, and yeomen farmers of Somerset, Devon, and Dorset.[75] For these men and women, a great many of whom were Dissenters, Monmouth's *Declaration*, with its promise of liberty of conscience, was good news for the godly. The Independent congregation at Axminster rejoiced to learn of Monmouth's "declarations to restore liberty to the people of God for the worship of God, to preserve the rights and privileges of the nation. . . . Now were the hearts of the people of God gladded and their hopes and expectations raised that this man might be the deliverer of the nation." Ferguson's use of antipapist rhetoric, which was the most effective element of Whig revolution culture, was also powerfully appealing. On June 25, the *London Gazette* reported that "the rabble at Frome, headed by the constable, had put up in the market-place the traitorous *Declaration*."[76] Joshua Lock's father, a tobacconist, testified that his son would never have "run over to Monmouth" had he not seen the *Declaration*. A Baptist named Lark reported that he joined Monmouth after he read the *Declaration*. A former soldier, Captain Walberton, was "ensnared" by the *Declaration* and was captured with a copy of it in his pocket. Samuel Storey of London knew parts of the *Declaration* by heart and warned members of the Church of England fearful of joining Monmouth that, though "we Dissenters shall be the first brought to the stake but depend upon it you will follow."[77]

73. BL, Add. 41,817, fol. 151.

74. *CSPD, James II*, 1:232, 260–63.

75. Clifton, *The Last Popular Rebellion*, 245–76; Earle, *Monmouth's Rebels*, 196–97.

76. *Ecclesiastica, The Book of Remembrance of the Independent Congregation of Axminster and Chard* (Barnstaple, 1874), 80; *London Gazette*, no. 2,046, for the direct quotations.

77. BL, Add. 41,819, fol. 15; BL, Lansdowne Collection, 1152A, fol. 238; BL, Add. 41,808, fol. 265; HMC, *The Manuscripts of Mrs. Stopford Sackville*, 1:26.

Monmouth's Rebellion did not fail because its accompanying manifesto was "a libel of the lowest class," but rather for a multitude of
reasons apart from the stated goals of Monmouth and his advisors. For
there was much about the *Declaration* that attracted followers to Monmouth's cause. Its appeal was demonstrated by the fact that much of its
content was echoed three years later in the prince of Orange's *Declaration of Reasons,* which accompanied his successful invasion of England in
1688.[78] Both Monmouth's and William of Orange's declarations maintain that James had violated his coronation oath; both call for a free and
legal Parliament to settle the matter of the succession and redress the
kingdom's manifold grievances; both contain long lists of the current
administration's crimes, including the appointment of papists to high
offices and the illegal usurpation of the city charters; and both proclaim
that their main concern is the restoration of England's constitution and
the subjects' invaded liberties.

Naturally, there are important differences between the two documents. William's *Declaration of Reasons* is a more controlled and conservative statement, a mark of the more moderate Whigs, both English and
Scottish, and the prince's Dutch advisors, who collaborated in its
production.[79] There were also new concerns and issues in 1688, such as
James's use of his suspending and dispensing powers, the trial of the
Seven Bishops, and the birth of the Prince of Wales. Yet the central
premise in both declarations is the same. The trust between subject and
sovereign was broken, the people's ancient rights and liberties trans-
gressed. The invader's sole purpose is to restore the equilibrium between the Crown and the people once again. Ironically, in response to
this endeavor, Ferguson twice styled Monmouth's cause "glorious"—a
word that never appears in William's declaration, yet a word that
became synonymous with his Revolution.

In the post-Revolution era, Monmouth's *Declaration,* the sole existing
manifesto of the radical Whig cause, was not forgotten. John Tutchin,
himself a Monmouth rebel, republished Monmouth's *Declaration* in its

---

78. Macaulay, *History of England,* 2:564, for the direct quotation; *The Declaration of His
Highness William Henry, Prince of Orange, of the Reasons Inducing Him to Appear in Arms in the
Kingdom of England* (1688).

79. Lois G. Schwoerer, *The Declaration of Rights, 1689* (Baltimore: Johns Hopkins University
Press, 1981), 106–8; Jonathan I. Israel, general introduction to *The Anglo-Dutch Moment: Essays
on the Glorious Revolution and Its World Impact* (Cambridge: Cambridge University Press, 1991),
13–15.

entirety in the 1693 and 1705 editions of his Whig martyrologies.[80] In 1701, the radical publisher John Dunton also reprinted the *Declaration* that had "prevailed" upon so many men to "assist him [Monmouth] with their lives and fortunes." Dunton hoped that the *Declaration* would remind his readers that "it is the cause and not the axe or the halter that makes the martyr."[81] Indeed, Monmouth's failure had made many new martyrs, including the credulous Protestant duke himself. In the aftermath of Monmouth's execution and Jeffreys's "bloody assizes" in western England, the sense of absolute defeat among Dissenters and the remaining radicals must have been awesome. As far as Whig activity is concerned, what the historian finds in the records for 1686 is a deafening silence—as silent as the ghostly limbs and carcasses that lined the western byways that year.

The New Regime

The failures of Monmouth's rebellion in western England and Argyle's in Scotland fed the increasingly vicious cycle between the promoters of a Protestant succession and the Stuart government—a cycle of Whig violence and Whig defeat. In the aftermath of the Rye House trials of 1683, Whig activists and Dissenters could still boldly voice and print their opinions, create larger-than-life martyrs out of their fallen heroes, and place all hope in the romantic Protestant duke, Monmouth, and the noble Scottish laird, Argyle. But the wake of the 1685 rebellions left radicals in complete disarray, with little to salvage from their defeat. True, the rebellions did produce a new pantheon of Protestant martyrs, heroes, and heroines: from the handsome Dissenting Hewling brothers, hanged in the west, to the Londoner, Elizabeth Gaunt, burned at the stake. Yet most of the stories of Protestant suffering associated with the "bloody assizes" were not widely known prior to 1689; it was only with the Glorious Revolution that rebel dying speeches and heroic last deeds became a part of Whig myth.[82]

---

80. Thomas Pitts (alias John Tutchin), *A New Martyrology*, 417–30; [Tutchin], *The Western Martyrology*, 155–62.
81. *The Merciful Assizes* (1701), 24–25, 17.
82. Zook, "The Bloody Assizes," 373–96.

Hence, the rebellions and their aftermath left radicals and Dissenters little to glorify, nothing to celebrate, and nowhere to place hope. James II had come into "his own" with a vengeance. The new king and his lord chief justice, George Jeffreys, were certainly not averse to spilling the blood or ruining the lives and fortunes of their enemies. In 1685 and 1686, they did just that with a number of beheadings, hangings, quarterings, deportations, whippings, pilloryings, humiliating confessions, extraordinary fines, and close imprisonments. The results of their campaign not only further truncated the radical Whig network and snuffed out its remaining leaders, it nearly silenced the radical voice.

Monmouth, "the people's darling," cut a poor figure in his last moments. Found munching peas in a farmer's field a few days after the defeat of his ragtag army at Sedgemoor, he was hauled back to London "starving and exhausted, filthy and friendless."[83] He was no Russell or Sidney. Parliament had already passed an act of attainder against his life, so there was no need for the formality of a trial before his execution. From the Tower, Monmouth scribbled, in a childlike hand, pathetic letters to James and the queen, begging for mercy, offering to convert to Catholicism, expressing willingness to name his former friends to the king. James did grant his nephew an interview at which Monmouth supposedly threw himself at the king's feet.[84] But it was to no avail. The king was disgusted by Monmouth's behavior, and he had not forgotten Monmouth's notorious manifesto: "To make me a murderer and poisoner of my dear brother, besides all the other villainies you charge me with in your declaration."[85] Monmouth blamed his misdeeds on the "knaves and villains," particularly Robert Ferguson, who had misled him, and maintained that he had never read the *Declaration*. Taking the title of king, he asserted, had been forced upon him.[86]

Monmouth's execution at Tower Hill on July 15 was a sad and morbid spectacle. In spite of the prattling pleas of the accompanying bishops, Monmouth now refused to confess any misdeeds, including the sin of rebellion. He made no speech: "he had come to die," as he told the

83. [Tutchin], *The Western Martyrology*, 154; Clifton, *The Last Popular Rebellion*, 227.

84. Earle, *Monmouth's Rebels*, 163–64; Clifton, *The Last Popular Rebellion*, 222–28.

85. Bramston, *Autobiography*, 187–88.

86. "An Account of what passed at the Execution of the late Duke of Monmouth, on Wednesday, the 15th of July, 1685, on Tower-hill," repr. in E. H. Plumptre, *The Life of Thomas Ken, D.D.*, 2 vols. (London, 1890), 2:218–22.

bishops. Further he was mindful of Russell's botched beheading and told the executioner not to "serve me as you did my Lord Russell." But instead, Monmouth's death was more horrible still, taking the executioner five strokes to finally severe the duke's head. Thus "Absalom," the great Protestant hope, died a "shameful death" and was more "pitied than lamented," according to Aphra Behn.[87] He did not leave behind a dying speech. In his last days, his behavior left little material out of which legends could be created. Even the fanciful pens of the Whig martyrologists in the post-Revolution era had to struggle to make a great martyr out of Monmouth: " 'Twas thought at first better to draw a veil before that unfortunate prince and say nothing at all of him."[88]

The earl of Argyle, who was beheaded only fifteen days before Monmouth in Edinburgh, made a less embarrassing death, although he too was willing to name his supporters and did so.[89] Perhaps it was fitting that in their ends, Monmouth and Argyle had forgotten the cause for which their manifestos so boldly declared and for which so many common men and women had staked and lost their lives. The favorite son of a king and the Highland chief had their own private aims and ambitions to consider and old scores to settle. But the Protestant cause was not forgotten by their followers, and many died reasserting it, demonstrating once again the power of the Whigs' revolution culture.

Colonel Richard Rumbold's dying speech, published shortly after his death, reminded the public of the abiding principles of the exclusion movement. Rumbold, a former Rye House plotter, had escaped to Holland in 1683, and joined Argyle's invasion of Scotland. He was hanged, drawn, and quartered in Edinburgh on June 26, 1685.[90] Upon the scaffold, Rumbold declared that he died in the cause of the nation's "just rights and liberties, against popery and slavery." He proclaimed

87. "An Account of what passed at the Execution of the late Duke of Monmouth, on Wednesday, the 15th of July, 1685, on Tower-hill," reprinted in Plumptre, *The Life of Thomas Ken, D.D.*, 218–22; Behn, *Love Letters Between a Noblemen and His Sister,* 460.

88. [Tutchin], *The Western Martyrology,* 154.

89. Argyle did deliver a paper at his execution, which was published in *The Western Martyrology,* 141–43. While prisoner, he was threatened with torture, which was still legal in Scotland. He named Mrs. Smith, the English woman in Holland who had helped fund both his and Monmouth's rebellions. John Willock, *A Scots Earl in Covenanting Times: Being the Life and Times of Archilbald, the Ninth Earl of Argyle* (Edinburgh: Andrew Eliot, 1907), 406.

90. Richard Rumbold, *The Last Words of Richard Rumbold* (1685). Rumbold's speech was particularly famous; see Douglas Adair, "Rumbold's Dying Speech, 1685, and Jefferson's Last Words on Democracy, 1826," *William and Mary Quarterly* 9 (1952): 520–31.

that the political powers he had fought were illegitimate. According to the "ancient laws and liberties of these nations," the king and the people are "contracted to one another. And who will deny me that this was not the just constituted government of our nation? How absurd it is then for men of sense to maintain, that though the one Party of this contract breakth all conditions, the other should be obliged to perform their part? No, this error is contrary to the law of God, the law of nations and the law of reason." Rumbold's last speech was radical Whig ideology, plain and simple. The ancient contract upon which England's government was built had been violated. The current government was illegitimate and hence resistance to it was both lawful and necessary. Rumbold was supposedly asked before his execution, "If he thought not his sentence dreadful?" He replied that he "wished he had a limb for every town in Christendom."[91]

Elizabeth Gaunt, the London Baptist burned alive for harboring a Monmouth rebel, made an equally powerful and provocative speech.[92] Her dying speech, which struck an extraordinarily defiant tone, was published in both English and Dutch in October 1685. Gaunt told the crowd that she was honored to be the first to suffer by fire in this reign of a Catholic monarch. She died, as the Marian martyrs had before her, not for any criminal offence, but because of her faith. She quoted Scripture, which commanded one to "hide the outcasts and betray not him that wanderth," and ended by laying her blood at the door of the "furious judge and unrighteous jury." Her message was clear. She had acted on the authority of a superior guide, Scripture, and was condemned by corrupted, unlawful powers.[93]

The gruesome exhibition of Elizabeth Gaunt's burning, the beheading of the ancient Lady Lisle for harboring rebels, and Chief Justice

91. [Tutchin], *The Western Martyrology*, 143–44.

92. Elizabeth Gaunt had hid James Burton. In 1683, Burton had participated in the Rye House Plot and had sought assistance from Gaunt after the plot's discovery. She gave him money and helped him seek transport to Amsterdam. When Burton was found at Gaunt's home in 1685, he won a pardon by informing against her. It was not without reason that London authorities were more interested in prosecuting Gaunt than Burton. She and her husband were involved in smuggling political and religious dissidents to and from Holland, and they were believed to be responsible for seeing Shaftesbury safely abroad in 1682 (Parry, *The Bloody Assize*, 267–69). Also on Mrs. Gaunt's activities in Holland in the summer of 1685, see BL, Add. 41,817, fols. 219, 225 .

93. *Mrs Gaunt's Last Speech who was burnt at London, October 23, 1685* (1685); [Tutchin], *The Western Martyrology*, 136–37.

Jeffreys's notorious campaign of vengeance that became known as "the bloody assizes" left vivid impressions on contemporaries and deep-rooted scars. In the west, more than two hundred executions in six towns were conducted in less than a month's time. The full punishment for high treason was carried out. Rebels were hanged until unconscious, disemboweled, beheaded, and quartered. Their remains were then boiled in brine, covered in black tar, and set up on poles and trees and lampposts. Green Ribbon brothers, London Whig lawyers, Rye House plotters, and nonconformist ministers were among the many who received this treatment.[94] In the west, residents and visitors found the sight of the exhibited body parts frightening and the smell nauseating. Only after a progress through the west the following year did James II himself, disturbed by what he saw, order the heads and quarters to be removed and buried.[95]

But the business of retribution was not yet over. The capture following the Battle of Sedgemoor of several Rye House conspirators, who turned king's evidence in order to save themselves, permitted the king to settle some old scores and complete some unfinished business. With the confessions of Nathaniel Wade and Lord Grey of Werk, and the testimony of Richard Goodenough, the king was able to pursue several of his former enemies. He proceeded against the former Whig sheriff Henry Cornish in October 1685. Cornish's real crime was the packing of juries in 1680 and 1681, hence allowing Whigs and Dissenters to escape justice. But on the perjured evidence of Richard Goodenough and John Rumsey, who wrongly accused Cornish of participation in the Rye House conspiracy, he was hanged and quartered. Charles Bateman, the late earl of Shaftesbury's surgeon, met the same fate in December.[96]

John Hampden, the younger, was next. The government was finally

---

94. Examples include John Ayloffe and Richard Nelthorpe, who were both members of the Green Ribbon Club, lawyers, and Rye House conspirators. Ayloffe was executed for his part in Argyle's rebellion; Nelthorpe, for Monmouth's. John Hicks and William Disney were Dissenting preachers. Hicks was captured at Lady Lisle's house and executed; Disney was executed for printing Monmouth's *Declaration*. Colonel Abraham Holmes was an old Cromwellian soldier who had participated in the Rye House conspiracy. He lost his son and his arm at Sedgemoor; he was hanged and quartered at Lyme. These men are discussed in Chapter 1.

95. Clifton, *The Last Popular Rebellion*, 240; Earle, *Monmouth's Rebels*, 175–77; Zook, "'The Bloody Assizes,'" 382–83.

96. *The Trials of Henry Cornish for conspiring the death of the King . . . and Elizabeth Gaunt . . . for harboring and maintaining Rebels* (1685); "The Trial of Charles Bateman, Surgeon, at the Old Bailey for High Treason," in *State Trials*, 11:468–80.

able to try him for high treason for his role in the Rye House conspiracy, since it now had two witnesses, Lords Howard and Grey. Hampden pleaded guilty and confessed but received a death sentence nonetheless. Yet James was more interested in embarrassing and discrediting young Hampden, the grandson and namesake of the Great Patriot, and commuted his sentence to a fine of six thousand pounds. As Hampden later let it be known, he had "lost his goods, his estate, his wife, and reputation" at the hands of James and Jeffreys. He never recovered from the psychological blow of his humiliation, and though he styled himself a great Protestant martyr after the Revolution, and became an active member of William and Mary's government, he was rumored to be quite mad at times. He committed suicide in 1696.[97]

In 1685 and 1686, James II struck several more blows to the Whig network in an attempt to silence the radical voice. Early in the first year of his reign, James moved to put the press under stricter supervision. His government was also quick to move against persons accused of distributing seditious papers or telling seditious tales. Bookstores were raided. Benjamin Harris's stocks were seized, wherein books were found with such titles as *English Liberties* (Henry Care's book) and *A Scheme of Popish Cruelties*. In December 1685, warrants to arrest anyone dispersing "seditious, scandalous, and unlicensed books, pamphlets, pictures, and papers" were issued. James's crackdown seems to have successfully hindered the production of radical books and pamphlets in England. The number of books printed in 1686 is the lowest of the entire decade. But the king could not eradicate the dissemination of oppositional propaganda completely or control his subjects' minds, many of which were already influenced by Whig revolution culture. Throughout his reign, persons were still arrested, charged with voicing seditious opinions or distributing seditious libels. Books promoting the Protestant cause were still smuggled in from Holland.[98]

James's government also pursued those individuals who had told tall tales during his brother's reign. In May 1685, Titus Oates, the initiator of the Popish Plot stories, was tried for perjury, condemned, fined, pilloried, and whipped from Aldgate to Newgate and from Newgate to

97. *State Trials*, 11:479–95; HMC, *Hastings*, 4:309; H. C. Foxcroft, ed., *The Life and Letters of Sir George Savile, Bart. First Marquis of Halifax*, 2 vols. (London, 1898), 2:93; HMC, *Seventh Report, part 1*, 482.

98. *CSPD, James II*, 1:142, 382, 401, 344; 2:378, 279.

Tyburn. Oates, however, was still a popular hero and received "much pity" from the "multitude," who "would cry to the hangsman . . . whose office it was to whip him, 'Enough!' 'Enough!' 'Strike easily!' 'Enough!' "[99] The Reverend Samuel Johnson suffered a similar fate. He had been a resident of King's Bench Prison since 1684, condemned for seditious libel for his pro-exclusion tract, the famous *Julian the Apostate* discussed in Chapter 2. While in prison, Johnson became friendly with another notorious member of the network, Hugh Speke of the Speke family of White Lackington. Speke had various prison liberties and was able to have Johnson's writings printed and distributed in the outside world. Hence Johnson was able to continue publishing antipapist, pro-resistance diatribes.

In 1686, Johnson and Speke decided to arouse the consciences of the Protestant soldiers serving in James II's army encamped outside London on Hounslow Heath. This was the very army with which James had crushed Monmouth's Rebellion and which the king seemed to have no plans to disband. Rather, by suspending the penal laws in individual cases, he filled the officer core with many fellow Catholics. Johnson's *Humble and Hearty Address to All English Protestants in this Present Army* exhorted the Protestant soldiers to come to the defense of their religion rather than assist their popish officers in erecting a "popish-kingdom of darkness and desolation." "Is it in the name of God and for his service," asked Johnson, "that you have joined your selves with papists, who will indeed fight for the mass-book, but burn the Bible; and who seek to extirpate the Protestant religion with your swords." Speke later claimed that he had twenty thousand copies of Johnson's address distributed.[100]

A Humble and Hearty Address had a noticeable effect on James's soldiers. Authorities were quick to suspect its source. As one observer noted, "Some libels have been spread among the soldiers and watermen exhorting them to stand for the Protestant religion against popery . . . no doubt but the author will be found to be that of *Julian the Apostate*, who lies in the gaol and must do something to merit his pension of forty

99. *A True Narrative of the Sentence of Titus Oates for Perjury* (1685); *The Proceedings upon the Second Trial of Titus Oates* (1685). Abraham de la Pryme, *The Diary* (Edinburgh, 1870), 9.

100. *A Humble and Hearty Address to all English Protestants in this Present Army* (repr. 1689), 160, reprinted during the Glorious Revolution as *A Letter of Advice to All Protestant Soldiers and Seamen* (1689); Hugh Speke, *The Secret History of the Happy Revolution of 1688* (1715), 14. Anthony Wood recorded that five hundred copies were found in "Speek's chambers" (*The Life and Times of Anthony Wood*, 3:178).

pounds from Lady Russell."[101] Johnson was convicted of high misde-
meanors, sentenced to pay five hundred marks, stand in the pillory for
three days, and be flogged from Newbury to Tyburn.[102] Johnson was
also degraded from the priesthood, an act that the church authorities
believed essential to avoid having a clergyman whipped through the
streets. Johnson's degradation and whipping made a profound impression on contemporaries. He was rarely mentioned after 1686, by either
friend or foe, without some reference to his public flogging and "great
suffering." Johnson also capitalized on his suffering for the Protestant
cause through a great deal of self-publicity after the Glorious Revolution.[103] But this new crisis landed Johnson back in jail from 1686 to
1688. Both he and Speke were silenced.

For radicals abroad, the period between the summers of 1685 and
1688 was frustrating and frightening. Many sued for pardons, and some
were even willing to betray their fellow refugees to obtain them.[104]
Others decided to turn their backs on the British Isles forever, or so they
thought, and make new lives for themselves in Europe. Still others, led
by the vociferous and hard-drinking Captain Edward Matthews, boldly
appeared in public, especially in pubs and taverns, boasting and toast-
ing to King James's eventual downfall. English spies reported that "the
gang" was still up to its old tricks, plotting and conniving against the
Crown.[105] But if so, who was to lead them? In 1686 and 1687, most of the
English and Scottish dissidents in Holland and Germany did not look to
the prince of Orange as a viable replacement for Shaftesbury or the
Council of Six or Argyle or Monmouth. Men like John Speke, who sued
for a pardon, or his brother-in-law, John Trenchard, who considered
buying an estate in Switzerland, were far too removed from the Hague

---

101. HMC, *Downshire* (1924), vol. 1, part 1, 172.

102. *State Trials*, 10:1336–54; *CSPD, James II*, 2:143, 313; *Journals of the House of Commons*,
10:193–94.

103. *Journals of the House of Commons*, 10:194; Zook, "Early Whig Ideology, Ancient Constitutionalism, and the Reverend Samuel Johnson," *Journal of British Studies* 32 (1993): 147.

104. For example, Monmouth rebel Joseph Tily agreed to undermine the efforts of fellow
Dissenting fugitives trying to establish a cloth factory in Lewarden in return for a pardon (BL,
Add. 41,813, fols. 150, 154, 203; 41,819, fols. 121–23). He also tried to help English spies
capture Robert Ferguson (BL, Add. 41,813, fols. 171, 199).

105. Matthews was the son-in-law of the "Whig bully," Sir Thomas Armstrong, who was
executed in 1684 for outlawry. The English spies referred to Matthews and his friends,
including Colonel Henry Danvers and Major John Manley, as the "ungodly party" (BL, Add.
41,819, fols. 19–20, 33, 164; 41,804, fols. 7–9; 41,813, fol. 129).

to foresee William's ultimate plans.[106] Any boasting and plotting on the part of the Whig fugitives prior to the spring of 1688 was irrelevant. Penniless and leaderless, they waited in a political wilderness.

With their leaders vanquished and their propagandists silenced, it may well have seemed to both friend and foe alike that Whiggism was either dead or dying. At first, the proponents of Filmerian ideology, passive obedience, and religious conformity may well have thought that they had found their champion in the new king. Presbyterian preacher George Trosse in Exeter noted that, "When K. James II came to the crown, the persecuting party presuming they should be able more fully to carry on their design of extirpating the Protestant Dissenters, and thereby ingratiate themselves with the court, now became very watchful of us." But Tories and High Churchmen mistook James. He was more artful and less predictable than they surmised, and as historians of his reign have noted, his policies shifted in 1687, and he began to court with favors and offices his former enemies, Whigs and Dissenters. He hoped to gain their support in his move toward liberty of conscience for Catholics and nonconformists. His reach even extended to the many hardened rebels skulking about Holland to whom pardons were liberally granted.[107] The promise of religious toleration was highly attractive to those who had been persecuted for their faith, and an increasing number began to reconcile with his administration. Many believed that there was simply no alternative. The days of green ribbons, bold manifestos, and conspiratorial politics were over. Their cause was lost, and it was time to return home to one's family, business, and estates.

So many of the king's former enemies were willing to live in peace with his administration and even take part in his government that James

---

106. BL, Add. 41,818, fol. 206. He was also thinking of investing in an English cloth factory (BL, Add. 41,818, fol. 235; 41,804, fol. 158).

107. *The Life of the Reverend George Trosse Written by Himself*, ed. A.W. Brink (Montreal: McGill-Queen's University Press, 1974), 126. For James II's courting of Whigs and Dissenters, see John Miller, *James II: A Study in Kingship* (London: Wayland Publishers, 1978), Chapter 12, "The King and the Dissenters (April 1687 to June 1688)," 165–87; Mark Goldie, "John Locke's Circle and James II," *HJ* 35 (1992): 557–86; "James II and the Dissenters' Revenge: The Commission of Enquiry of 1688," *The Bulletin of Historical Research* 66 (1993): 53–88; J. R. Jones, "James II's Whig Collaborators," *HJ* 3 (1960): 65–73; and "James II's Revolution: Royal Policies, 1686–92," in Jonathan I. Israel, ed., *The Anglo-Dutch Moment* (Cambridge: Cambridge University Press, 1991), 41–71. Among those within the network who received pardons were John Speke, Edward Norton, John Trenchard, Joseph Tily, and Samuel Barnardiston, the younger. Robert Peyton and Slingsby Bethel applied for pardons but were denied (BL, Add. 41,819, fols. 51, 183, 45, 97, 166, 135; 41,813, fol. 96).

II's courtship of Whigs and Dissenters in 1687 and 1688 was even more damaging to Whig politics and solidarity than the failed rebellions of 1685 and their aftermath. His policy of reconciliation and liberty of conscience in the last two years of his reign was more effective than the brutality and oppression of his first two years. Yet James carried his policies too high, too far, too fast. He alienated those whose support he needed most. As the diarist John Stout observed, the king's granting of liberty of conscience was happily accepted by most Dissenting Protestants, "but this very much offended the bishops and clergy who soon perceived that all his pretended liberty was only intended to introduce a papist government." Presbyterian George Trosse refused James's liberty to preach, believing his true aim was to "so weaken the party of the Church of England" that the Dissenters would soon be "easily crushed" and popery reestablished. The Anglican Ralph Thoresby also knew the king's declaration was "a snake in the grass."[108] James's pro-Dissent policies and the increasing prominence of Catholics at court and within the government, universities, and army frightened Tory elites and the Anglican establishment. Had the predictions of the radicals come true after all?

When the prince of Orange landed at Torbay on November 5, 1688, James found that his new Whig and Dissenting friends were few and fickle. With very few exceptions, they failed to support him. When yet another Protestant deliverer appeared, Whig and Dissenting lords, gentlemen, lawyers, soldiers, publishers, and preachers hastened to his side. From Cheshire, Henry Booth, Lord Delamere, whose strident Whig politics had landed him in prison twice under Charles II and again under James, galvanized his tenants to arm themselves and follow him to meet the prince. "I am of the opinion," he declared, "that when the nation is delivered, it must be by force or by miracle; it would be too great a presumption to expect the latter and therefore our deliverance

---

108. See J. R. Jones, "James II's Whig Collaborators," 68–70, and Mark Goldie, "John Locke's Circle and James II," 568–77. Twenty Whigs within the network reconciled with James II's government: William Atwood, James Burton, Henry Care, John Freke, Lord Grey, Richard Goodenough, John Hampden, the younger, Nathaniel Hooke, Lord Howard, Matthew Mead, Stephen Lobb, William Rumbold, Colonel John Rumsey, John Speke, Edward Strode, William Strode, Joseph Tily, Henry Trenchard, John Trenchard, and Nathaniel Wade. Quotations are from William Stout, *The Autobiography of William Stout of Lancaster, 1665–1752*, ed. J. D. Marshall (New York: Barnes & Noble, Inc., 1967), 91; *The Life of the Reverend George Trosse*, 125; and Thoresby, *Diary*, 186.

must be by force."[109] The Protestant cause was not forgot, nor the blood of Whig radicals spilt for naught. In 1688, the ideology that permitted resistance, and the revolution culture that disseminated it, triumphed. The cycle of Whig defeat was broken.

109. An example of the fickleness of James II's new friends is Lord Grey to whom James II was very generous and who had turned king's evidence following Monmouth's Rebellion. Yet Grey failed to come to the king's side in November 1688, sending the excuse that he had recently fallen from his horse. See his pathetic letter (BL, Add. 30,277, fol. 10). Henry, Lord Delemere, Booth, *Lord Delamere's Speech* (1688), broadside, for the quotation.

6

Revolution Justified:
The Radical Response to 1688

The Return of the Plotter

Perhaps the greatest asset of the fugitives in exile during James's reign was the presence among them of the archconspirator and propagandist, Robert Ferguson. He had escaped from the battlefield at Sedgemoor, and after hiding in a hayloft for several weeks, took a ship to Amsterdam. The capture of Ferguson was the first priority of the English spies in the Netherlands, and he lived in constant fear for his life. He was also flat broke, seen in tattered clothes, and rumored to be starving.[1] Still, even from these dire circumstances, the Plotter recovered, and by the winter of 1687, he was once again churning out propaganda. Whether his efforts were commissioned or rewarded by the prince of Orange is

---

1. BL, Add. 4,460, fol. 52; 41,819, fol. 20v.

unknown. What is certain is that Ferguson now saw the prince as the new leader, "the head of the Protestant interest."[2]

Ferguson reentered public debate in 1687, in reaction to James II's *Declaration of Indulgence*. In *A Representation of the Threatening Dangers impending over Protestants in Great Britain*, which was published in both English and Dutch, Ferguson strove to warn nonconformists of the dangers belying James's promise of liberty of conscience. Though he "may hug and carressth" Dissenters now, his true desire was to open the kingdom to popery. They count them "pious and meritorious acts" in Rome to murder Protestants, and if the example of Mary I may be remembered, the Smithfield fires were exactly what lay in England's future. Ferguson's harsh language and frightening images were reminiscent of his earlier tracts. But *A Representation* was far more sophisticated than anything he had written before. In it Ferguson set forth his ideas on toleration, which he expressed through the language of natural law. He argued that freedom of conscience was a natural right that could not be alienated from the people because they "cannot divest themselves" of it. Liberty of conscience does not "lie under the power of the sovereign and legislative authority to grant or not to grant; but it is a right settled upon mankind antecedent to all civil constitutions and human laws, having its foundation in the law of nature, which no prince or state can legitimately violate and infringe." Persecuting people over matters of faith was "repugnant to the light of nature, inconsistent with the fundamental maxims of reason," and contrary to "the rules of the gospel." Ferguson declared that "God has reserved the empire over conscience to himself."[3]

Ferguson's next tract also addressed the question of toleration. His *Reflexions on Monsieur Fagel's Letter* was written as a companion piece to a tract by Caspar Fagel, pensionary of Holland, who published a description and defense of the prince and princess of Orange's response to James II's *Declaration of Indulgence*.[4] Ferguson's *Reflexions* was specifically addressed to all Dissenters tempted to support James's indulgence. He began by describing the character of the prince of Orange, whom he believed would one day inherit the throne of England: "Their High-

2. Ferguson, *Reflexions on Monsieur Fagel's Letter* (1688), 2.
3. *A Representation of the Threatening Dangers impending over the Protestants in Great Britain* (1687), 9, 36–37.
4. *A Letter Writ by Mijn Heer Fagel, Pensioner of Holland . . . giving an Account of the Prince and Princess of Orange's Thought concerning the Repeal of the Test and the Penal Laws* (1687).

nesses [the Prince and Princess of Orange] . . . are predestined . . . to make us happy in putting an end to our differences and in fixing the prerogative and in recovering the nation." Yet Ferguson's portrait of Prince William was far from hagiographic. He understood the skepticism his intended audience might harbor for William or any prince: "I am as apt as you to mistrust Princes' promises," he wrote, "human infirmities are great, temptations to arbitrariness are strong, and often both the spirit and the flesh are weak."[5]

But Ferguson's friends were not to worry. Prince William would not be a hereditary prince, and the more tenuous nature of his claim would surely make him a more responsible prince, attentive to the needs of this people and anxious not to exceed his bounds. Ferguson also warned his audience of James II's true intention of reestablishing popery. If they supported him, the Church of England would be lost, and in the end, they would have traded their civil liberties away for "a precarious, pretended liberty of conscience." The "ruin of the Church," Ferguson declared, was at issue. The Church of England was the only "bulwark" against popery. If the Dissenters abandoned their conformist brethren, James and his Catholic supporters would carry the day and reduce England and Scotland "to the miserable condition of those of our [French Protestant] neighbors."[6]

The birth of James II's son, James Edward, in June 1688, became the catalyst for the Revolution. The English could now look forward only to a succession of Catholic kings. Promised support within England by a cadre of Tory and Whig elites intent on establishing a Protestant succession, the prince of Orange landed an army at Torbay on November 5, 1688. King James flew into a panic as he watched both his officer core and even members of the royal family defect to the prince's camp. On December 22, in fear of his life, James fled to France.

In the months prior to William of Orange's invasion of England, a new mood of confidence was clearly evident among the English and Scottish dissidents in the Netherlands. They now boldly congregated on the streets and in the taverns. No longer the half-starved fugitive, Ferguson also appeared publicly in Amsterdam in October 1688, and was reported to have declared that, whereas Monmouth "went altogether upon hopes . . . now there is all the assurances [from England]

---

5. *Reflexions on Monsieur Fagel's Letter,* 2; 1–3.
6. *Reflexions on Monsieur Fagel's Letter,* 3, 4.

that can be desired."[7] Ferguson's assistance may have been enlisted by the prince of Orange's Dutch and English advisors as they prepared William's English and Scottish declarations.[8] Meanwhile, propaganda in England promoted the idea that William's cause was supported by "some loyal Rye-House and Sedgemoor men, true disciples of honest old Rumbold and Robin Ferguson."[9] Although honest old Richard Rumbold was long dead, Ferguson, the survivor, was once again at the very heart of the storm. He sailed to Torbay with the prince and his army, and on November 10, kicked down a church door, and with sword in hand proclaimed, "cursed be he who keeps back his sword from blood."[10]

Lord Macaulay believed that Ferguson "was generally distrusted and despised by William's supporters."[11] Perhaps this was the case, although Macaulay's own bias against Ferguson was probably far stronger than those of William's associates, who allowed him to accompany the prince in November, and rewarded him for his services after the Revolution. Ferguson deserved his reward. In justification of William's cause, Ferguson penned his finest piece of Whig polemic. A *Brief Justification of the Prince of Orange's Descent into England* was certainly one of the most influential tracts published during the Revolution. It not only promoted and defended William's claim to the throne, it gave the Conventioneers, who met in January of 1689 to solve the current crisis, an interpretative framework. It provided them with a verbal and a historical context in which to place, discuss, and explain the final months of 1688.

In *A Brief Justification*, Ferguson set forth a contractarian theory of government, which he claimed was the basis of England's ancient constitution. The tract began in the same vein as the printed version of Monmouth's *Declaration*: government "derives its ordination and institution from God" but owes its particular form to the people, who "prescribe and define what shall be the measures and boundaries of public good, and unto what rules and standard the magistrate shall be restrained." The articles of the agreement between the ruler and the people become the "fundamentals of the respective constitutions of

7. BL, Add. 41,815, fols. 124–25; 41,816, fol. 26, fol. 228 for the quotation.
8. Schwoerer, *The Declaration of Rights*, 117; BL, Add. 34,512, fol. 113.
9. Broadside quoted in James Ferguson, *Robert Ferguson*, 257–58.
10. Roger Morrice, "Ent'ring Book, Being a Historical Register of Occurrences from April, Anno. 1677 to April 1691," 4 vols. 2:320.
11. *History of England*, 3:1103.

nations." All legal governments have their origins in such "compacts, stipulations, compromises, and agreements." Ferguson's rulers were not to be divinely ordained but chosen by the people: "One person becomes advanced from the common level to the title and authority of a sovereign, and all others are by their own consent reduced and brought down to the condition of subjects." Subjects owe their allegiance first to the constitution and only second to the sovereign. With the Rye House martyrs in mind, Ferguson claimed that "they neither are nor can be traitors who endeavor to preserve and maintain the constitution." Should the ruler invade the fundamental laws of the constitution, the people are restored "to their state and condition of primitive freedom."[12]

Having set out the principles that govern all societies, Ferguson proceeded to examine the English nation's first agreement with its rulers. Drawing upon the ideas of the Whig constitutionalists, Ferguson asserted that the Magna Carta and other such charters were merely "recognitions of what we had reserved unto ourselves in the original institution of our government, and of what we had always appertained unto us by common law and immemorial customs." The original agreement between king and people, which dated back to Saxon times, was "revised, repeated and confirmed by the Confessor," was ratified by "William, the first Norman king," and remained the "birthright of every Englishman." Part of this birthright was the people's "share in the legislation" and the right "of being . . . governed by such laws as we ourselves shall choose." The people may further "relieve ourselves from and against anything that either threatenth, endangerth, or oppressth us."[13]

Applying the principles of civil government set forth in the first part of his text, Ferguson justified the revolutionary events of 1688 in the second half. His argument was predictable but contained a bit of a twist. Through his subversion of the constitution and invasion of the people's rights and liberties, James II had "unqualified himself" from his position as king. It was, therefore, the "duty of every Protestant and Englishman" to take up arms against him. Yet, in the end, force was not necessary. Perhaps it was a "sense of his own guilt" that "chased him from his throne." But it was more likely his "fear of a free parliament," as called

12. *A Brief Justification*, 5–6, 8, 9–10.
13. *A Brief Justification*, 13–14.

for by the prince of Orange. Regardless, James II did the nation a "kindness" by "retiring across the sea."[14] Ferguson's forfeiture theory, the assertion that resistance to James was not necessary, since he himself had forfeited the throne, is crucial.[15] This is the interpretation of the Revolution later adopted by the convention and asserted in the *Declaration of Rights*. Conventioneers agreed that James had simply "vacated" the throne and thus "abdicated" his position. Ferguson used the word "abdicate" throughout *A Brief Justification* and pointed to historical examples of kings who "abdicate themselves."[16]

Ferguson also believed that once the throne became "empty and vacant," political power devolved to the people's representatives in Parliament, whose ancient right it was to settle the royal succession. In *A Brief Justification,* he did not deny the right of the people to choose any form of government they wished, but he recommended monarchy, for "the mercurial and masculine temper of the English people is not to be molded and accommodated to a democracy." Furthermore, kingship was essential to the constitution: "it is woven into our laws"; "the government of England is imperfect without a king." Since the "disposal" of the Crown had fallen to the people, they were free to choose the next successor. They were not bound by any restrictions nor need they worry about inheritances or "proximity of blood." Their sole condition was to be "the public good."[17]

Ferguson concluded *A Brief Justification* by recommending that Parliament endow the prince of Orange with "sovereign and legal power," while allowing his wife, the princess of Orange, to be "named with him in all leases, patents and grants." This formula, which placed both William and Mary on the throne while investing administrative power in William alone, was the one adopted by the convention. Ferguson listed many reasons why Prince William was the best choice, including "gratitude." "His vindicating our liberties and laws deserves his being trusted with the execution of the one and with the defense of both." By choosing William, the "nation hath in its whole political body exercised

14. *A Brief Justification*, 9, 21–22.
15. Burnet made the same argument in *An Enquiry into the Measures of Submission* (1688, repr. 1688, 1693).
16. *A Brief Justification*, 18.
17. *A Brief Justification*, 23–24, 34.

the power belonging to it" and restored "the government upon its primitive and original foundation."[18]

The Conventioneers who met in January of 1689 to settle the crisis of King James's exodus and the prince of Orange's invasion did choose William to reign as the new king of England. Were they influenced by the ideas spun by radical propagandists over the past decade? Had they read *A Brief Justification*, published just prior to their sitting? Both seem probable. Many were members of the radical network and knew Ferguson himself, including City Whigs, Sir Patience Ward, Sir Thomas Pilkington, and Ferguson's former patron, Thomas Papillion; Rye House plotters, John Hampden, the younger, John Trenchard, and John Wildman; and Monmouth rebel Major John Manley. Even if the Conventioneers had read *A Brief Justification* and nothing else published by radicals since the Exclusion Crisis, they would have received through it alone all the basic principles of radical Whig thinking. For Ferguson echoed the tenets of the constitutionalists, William Petyt, William Atwood, and Edward Cooke, as well as the more rational theorists, Thomas Hunt and the Reverend Samuel Johnson. He harmonized concepts gathered from both ancient constitutionalism and the more abstract politics of natural law, bringing together two traditions within Whig polemic. He was no inventor but rather a collector and synthesizer of political ideas. His genius lay in his ability to weave together the rhetoric of Whiggism since the early days of the Exclusion Crisis. His thinking was never rigid or dogmatic. He had an agility of mind that allowed him to pick and choose his ideas and fit them for the occasion. He was first and foremost a pragmatist, unbound by principle.

Though it was a radical defense of the Revolution that both justified the use of force and asserted the concept of devolution of power to the people, many of the ideas in *A Brief Justification* were consistent with the thinking of the Conventioneers. Ferguson had a good understanding of the minds of the more timid members of the convention and gave them an easy escape from the radical implications of popular resistance. Kings could also abdicate themselves and do everyone a great favor by vacating their thrones, as did James II. Ferguson was a master politician; *A Brief Justification* was a mirror image of the Revolution itself, of compromise and conciliation. Yet the tract was Ferguson's last contribution to Whig ideology. By the end of 1689, he was already highly

18. *A Brief Justification*, 36–37.

critical of William III's policies and had begun writing in the service of disaffected Scottish Whigs whose ambitions had not been realized under the new regime. By 1694, Ferguson was fully converted to Jacobitism, plotting on behalf of James II and propagating his cause. In the 1690s, Ferguson's tracts not only vehemently attacked the Dutch interest, King William's War, and William's administrators but also the Revolutionary Settlement of 1689—the very event that Ferguson had helped to establish.

The Revolutionary Settlement

The months following the proclamation of William III and Mary II, in February 1689, were a time of national reflection on the past decade. From the press poured an avalanche of antipapist satire; reprints of pro-Exclusion literature; the dying speeches of Rye House and Monmouth rebels; and, of course, a flood of pamphlets justifying the prince of Orange's invasion and ascent to the throne of England. This preoccupation with the immediate past had, quite naturally, everything to do with the present moment. The Revolution unleashed the voices of the opposition that had been muffled or silenced altogether since the ascension of James II in 1685. It was their turn to vindicate Whig ideas and actions, justify their past politics, and apply their principles to the recent revolution. It was their turn to tell tales—stories of hardship, suffering, heroism, and martyrdom. Whig history was born.

The press was not the only forum for revision. Parliament also sought to examine the past so as to punish the guilty and reward the sufferers for the Protestant cause. John Hampden, the younger was called before the special committee of the House of Lords investigating the trials and executions of William, Lord Russell, Colonel Algernon Sidney, and other supposed Rye House plotters in 1683. "The method of revolt," Hampden confidently told the committee, "was the old English form of protest against tyranny and the expedition of William [of Orange] but a continuation of the Council of Six." Monmouth's Rebellion in 1685 was but "another struggle for liberty."[19] Hampden himself had been a member of the so-called Council of Six, the upper echelon of Rye

---

19. H. C. Foxcroft, ed., *Halifax*, 2:95.

House conspirators in 1683. He had good reason to frame the council's actions, which included a design for insurrection and the assassination of the royal brothers, within an "old English" struggle against tyranny. The Rye House plotters and the Monmouth rebels were, after all, doing nothing more than what the barons at Runnymede had before them.

Hampden's Whig vision of the decade preceding the Revolution signifies three important aspects relating to how the "first Whigs" envisioned their struggles in the 1680s. To the committee, Hampden's tale was probably an increasingly familiar story, one furiously propagated in pamphlets and weeklies justifying the revolution. But Hampden's remarks remind scholars that narratives are imposed upon the past, often by persons who make themselves the heroic protagonists of their stories. Hampden chose to label his dead friends as liberators and the forces that brought them to the scaffold as tyrannous. He further justified the violence discussed by the Council of Six and that taken by Monmouth's followers within a historical discourse. Rebellion was customary practice, as English as Magna Carta. Finally, he linked together the Rye House Plot, Monmouth's Rebellion, and the successful invasion of the prince of Orange. Each became a struggle for Protestantism and liberty. Each shared the same goal of emancipating the nation from popery and slavery. As Hampden put it before the committee, "the foundation of this glorious revolution was laid in the Council of Six."[20]

Hampden's retelling of the Revolution ignored the official interpretation set forth by the Conventioneers in January 1689. They had tried to find a middle course between radical Whig principles, which they saw as granting far too much power to "the people" (whoever they might be) to make revolutions and establish governments, and the opinions of archconservatives, usually High Churchmen, who believed that the convention itself was illegitimate and that the rightful king, James II, should be immediately restored. The task of the Conventioneers was certainly not an easy one. Their solution was to accept the "Revolution," crown William and Mary, but deny that "the people" had anything to do with the making of the events of 1688. Providence had brought forth a Protestant deliverer, and James II himself had decided to "abdicate."[21] A

---

20. Foxcroft, ed., *Halifax*, 2:95.

21. *The Declaration of Rights* (February 12, 1689) reads, "And whereas the said late King James the second having abdicated the Government and the throne thereby being vacant" (Schwoerer, *The Declaration of Rights*, Appendix 1, 295–98).

bizarre twist of events, no doubt, and one that was unlikely to be repeated. It was an interpretation without revolutionary implications. The people had no part in the events; they were but passive recipients of divine Providence. It was more of a revelation than a revolution. The minimalist interpretation of 1688, hammered out by the Convention-eers, sought to please everyone. In fact, it pleased almost no one.

All sides criticized the convention's efforts to steer a moderate course. Radicals like Reverend Samuel Johnson scorned any interpretation of the Revolution that did not admit that the people had dethroned James II for violating the nation's established laws, and had promoted William and Mary in his place. Moderate Whigs like Bishop Gilbert Burnet began to advocate acceptance of William as a king de facto (in possession) though not de jure (by right).[22] Nonjuring clerics, who refused to take the oath of allegiance to William and Mary, maintained that the oath they had sworn to James II was not invalidated. They would live in peace under the new regime but would not acknowledge William and Mary as their legitimate sovereigns. As a result, they lost their liveli-hoods.[23] Others, including Jacobites, attacked the Revolution from a constitutional perspective. The newly converted Robert Ferguson argued in 1695, that under "no circumstances" did the constitution ever "permit" or "empower" the people "to rebel against the King."[24]

Still other interpretations of the Revolution flourished. A wave of literature flowed from London bookshops defending, rejecting, and reinterpreting the Revolution. What had transpired in a few short months in 1688 and 1689, continued to be fought out in the press by Tories, Trimmers, nonjurors, Jacobites, Williamite Whigs, and radicals throughout the 1690s and into the early eighteenth century. As one anonymous pamphleteer put it, "one submits to Providence, another to an usurper, another to a king de facto, another a conqueror: one says King James left us; another, we turned him out."[25] Radical Whig

---

22. Johnson's and Burnet's views are discussed below; Burnet, *A Pastoral Letter Writ by the Right Reverend Father In God Gilbert, Lord Bishop of Sarum* (1689).

23. On the nonjurors, see T. Lathbury, *A History of the Nonjurors* (London, 1845), and G. V. Bennett, "Conflict in the Church," in G. Holmes, ed., *Britain after the Glorious Revolution* (New York: St. Martin's Press, 1969), 155–75.

24. *Whether Preserving the Protestant Religion was the motive . . . the late Revolution* (1695), 8. Also see Paul K. Monod, *Jacobitism and the English People, 1688–1788* (Cambridge: Cambridge University Press, 1989), 23–27.

25. N.N., *A Letter from Oxford concerning Mr. Samuel Johnson's Late Book* (1693), 10.

propagandists defended the Revolution while reinterpreting it based on the principles they had developed during the 1680s. The Revolution gave the polemical careers of the lawyer and antiquarian William Atwood and the notorious Whig martyr the Reverend Samuel Johnson new leases. They had to tell the real story of the Revolution. Their brethren had not fought and died over the preceding decade so that James might one day pick up and leave on his own accord. He was pushed out; such was the will of the people.

William Atwood and the Triumph of Law

> The brown-hair'd coming with hawk-nose to fight
> Shall put his baffled enemy to flight;
> The exile to the land he shall restore
> Placing the stoutest of them next to the shore.
> —Atwood, *Wonderful Predictions of Nostradmus*
> (1689)

The years between 1683 and 1689 had marked a hiatus in Atwood's polemical career. He published merely one versified translation.[26] Considered an opponent of the court, he moved to the countryside during the reign of James II and did not publish his political views again until after the Glorious Revolution.[27] Moreover, like many Whigs, Atwood reconciled with James's administration in its final eighteen months and accepted a position as a magistrate in Essex in 1687.[28] But with the Revolution, both he and Johnson began publishing tract after tract of Whig rhetoric. Naturally, they felt a strong sense of righteousness. After all, had they not been correct all along? Atwood's post-Revolution propaganda burst with enthusiasm for the new regime. While his style had always exhibited a generous amount of self-confidence, he had formerly been too timid to sign his tracts. But with

---

26. *Grotius, His Arguments For the Truth of Christian Religion rendered in plain English verse* (1686).

27. The earl of Danby placed Atwood on a list of "lawyers in the country in opposition in James II's reign," along with Sir Richard Atkyns, Richard Wallop, and Sir William Williams (Browning, *Thomas Osborne, Earl of Danby*, 3:163).

28. John Bramston, *Autobiography*, 304; Mark Goldie, "John Locke's Circle and James II," 573.

the Revolution, he felt vindicated. He signed his new pieces and acknowledged his old.[29] He even began to dedicate his tracts to various prominent Williamite Whigs, hoping to be noticed and favored.[30]

Atwood's extraordinary confidence was not the only characteristic of his work that carried over from the 1680s to the 1690s. His bold and strident anticlericalism became even sharper after the Revolution. He believed Anglican divines like George Hickes and William Sherlock, who had preached and propagated such "destructive" opinions as passive obedience, were responsible for the people's suffering over the past decade. Even during the Revolution, the clergy had sought to delay and undermine "our settlement." Nothing infuriated Atwood more than clerical interference in statecraft and law, the true domain of lawyers. "The greatest unhappiness of this nation," he declared, "is that divines are not only set up for great statesmen, but will pretend to be the best lawyers and casuists in these points." Atwood had come to the conclusion, which Samuel Johnson had pointed out in 1683, that in political matters Scripture was too easily "employed" for "mischievous applications for the future." In 1691, he wrote that Hickes had used Scripture to fortify his politics, where he should have consulted the law: "In the room of Law, he set up Scripture and Reason, without regard for law, but abuses Scripture and perverts it."[31] Since Scripture was open to abuse and misapplication, it could not be treated as a legitimate

29. See the advertisement in *A Complete Collection of Papers in Twelve Parts* (1689), which lists all of Atwood's pre-1689 tracts and acknowledges him as the author. After 1689, Atwood put his name to all of his tracts except one, *Dr. Sherlock's Two Kings of Brainford brought upon the stage in a Congratulatory letter to Mr. Johnson* (1691), which defended Samuel Johnson and attacked William Sherlock, one of Atwood's favorite targets of abuse. The tract was filled with the most obvious characteristics of Atwood's work, including an utter disdain for the clergy, a vindication of the Revolutionary Settlement, and a celebration of the role of law and lawyers. Atwood probably decided to print it anonymously because he understood that Johnson was seen by many within William's government as a fanatic whose principles were far too extreme for their tastes. Atwood was a cautious man; he wished to build a career for himself. On the other hand, his championing of Johnson, albeit anonymously, displays his more radical side. Atwood and Johnson were probably friends. In the early 1680s, the royalist William Hopkins believed that Thomas Hunt, Johnson, and Atwood were part of a "club" and that Atwood and Hunt had supplied Johnson with material for *Julian the Apostate* and its defense, *Julian's Arts to Undermine and Extirpate Christianity*. See Hopkins's furious attack on Johnson, *Animadversions on Mr. Johnson's Answer to Jovian* (1691).

30. For example, Atwood's *Antiquity and Justice of the Oath of Abjuration* (1694) was dedicated to Sir John Somers; *Reflections upon a Treasonable Opinion, industriously promoted against the Signing the National Association* (1696) was dedicated to Charles Talbot, earl of Shrewsbury.

31. Atwood, *Dr. Sherlock's Two Kings of Brainford* (1691), 4, 6, and *The Fundamental Constitu-*

authority in the temporal world of politics. Government was a strictly human affair and could only be understood by sources which, like itself, were also man-made.

Atwood first set out his defense of the Revolution in the preface of his versified translation of Nostradamus, which he believed foretold the Revolution. He vindicated the decisions of the Conventioneers and directed his readers to Ferguson's *Brief Justification* if they desired a fuller explanation of the events of 1688. Atwood also argued that James had uncrowned himself. But unlike the Conventioneers, Atwood maintained that it was not the king's flight to France that had ended his reign. James's abdication was the result of his breach of the "original contract" between himself and the people. Thus "the people" had promoted William and Mary in his place, exercising a power that was rightfully and legally theirs. The original contract, which James had abrogated by his arbitrary actions, was embodied in the coronation oath in which he had sworn to uphold the Laws of Edward the Confessor. There was nothing mystical or sacramental about the oath; it was instead a legal contract: "The King's oath is the real contract on his side; and his accepting the government as a legal King."[32]

A year later in 1690, Atwood elaborated upon these arguments in *The Fundamental Constitution of the English Government*. Here was a thoroughgoing declaration of the ancient constitution. Prior to the Revolution, Atwood and his mentor, William Petyt, had defended component parts of ancient constitutionalism, mainly the antiquity of the parliamentary commons and William of Normandy's supposed "nonconquest" of England. With the Revolution, Atwood became a zealous professor of ancient constitutionalism. The crux of his political philosophy revolved around the image, so marvelously depicted on the frontispiece of Edward Cooke's *Argumentum Anti-Normanicum*, of William I accepting the Laws of Edward the Confessor. Constitutionalists believed that Holy Edward's Laws embodied the liberties and privileges of every freeborn

---

tion of the English Government (1690), 3; Johnson, *Julian the Apostate*, 53; and Atwood, *Dr Sherlock's Two Kings of Brainford*, 19, for the quotations.

32. Preface to *Wonderful Predictions of Nostradamus, Grebner, David Pareus and Antonius Torquatus. Wherein the grandeur of their present Majesties, the happiness of England . . . are foretold* (1689), pages unnumbered. Also see the stanza at the beginning of this section. Atwood also believed that James's desertion violated the original contract: "This alone would have been enough to set him aside; he deserted us and went to our enemy" (preface to *Wonderful Predictions*).

Englishman, and that each successive monarch vowed to uphold those laws at the swearing of the coronation oath. This was England's ancient heritage, and it was exactly this that James II had violated.

"All civil societies," Atwood argued, "are founded on contracts and covenants made between them." It is "warranted by that noble transcript of the original contract that if a king does not answer the true end for which he was chosen, he looses the name or ceases to be king."[33] In such cases, the people are discharged of their allegiance and must resist this self-abdicated king. Atwood maintained that the contract between James II and his people had dissolved. But this raised many troubling questions. Had not the government also dissolved? And, if so, had the people returned to the state of nature?

Atwood was well aware that the anonymous author of *Two Treatises of Government* had recently argued that all civil power did return to the people who were themselves returned to their original precivil state of nature. Furthermore, under certain conditions, the people were at liberty to set up any form of government they pleased.[34] Atwood had no qualms with Locke's argument that power devolved to the people. Ferguson, whose *Brief Justification* he had recommended, also argued as much. But no ancient constitutionalist could countenance the idea of a full dissolution of the government. The ancient constitution never dissolves. If it did, every subject's rights and liberties would be lost. The ancient constitution had to remain an unbroken continuum. This being the case, what had happened between December 22, when James had fled, and February 13, when William and Mary were proclaimed king and queen? Atwood argued that the "dissolution of the contract between the immediate prince and people" did not "destroy the form of government." True, James's flight had produced "a vacancy," but not an interregnum.[35] There "was and is an established judicature for this, without need of returning to the equity which people are supposed to have reserved." Atwood was referring to Parliament's ability to designate the next successor. The government had not dissolved in December 1688; rather, power had devolved "to the people of legal interests in

33. *The Fundamental Constitution*, 4, iv. In the first passage, Atwood was quoting Edward Stillingfleet, *Irenicum* (1659), 132.

34. Atwood cited passages from Locke on the dissolution of government. See Atwood, *The Fundamental Constitution*, Chapter 10, and John Locke, *Two Treatises of Government*, Chapter 19, "Of the Dissolution of Government," 406–28.

35. *The Fundamental Constitution*, 79.

the government" and they had chosen a successor. For Atwood, the legality of the Convention was beyond question. Parliament was the "organ of continuity" linking the past with the future, bridging any kind of a vacancy of the Crown.[36]

Atwood defined exactly what he meant by "the people," something neither Ferguson nor Locke had felt compelled to do. He declared that political power did not return to all the people "wherein everybody has an equal share in the government . . . even servants." Such a situation would "make a quiet election unpractical" and perhaps even return the state to "absolute anarchy."[37] Thus power devolved only to a limited number of people, "the people with legal interests in the government," whom Atwood defined as all freeholders and masters of families. These men were the nation's true "citizens." It was their right to choose a new king. Atwood believed that England was an elected, limited monarchy and unless utterly impossible, "the people" should elect only members of the royal family.[38]

Richard Ashcraft argues that Atwood feared the "social implications" of Locke's full dissolution of the government and the return of the people to a state of equality, but this is an oversimplification of Atwood's objections to Locke. Motivating Atwood was not simply a status-conscious fear of the common crowd but a strong desire to see the ancient constitution upheld. Everyone's liberties, regardless of social status, were lost if the ancient constitution were destroyed. Atwood was afraid of anarchy not simply because he feared "the rabble," but because he believed that tyranny was the more likely offspring of such chaos.[39] Atwood's constitutionalist defense of the Revolution was more moderate than Ferguson's and Locke's. He clearly sought to limit the possible political players and the political responses open to those players should the English contractarian government break down. Although he admired the *Two Treatises* and felt they were an effective antidote to Filmerian patriarchalism, Atwood was plainly responding to what he believed were the more dangerous implications of some of Locke's

36. Preface to *Wonderful Predictions*. J. P. Kenyon uses the phrase "organ of continuity" (*Revolution Principles*, 18).

37. Preface to *Wonderful Predictions*.

38. *The Fundamental Constitution*, 9, 98, xvi.

39. Ashcraft's reading of Atwood is anachronistic, in that it fails to acknowledge that Atwood, as well as most of his late seventeenth-century contemporaries, had good reasons to fear disorder (*Revolutionary Politics*, 587–88).

ideas, just as he had responded to those of fellow Whig Thomas Hunt in 1683. Atwood defined exactly who "the people" were and what their political options were with a precision utterly lacking in Locke.

Despite Atwood's fears over some of the more ambiguous concepts promoted in the *Two Treatises*, his ideas represented the basic tenets of radical Whig ideology as developed in the 1680s. First and foremost, Atwood sought to desacralize both the political discourse and the political process itself. For Atwood and other constitutionalists, maxims about the king (such as "the king can do no wrong" and "the king never dies") were really about the law. For it was the law that was never wrong and never died. Atwood found the public statement of the cleric George Hickes, that he sucked in the doctrine of passive obedience with his mother's milk, outrageous. Hickes, Atwood blasted, should have *"suck'd in law* with his *milk.*"[40] The law, whose interpretation was the domain of lawyers alone, was the yardstick by which all political action should be measured. But whose law was it? Both royalist and parliamentarian, Tory and Whig, had used "the law" to support their arguments. For the Whig constitutionalist, the law was the common law: the people's law formed over centuries, to be interpreted historically only by those properly trained to do so. The new politico, championed by Atwood, was not simply the lawyer, but the lawyer-historian.

The Protestant Martyr: The Reverend Samuel Johnson

Although Atwood tempered his own principles, he was a great admirer of one whose politics were far less cautious. In 1691, Atwood published yet another defense of the Reverend Samuel Johnson.[41] This time Johnson's critic was Anglican divine William Sherlock. Sherlock, a nonjuror, scolded Johnson for his enthusiasm for the Revolution and rejection of James II. Sherlock accused Johnson of having "renounced the merits of your suffering, forefaulted your right of compensation, abdicated your religion together with your King . . . and almost justi-

---

40. *The Fundamental Constitution*, 77, xix, for the direct quotes. On the law, also see Samuel Johnson, *Julian's Arts*, 108.
41. *Dr. Sherlock's Two Kings of Brainford* (1691).

fied the inhumanity of your sentence."[42] In response to Sherlock, Atwood eulogized Johnson, whom he called "the real martyr for truth." "Every lash you bore," Atwood exclaimed, "for the sake of English liberties shall rise about you in circles of glory."[43] The remaining members of the network were particularly generous. As an anonymous critic put it in the eighteenth century, "Johnson's friends found means to make his whipping very favorable."[44] In the 1693 edition of John Tutchin's Whig martyrology, "the pious, reverend, and learned Mr. Johnson" was applauded for doing more than "any man in the world" to promote the acceptance of "our great and happy Revolution."[45]

Johnson was finally released from prison in the spring of 1689. On June 11, the House of Commons resolved that the sentence passed against him in 1686 should be deemed "cruel and illegal." Johnson's degradation was also reversed, and he was reinstated as the rector of Corringham.[46] All of Johnson's tracts were also republished, including *Julian the Apostate*, which was reissued in the crucial month of December 1688. In January 1689, the formerly suppressed *Julian's Arts to Undermine and Extirpate Christianity* appeared in print for the first time. Hoping to capitalize on Johnson's new fame, Whig publisher Richard Baldwin brought out a collection of Johnson's works, *A Second Five Year's Struggle against Popery and Tyranny* (1689), mostly written during his imprisonment and dedicated to William III. The collection included headnotes to each tract written by Johnson, wherein he styled himself a great sufferer and martyr for the Protestant cause.

Johnson expected, after all his suffering and service for the cause prior to the Revolution, to be rewarded by the new regime. His supporters, including the Reverend John Tillotson, a close friend of Lady Rachel Russell, reported that the new king was "well inclined" toward the Whig divine. Yet William III persistently avoided making

---

42. Sherlock was referring to Johnson's flogging in 1686. See his *Observations upon Mr. Johnson's Remarks upon Dr. Sherlock's Book of Non-Resistance* (1689), 6, which was a response to Johnson's *Remarks on Dr. Sherlock Book, intitled [sic] the Case of Resistance of the Supreme Powers Stated and Resolved*.

43. *Dr. Sherlock's Two Kings*, 3, 4. In *The Fundamental Constitution*, Atwood wrote that Johnson was the only Anglican cleric who was "not filling all places with their pulpit-law [passive obedience] and the dictates of their guide Sir Roger [L'Estrange]" during the Exclusion Crisis (13–14).

44. *A Vindication of the Royal Family of the Stuarts* (1734), 5.

45. [Tutchin] *The New Martyrology*, 149–53

46. Grey, *Debates*, 9:289; *Journals of the House of Commons*, 10:193–94 .

particular arrangements for Johnson. At one point, there was talk of sending Johnson to an Irish bishopric in order to "stop many mouths as well as his." Finally in 1695, Johnson was simply pensioned off, given a thousand pounds in "ready money" and three hundred pounds per year for his life and his son's.[47]

In the early 1690s, despite his exclusion from favor, Johnson continued to be a public figure. He wrote numerous tracts instructing the new government on the genius of England's ancient constitution. Though Johnson never directly attacked William III, he was not always pleased with the direction of the new king's policies. But even as Johnson's prospects for preferment grew dim, he wrote, "No court-neglects or disappointments have altered me; and I will love this Court whether they will or not, for I am sure I laid the bridge that brought them over, and I am pretty sure they did not come thither by virtue of passive obedience."[48]

Johnson was extremely critical of the interpretation of the Revolution adopted by the convention. In 1692, as the controversy over the Revolution still raged in the press, Johnson published what he hoped would be recognized as the quintessential interpretation of the events of 1688. His pamphlet, *An Argument Proving that the Abrogation of King James by the People of England . . . was according to the Constitution of the English Government*, went into five editions in 1693 alone and was translated into Dutch. Even Johnson's enemies recognized that this latest "pamphlet of renown filled every tongue in town." Here Johnson declared that the convention's abdication/vacancy formula was mere terminological camouflage used to mask the simple fact that the people had dethroned James II for his violation of the nation's established laws and promoted William and Mary in his place. Johnson wished to expose the Conventioneers' efforts to sustain the myth of public nonresistance to James. The abdication/vacancy formula was created "to cover the doctrine of passive obedience and to keep that safe and sound notwithstanding the Prince and the whole nation engaged in resisting oppression and defending their rights."[49]

---

47. Both Tillotson and the earl of Sunderland reported that William III was "well inclined" toward Johnson. In September 1689, Tillotson wrote to Lady Russell that "a good bishopric in Ireland" might appease Johnson. *The Letters of Lady Rachel Russell* (1854), 146, 153; HMC, *Downshire*, vol. 1, part 1, 158; Luttrell, 3:559.

48. *An Essay Concerning Parliaments at a Certainty; or The Kalenders of May* (1693), 293.

49. *The Canonical Statesmen's Grand Argument Discussed* (1694), 3, and Johnson, *An Argument Proving*, 262, for the direct quotations.

Johnson was further infuriated by the providential theories used to sanction William's arrival. He sneered at reverence to the "Protestant wind," taunting those who believe that "the Revolution is proved to be right because at Torbay the wind chopped about." "Even God," he scoffed, "cannot make wrong be right." Johnson was also quick to denounce the justification of the accession of William and Mary based on the right of conquest. Jacobites and nonjurors alike often argued that William of Orange's "conquest" of England had resulted in the loss of all English liberties and rights. Johnson asserted that it was obvious that England had not become a "new Dutch colony." The prince of Orange was invited to England. His *Declaration of Reasons* made it clear that he had come to protect English liberties; it sounded like "Gospel" to Johnson. William's crown was bestowed upon him by the people. A conqueror, on the contrary, illegally usurps the throne and "no after-treaties nor consent can ever make [him] a King."[50]

Closely related to the right of conquest argument was the concept of de facto kingship. Many hoped, including Bishop Gilbert Burnet, that recognition of William as king by possession rather than by right (king de jure) would make the settlement more widely acceptable.[51] But what Burnet did not understand, and what Johnson saw all too clearly, was that kingship based on the "present prevailing powers" nullified any discussion of immemorial rights. As J. G. A. Pocock states, "to discuss what was ancient was by definition to discuss what was *de jure*." Thus for Johnson, since William and Mary's accession was only justifiable within the construction of the ancient constitution, their title was necessarily de jure. Moreover, the idea that the people were merely "subject to the powers that are" was a "wretched foundation for allegiance." Upon this supposition obedience is only due to the present prevailing powers; it is but "a shifting of the guards, and in an instant all the people's allegiance bid their king goodnight." In 1694, Johnson penned a bitter reply to Burnet: "If I were a bishop of King William's making," and Johnson certainly wished to be a bishop of William's making, "I would never for my own sake call my founder a king *de facto*," for a de facto king can only make *de facto* bishops![52]

Like Atwood, Johnson promoted his politics within the framework of

---

50. *An Argument Proving*, 271, 262, 267, 264, 270.

51. *A Pastoral Letter Writ by the Right Reverend Father In God Gilbert, Lord Bishop of Sarum.*

52. Pocock, *The Ancient Constitution*, 325; Johnson, *An Argument Proving*, 270, 264; Johnson, *Notes upon the Phoenix Edition of the Pastoral Letter* (1694), 301, for the quotations.

the ancient constitution. Johnson continued to scorn the use of Scripture in political debate, since "government is the ordinance of man and of human extraction." The customs and the deeds of men were the true stuff of politics. "The passive obedience nation excuse themselves for a very good reason from the intricate labyrinths of law and history which are the rule that I go by; and which are the standard in this affair as Gospel is of Christianity."[53]

Johnson, the historian, reiterated the familiar story of England's "ancient and approved laws," which had "passed through all the British, Roman, Danish, Saxon and Norman times with little nor no alternation in the main." Johnson also celebrated Holy Edward's Laws whose "inviolable observation" was sworn to by "King William the First (falsely and flatteringly called the Conqueror)." Magna Carta was no "invention or innovation," for it affirmed ancient liberties, and though born in 1215, had "a grey beard."[54] Like Ferguson and Atwood, Johnson believed the coronation oath represented that contract between king and people. He called the oath a "fundament contract," the "covenant of the kingdom," and a "downright English bargain."[55] Should the king dispense with or violate the law, the Crown reverted to "the people of England, who had always had the disposal of it until they invest a new king with it." William III "is the rightfullest king that ever sat on the English throne. For he is set up by the same hands which made the first king, and which have always unmade all tyrants as fast as they could."[56]

Johnson addressed the issue of legislative authority that Atwood, the lawyer, curiously did not. In 1683, Johnson had backed away from Thomas Hunt's radical vision that the power to make law resided in Lords and Commons, sans king. Johnson did assert in *Julian's Arts* that the law was the supreme authority on earth and that kings "suffer the law as others of his people"; and that kings have "no power beyond the law." Sometime after 1683, Johnson decided that "the people" also had the right to "repeal, alter, and explain" the law. The laws "bind every man because every man's consent is involved in their creation." Law-

53. *An Argument Proving,* 271.

54. *The Second Part of the Confutation of the Ballancing Letter: Containing an Occasional Discourse in Vindication of Magna Carta,* 340–41.

55. *Remarks upon Dr. Sherlock's Book, intitled [sic] The Case of Allegiance due to Sovereign Princes, Stated and Resolved* (1690), 238–39.

56. *A Confutation,* 337; *Remarks upon Dr. Sherlock's Book, intitled [sic] The Case of Allegiance,* 237.

breakers, those who seek to infringe, violate, or dispense with the laws (including kings), were to be resisted by force. For Johnson, resistance was not simply a matter of self-defense. Anyone who broke the law was a "publick enemy," and the active use of force against them was justifiable.[57]

Johnson was also very specific about the civil rights that England's ancient constitution guaranteed every freeborn subject. "Every liege subject," he wrote, "has a legal property in life, liberty, and estate and the free exercise of the Protestant religion." Johnson never defined whom he meant by "the people," to whom he gave considerable rights and responsibilities. The king "received his power from his people"; they were the true custodians of the law and have the power to make princes and destroy tyrants. He plainly excluded minors and slaves from his concept of "the people," because he believed they could not "be party to a contract." He probably excluded servants and women as well. On the other hand, Johnson's concept of "the people" was broader than simply the electorate. He believed that "everyone above sixteen" should swear to the oath of allegiance, and that "all men" have both a "natural and civil right and property in their country."[58]

What Johnson clearly did not mean by "the people" was merely their representatives in Parliament. While Johnson advocated annual Parliaments and defended the antiquity of Parliament, it was in the "good, ancient and approved laws of the realm" that Johnson believed English liberties were ultimately entrusted. Johnson was disillusioned with Parliament, especially after the "slight-of-hand" performed by the convention of January 1689, when it was declared that James II had fled, abdicating the throne.[59] Johnson considered the abdication/vacancy formula a betrayal of the Revolution, and he may have come to the conclusion that the men of power were insincere and easily corrupted, whereas the old English Constitution was beyond reproach. Johnson was the consummate purist. Ferguson, happy with the results alone, could compromise his principles for the Revolution. Atwood, eager for self-promotion, could bend his ideas a bit and thus lavishly celebrate the events of 1688–89. But for Johnson, there was simply one authentic

57. *Julian's Arts*, 103; *Of Magistracy* (1689), 153, 156.
58. *Remarks upon Dr. Sherlock's Book, intitled [sic] The Case of Allegiance*, 224; *An Argument Proving*, 264; *Notes upon the Phoenix Edition*, 301.
59. *An Argument Proving*, 260.

interpretation of the Revolution, the one Richard Rumbold had spoke from the scaffold: the original contract had been violated and broken by the king; resistance to his tyranny by the people had been both lawful and necessary.

The Revolution of 1688–89 signaled the demise of the radical Whig network. Its objective had been achieved. The Catholic James II was removed from the throne and a Protestant succession was established. Many, pleased with the new regime, were rewarded for their past services and appointed to various positions within William's administration. Lord Delamere and Lord Grey were appointed to the king's Privy Council and held various offices under William as well.[60] John Trenchard was knighted by William III and appointed secretary of state in 1692. Even many among the lower cabal of Rye House conspirators were rewarded and brought into the government. Zachary Bourne became a messenger to the chamber; Edward Norton received a commission in the infantry. Aaron Smith became the solicitor to the treasury in 1689. All in all, at least twenty members of the Whig network were rewarded with offices or honors after the Glorious Revolution.[61]

Others, dissatisfied with the Revolutionary Settlement and the new government, remained part of a restless, disaffected faction of the Whig party. Their sentiments were neatly summed up by a pamphleteer in 1693, who wrote, "It pleased God to stir them up a Deliverer, who indeed they accepted at first with open arms, though some of them thought afterwards he delivered them more than he needed."[62] The Reverend Samuel Johnson and former Monmouth rebel John Tutchin, a prolific journalist, poet, and primary author of the Whig martyrologies, belong to this group.[63] Mark Goldie has called them "the shocktroops on the left wing [who] served both to recall Whigs to their old loyalties and to denounce them and the establishment for dereliction of principle."[64] Other members of the network simply retired into obscurity. Still

60. Delamere was elevated to the earl of Warrington in 1690; Lord Grey became the earl of Tankerville in 1695.

61. See "Select List of Offices and Honors Received by Radicals in the Aftermath of the Revolution of 1688–89," in Richard Greaves, *Secrets of the Kingdom*, 350–54.

62. N.N., *A Letter from Oxford concerning Mr. Samuel Johnson's Late Book*, 9.

63. On Tutchin, see Zook, "The Bloody Assizes," 381–82.

64. "The Roots of True Whiggism," 197.

Conclusion: Radical Whig Legacies

> I am perfectly lost in wonder when I think of this
> Revolution. To us, that knew it, it looks like a dream, but
> to posterity it must certainly seem like a romance . . .
> that all the politics of several years last past should be
> unraveled in three months.
> —*A Dialogue Between Dick and Tom* (1689)

The Revolution for which radicals had fought and died over the preceding decade was over so quickly, unraveling in less than four months, that it was little wonder that the anonymous author of *A Dialogue Between Dick and Tom* thought it seemed like a "dream." Yet this scribbler also knew that "all the politics of the several years last past" had something to do with it, though he feared the politics would be forgotten and the Revolution would appear to "posterity" as a "romance." His words were prophetic. For indeed we know that, while radicals did their best to keep the stories of their suffering and heroism alive, their tales faded with time. By the nineteenth century, an English schoolboy or girl might very well learn about the martyrdoms of the noble Russell and the brave old soldier Sidney. But the whipping of the Reverend Samuel Johnson would be forgot. Memories of the "bloody assizes" in western England might linger, but the radical politics preached from the gallows would be erased. Voices so loud in the 1680s were nearly silenced by the nineteenth century, and the Revolution for which they fought became like a "romance," no longer simply "glorious," but bloodless as well. The ideas of Hunt and Atwood, Ferguson and Johnson, would come to be labeled "Lockean." Their names would be lost, written out of history, while Locke's *Two Treatises,* arguing in the far more universalist language of natural law, would go on to inspire revolutionaries in America and France, although it had little impact in the making of the English Revolution of 1688. Locke, traditionally cast as the philosopher above all the petty wrangling of the Exclusion Crisis, fit far better into the liberal vision of English history than the likes of Ferguson.

Stories of Whig suffering in the 1680s—the execution of the "Protestant Joiner," the "killing" of the earl of Essex in the Tower, the "judicial murders" of Russell and Sidney, the barbarity of Jeffreys's "bloody assizes," the flogging of Oates and Johnson—were kept alive in the 1690s and early eighteenth century by the Whig martyrologists and other, mostly radical, propagandists, antiquarians, and politicians.[1] They served to sensationalize Stuart violence and sanctify Whig activity. They helped future English historians depict the Catholic king as deserving his fate, while further highlighting the virtues of an ostensibly peaceful Protestant Revolution. But the liberal Whig interpretation of history would eventually leave the radical principles and escapades of the Whig sufferers to the wayside.

Even in the 1690s, not all Whigs found the tactics of their brethren in the 1680s something they wanted to remember or celebrate. The clubbing and petitioning, the packed juries and the sheriff's riot, the assassination plots and the Monmouth episode were, for many Williamite Whigs of the new order, something best forgotten. Even the Whig martyrologists, who eulogized seventy-two Whig and Dissenting heroes and heroines, were silent with regard to the Whig leader Lord Shaftesbury and his aid-de-camp, Robert Ferguson.[2] Their crafty careers and clandestine politics were written out of the newly sanitized Whig history. Just as the Settlement had denied the popular will, so Whig historians of the new order cleansed the pre-Revolutionary era of its messy politics. What Whig radicalism needed, if it were to remain an influential voice in the political discourse and ideology of the immediate post-Revolution era, was respectability. Samuel Johnson's fame and notoriety and William Atwood's more moderate constitutionalism helped maintain the radical voice. But it found an even more successful spokesman in James

---

1. There are hundreds of examples; a few, first published during the Revolution, include *An Account of the Pretended Prince of Wales* . . . *[and] A Short Account of the murther of the earl of Essex* (1688); Henry Booth, Lord Delamere, *The Late Lord Russell's Case* (1689); John Hawles, *Remarks on the Tryals of* . . . *Stephen Colledge,* . . . *The Lord Russel, Colonel Sidney, Henry Cornish* (1689); Robert Atkyns, *The late Lord Russell's Innocency further defended* (1689); *Sidney Redivivus* (1689); *The Dying Speeches, Letters and Prayers of those Eminent Protestants who suffered in the West* (1689); *The Protestant Martyrs, or the Bloody Assizes* (1689); and [John Tutchin] *The Bloody Assizes, or the Compleat History of the Life of George, Lord Jefferies* (1689, enlarged and reprinted in 1693 and 1705).

2. [Tutchin] *The Western Martyrology.*

Tyrrell. A gentleman and scholar, Tyrrell was the kind of man Atwood had in mind as the new politico: a lawyer-historian, trained in the common law, steeped in the artifacts of the past.

James Tyrrell: The Gentleman Scholar

Tyrrell came from a social level—the men of "legal interests," the gentry—whose members Atwood admired and wished to influence. Although he never practiced, Tyrrell had studied law at Gray's Inn and the Inner Temple. He spent most of the 1680s on his country estate, aloof from the turbulent City politics of Whigs and Tories. He spent the 1690s reiterating the radical Whig principles developed in the previous decade, and the early eighteenth century, until his death in 1718, rummaging through libraries and writing a mammoth multivolume history of England that would demonstrate, once and for all, the truth of Whig constitutionalism.

Tyrrell was the grandson of the famous James Ussher who had faithfully served both James I and Charles I as the archbishop of Armagh and primate of all Ireland. Ussher had dominated the Protestant Church in Ireland from 1620 to 1645. He was a strong opponent of popery and a thoroughgoing Calvinist with moderate views on episcopacy and ceremonialism.[3] He was also one of "the giants of Jacobean scholarship." He produced more than twenty-five treatises on history, theology, and politics, and was engaged—as his grandson would be—in many of the great historical controversies of his age, seeking the truth in the artifacts of the past.[4] Ussher was profoundly shocked and disgusted by the civil wars and the execution of Charles I. His treatise, *The Power Communicated by God to the Prince and the Obedience Required of the Subject*, published posthumously in 1661, was written in reaction to the chaos and disorder created by the wars. The only remedy against such anarchy, according to Ussher, was recognition of the supreme authority of the king and the absolute obedience of the subjects to God's appointed

3. Bernard Nicholas, *The Life and Death of . . . Dr. James Ussher* (1656); Richard Parr, *The Life of the Most Reverend Father in God, the Late Lord Archbishop of Armagh, Primate and Metropolitan of all Ireland* (1686); R. Buick Knox, *James Ussher, Archbishop of Armagh* (Cardiff: University of Wales Press, 1967).

4. Pocock, *The Ancient Constitution*, 92; *DNB*.

ruler. Kings were accountable to God alone; they "derive their power and hold their crown from God," and disobedience to a king, even one turned tyrant, was equivalent to disobedience to God himself.[5]

The Power Communicated by God justified the very principles that the radical Whigs had so stridently opposed in the 1680s. Yet when the treatise was published in 1661, and again in 1683 and 1710, it contained a laudatory preface by the famous archbishop's grandson, James Tyrrell. He had safeguarded and seen to the publication of the *Power Communicated by God*.[6] He and his grandfather did not share the same politics, but they did share the same appreciation for the authority and plasticity of history and political theory. Ussher remained a powerful and ever present force in Tyrrell's political and historical works. Tyrrell even applied several of his grandfather's theoretical models and idioms to Whig theory. As Ussher had used the language of God's laws and right reason (natural law) to support his politics, so Tyrrell, particularly in his earliest works, emphasized the "divine authority of those dictates of right reason, or the rules of life, called the laws of nature."[7] Tyrrell also agreed with Ussher that God was the "principle" behind the ordination of government, though as Ussher himself pointed out, "the particular forms of government were instituted by the choice and counsel of man."[8]

Tyrrell's first piece of Whig polemic, *Patriarcha non Monarcha* (1681), was a long and complicated response to Filmer's *Patriarcha*, in which Tyrrell strove to answer the analogy drawn by both Filmer and Ussher between the patriarchal family and the patriarchal state. Ussher had declared that the rule of the father/husband within the family "established a headship" that "laid the foundation of political government."[9] Tyrrell wanted to demonstrate that fathers had no such absolute authority within the family to permit them to take the lives of their dependents. He argued that lunatic, violent, or drunken fathers, like tyrannical

---

5. *The Power Communicated by God to the Prince and the Obedience Required of the Subject,* dedicated to Charles II by James Tyrrell (2d ed., 1683), 42, 111–12.

6. In the preface of *The Power Communicated by God,* Robert Sanderson, bishop of Lincoln, wrote that the manuscript was brought to him by "a gentleman of great hopes and ingenuity and the grandchild of the said author [Ussher] in whose custody it then was."

7. James Tyrrell, preface to *A Brief Disquisition of the Law of Nature* (1692).

8. Ussher, *The Power Communicated by God,* 12; Tyrrell, *Patriarcha non Monarcha,* 119.

9. *The Power Communicated by God,* 14.

kings, may be resisted by their wives and children in self-defense.[10] Tyrrell's affirmation of the right of resistance probably influenced his friend John Locke, who was also busy writing a reply to Filmer, which later became the *First Treatise*.

Tyrrell did not publish again until after the Revolution. Throughout most of the 1680s he lived a sedate existence on his Buckinghamshire estate, Oakley. Though Tyrrell lived the life of the country gentleman and scholar, he maintained numerous connections with Whig radicals in London and was considered "disaffected" by the authorities.[11] Tyrrell had made John Locke's acquaintance at Oxford in 1658, and although he was Locke's junior by ten years, they became life-long friends, affectionately referring to each other by the nicknames "Musidore" for Tyrrell and "Carmeln" for Locke in the early years of their correspondence.[12] Through Locke, Tyrrell met the earl of Shaftesbury, and together with a circle of intellectuals, they frequently met at Shaftesbury's London house in the 1660s and 1670s.[13]

Tyrrell also corresponded with William Petyt, whom he admired and to whom he often deferred with regard to historical controversies. Tyrrell and Petyt shared information and historical sources in the 1680s and 1690s, especially as they both prepared to attack the ideas of Filmer.[14] Tyrrell was friendly with the Whig constitutionalists Edward

10. *Patriarcha non Monarcha* (see especially 102–17). Also see *Bibliotheca Politica* (1694), First Dialogue, 21, wherein Tyrrell declares that parental and civil government cannot be compared.

11. *CSPD*, 25:110.

12. On the relationship between Tyrrell and Locke, see, J. W. Gough, "James Tyrrell, Whig Historian and Friend of John Locke," *HJ* 19 (1976): 581–610, and Mark Goldie, "John Locke's Circle and James II," 557–86.

13. Gough, "James Tyrrell, Whig Historian," 583. Tyrrell was present when the ideas behind Locke's *Essay Concerning Human Understanding* were first discussed at Shaftesbury's house. In the preface of the *Essay*, Locke recalled his discussions with his friends at Shaftesbury's. In the margin of a 1690 edition of the *Essay* (in the British Library), Tyrrell noted the following next to Locke's reminiscing: "This was in the winter of 1673 as I remember being myself one of those that then met there when the discourse began around the principles of morality and revealed religion" (Tyrrell's marginalia in the preface of *The Essay Concerning Human Understanding* (1690), pages unnumbered.

14. Pocock noted that Tyrrell wrote to Petyt in 1680, "addressing him as his superior in historical learning." The letter is published in *The Ancient Constitution*, 346. Tyrrell acknowledged his gratitude to Petyt in the preface of Dialogue 6 of his *Bibliotheca Politica*, wherein he wrote "that having had the happiness of a long and familiar acquaintance with Mr. Petyt, I have been furnished by him with divers authorities (both manuscripts and printed) not hitherto taken notice of by any on this subject." Tyrrell also referenced Petyt's work in Dialogues 5, 7,

Cooke and William Atwood, and made numerous references to their work.[15] It is less certain whether Tyrrell met the infamous public figures Robert Ferguson and the Reverend Samuel Johnson, although it seems likely that he could have met one or both at Shaftesbury's London house. Tyrrell never mentioned Ferguson in his work, but since the bulk of Tyrrell's writings were produced after Ferguson had converted to Jacobitism, this is no surprise. Tyrrell did make numerous references to Johnson, whom he clearly saw as a Protestant hero and martyr. With regard to the controversy between Johnson and George Hickes over the right of resistance and passive obedience, Tyrrell declared in 1694, that his readers should "choose whether Johnson or Hickes won the argument," keeping in mind which man "suffered" and which tried to introduce "arbitrary imperial power." "I had much rather have that man's [Johnson's] reputation who he [Hickes] opposed though with all his suffering than this gentleman's though attendant with all his learning."[16]

Tyrrell's family was also intimately connected with the ardent Whig, deist, and freethinker, Charles Blount. Blount married Tyrrell's sister Eleanora in 1672. He was also a gentleman and, like Tyrrell, intellectually curious and drawn to Whig politics. A member of the Green Ribbon Club, he was probably the author of the radical and violently antipapist *Appeal from the Country to the City* (1679), which argued that Monmouth would make the best successor to Charles II, since he had a weak claim to the throne: "He who hath the worst title, ever makes the best king," Blount declared. For instead of asserting his Crown by "God and by

---

8, and 10, in *Patriarcha non Monarcha*, 124, 188, 190, and reviewed his arguments in the appendix of his *General History of England* (1704), vol. 3.

15. In *Patriarcha non Monarcha*, Tyrrell cited Atwood's *Jani Anglorum* as "written by a young gentleman of great learning and ingenuity" (124). Tyrrell also referenced Atwood's work in Dialogues 6, 7, and 10 of *Bibliotheca Politica*, and in *A Brief Enquiry into the Ancient Constitution and Government of England* (1695), preface and 34. In addition, he reviewed Atwood's historical arguments in the appendix of *The General History of England* (1703), vol. 3. Atwood called Tyrrell his "learned friend" in *The Fundamental Constitution*, 4. Tyrrell and Atwood had a rocky relationship. William Nicolson, bishop of Carlisle, noted in his diary for January 1706, that Tyrrell was "in an uneasy wrath at Mr. Atwood" (*The London Diaries of William Nicolson, Bishop of Carlisle, 1702–1718*, eds. Clyve Jones and Geoffrey Holmes [Oxford: Clarendon Press, 1985], 345). Tyrrell cites Cooke's *Argumentum Anti-Normannicum* several times in his *General History of England*. He also lobbied Bishop Nicolson for support for "his friend Mr. Cooke, author of *Arg Anti Norm*" (*The London Diaries*, 482).

16. *Bibliotheca Politica*, Dialogue 4, 294.

right, his motto may be, by God and my people." Initially Blount, like Ferguson and Atwood, used the forfeiture theory to interpret the Revolution. In his poem "A Dialogue Between King William and the late King James" (1690), Blount had William III remind James II that, "Titles to crowns from civil contracts spring, / And he breaks the law dissolves the king."[17] In 1693, however, Blount created controversy by arguing that William and Mary owned their crowns by right of conquest. So offensive did the strongly Williamite House of Commons perceive conquest theory that they ordered Blount's *King William and Queen Mary Conquerors* be burned by the common hangman, and the Tory licenser of the press, who had authorized the tract's publication, dismissed.[18] Blount's life ended tragically. After his first wife's death, he fell hopelessly in love with her sister. He had asked her to marry him, but she refused as such a match would have been considered incestuous. Blount defended the legality of marriages between two so intimately connected, but in despair fatally shot himself in 1693.[19]

Tyrrell and the Historians

Tyrrell is not served well in the existing scholarship. Overshadowed by his famous friend, he is represented either as a mediocre antiquarian whose histories were mere party propaganda or as a mediocre propagandist whose Whiggism was far more tempered and tangled than that of the illustrious Locke.[20] But these indictments of Tyrrell's work fail to appreciate the purpose of his propaganda and historical studies, as well as the implications of his political principles. Locke's *Two Treatises* have become the "classical constitutional statement of the period." Yet, in its

17. [Charles Blount], *An Appeal from the Country to the City*, 409; Charles Blount, "A Dialogue Between King William and the late King James," (1690), lines 25–26, in *POAS*, 5:525–27.

18. Mark Goldie, "Charles Blount's Intention in Writing "King William and Queen Mary Conquerors" (1693)," *Notes and Queries* 223 (1978): 527–32.

19. McDonald and Murphy, *Sleepless Souls*, 150–51.

20. On Tyrrell as a historian, see Gough, "James Tyrrell, Whig Historian," especially 605, and D. W. L. Earl, "Procrustean Feudalism: An Interpretative Dilemma in English Historical Narrative," *HJ* 19 (1976): 33–51. On Tyrrell as a Whig propagandist, see Caroline Robbins, *The Eighteenth-Century Commonwealthman*, 73–78. Tyrrell fares better in Pocock, *The Ancient Constitution*, 346–48; Kenyon, *Revolution Principles*, 36–37, 47–50; and Weston and Greenberg, *Subjects and Sovereigns*, 131–32, 138–39.

time, contemporaries were more influenced by Tyrrell's brand of politics, which had more in common with the ideas of the Whig ancient constitutionalists (Petyt, Atwood, Cooke, and Johnson) than with Locke's.[21]

Caroline Robbins looked upon Tyrrell's work as "very mediocre Whiggery," "aristocratic" in tone and character. The interpretation is understandable. Tyrrell filled his writings with numerous disclaimers and apologies, asserting time and again that he was "no commonwealthman." "I am not what the world calls a republican or commonwealthman," he declared. Rather, he described himself as "a zealous asserter and defender of the government established by law." "None can admire our excellent constitution more than myself," he proudly exclaimed.[22] The same words could have been penned by Atwood or Johnson or any of the other Whig constitutionalists. They were all monarchists and ardent admirers of an English constitution of their own creation.

Tyrrell's work also appears conservative when compared to Locke's because it lacks the more ambiguous character of the Second Treatise. Tyrrell defined his terms. He repeatedly stressed exactly what he meant by "the people." He feared that his audience might think that he was referring to the "mere vulgar and mobile" when he used the words "the people" in his collection of political dialogues, Bibliotheca Politica (1694). Tyrrell used the term to mean "all degrees of men" and defined "the people" most eloquently in the preface of the First Dialogue: "I desire always to be understood that when I make use of the word people, I do not mean the vulgar or mixed multitude, but in the state of nature the whole body of freemen and women, especially fathers and masters of families; in the civil state, all degrees of men, as well as the nobility and clergy, as the common people." By this definition, only women and slaves were excluded from political rights and responsibilities within the civil state, or as Tyrrell had put it in 1681, "there never was any government where all the promiscuous rabble of women and children had votes as being not capable of it."[23] Yet Tyrrell's definition of "the

---

21. Judith Richards, Lotte Mulligan, and John K. Graham argue that the works of Tyrrell and Algernon Sidney were seen as "more effective defenses of the Whig position" than Locke's work. See their " 'Property' and 'People': Political Usages of Locke and Some Contemporaries," *Journal of the History of Ideas* 42 (1981): 31.

22. Robbins, *Eighteenth-Century Commonwealthman*, 75; Tyrrell, preface to *Bibliotheca Politica* (1718 ed.), v, and preface to *Patriarcha non Monarcha*.

23. Advertisement to *Bibliotheca Politica; Patriarcha non Monarcha*, 83. Tyrrell believed that a wife's vote was included in that of her husband's.

people" was far broader than that of William Atwood and most of his contemporaries.[24] Richard Ashcraft argues that Locke, a gentleman and scholar like Tyrrell, had the broadest possible vision of "the people" in mind when he used the term. But because Locke never defined exactly what he meant by "the people," Ashcraft is merely speculating.[25] More likely, Locke's conception of "the people" was no more radical than either Atwood's or Johnson's, nor any more inclusive than Tyrrell's.

Unlike Locke's *Two Treatises* and the work of Thomas Hunt, Johnson, and Atwood, the bulk of Tyrrell's writings are a product of the 1690s rather than the 1680s. They lack the sense of urgency that permeated so much of early Whig ideology. After all, Tyrrell was writing when the object of Whig aims, the establishment of a Protestant succession, was already accomplished. There is a terseness, clarity, and immediacy in the writings of Ferguson and Hunt that is missing in Tyrrell. He had time to ramble, to restate his ideas in a variety of manners and forms. The sheer volume of Tyrrell's work after 1689 is daunting. Yet his main objective was to condense and summarize the major tenets of 1680s Whiggism and package this material in various forms intended for diverse audiences. In this he was successful, propagating Whig ideology in his *Bibliotheca Politica* (composed of fourteen dialogues), his multivolume history of England, and his *Brief Enquiry into the Ancient Constitution* (1695), a single dialogue written for the "meaner sort."

Tyrrell and the Ancient Constitution

In the epistle dedicatory of *Bibliotheca Politica, or An Enquiry into the Ancient Constitution . . . in Thirteen Dialogues* (1694), Tyrrell claimed to have "carefully perused all treatises of any value that have been published of late years concerning the original and rights of civil government as well as of monarchy." Having found it necessary to write down "the most considerable arguments on both sides," Tyrrell showed his notes to "some friends" who suggested that he publish the arguments to help convince others of the lawfulness of the late Revolution. Thus through a series of dialogues between Mr. Meanwell, a gentleman, and

24. Richards, Mulligan, and Graham, " 'Property' and 'People,' " 41–51.
25. See his argument in "A Radical Manifesto," Chapter 11 of *Revolutionary Politics*, 521–89.

Mr. Freeman, a lawyer, Tyrrell presented the "arguments fairly on both sides" of the most heated public controversies of the 1680s "without interposing my own judgement, but to leave it to the intelligent and impartial reader to embrace that side on which where he found the most rational and convincing arguments."[26] The "intelligent and impartial reader" would undoubtedly find that Mr. Freeman, the lawyer, consistently voiced the "most rational and convincing arguments." Mr. Meanwell earnestly presented the major arguments of Sir Robert Filmer, Dr. Robert Brady, George Hickes, and other proponents of divine right and patriarchal theories of government. But Mr. Freeman always won the debate. He, after all, had as his authorities the works of none other than William Petyt, William Atwood, Samuel Johnson, Edward Cooke, John Locke, and Tyrrell's own *Patriarcha non Monarcha.*

Despite Tyrrell's declared impartiality and his statement that he "declined showing myself a party or giving my own opinion in any question," his politics were abundantly clear from the outset. He could not resist glorifying "the late wonderful happy Revolution," or viciously attacking his ideological opponents, particularly the clergy. Tyrrell hoped his readers would not "slight" the first two dialogues, dealing with divine right and patriarchalism: opinions that he knew were "at present out of fashion." Though it was not too long ago "that our pulpits and presses would scarce suffer any other doctrines either to be preached or published than on these subjects." These ideas were still a threat so long as unscrupulous men about the court were willing to expound such ingratiating and self-serving doctrines: "It faring with some political opinions, as with fashions, which are never so generally received and worn as when they have been in vogue at Court. Those divines and lawyers who were the first inventors or new vampers of them, commonly receiving the greatest rewards and preferments, who (as the Court-taylors did fashions) could invent such doctrines and opinions as were most burdensome and uneasy to all sorts of people, except a few great ones, who were to gain by them."[27] Tyrrell held those "clerics and laity" who embraced Filmerian patriarchalism in the highest contempt, admitting in his preface of the 1718 edition of *Bibliotheca Politica* that he had presented the case "pretty stiffly against the divine right of monarchy and indefeasible hereditary succession to crowns." "I had one of my

---

26. Epistle dedicatory to *Bibliotheca Politica.*
27. Epistle dedicatory to *Bibliotheca Politica.*

disputants [Mr. Freeman] shew the absurdity and fatal consequences of Sir Robert Filmer's principles."[28] Like Hunt, Atwood, and Locke, Tyrrell also believed that the major propagators of these absurd opinions were clerics, and he reiterated the argument of his fellow Whigs that neither Scripture nor the clergy should have anything to say about secular concerns. In the Third Dialogue, Mr. Freeman accuses Mr. Meanwell of taking "refuge under the covert of Holy Scripture to impose an opinion contrary to the common sense and natural notions of mankind." But in fact "our Savior made no alternation in civil government." "The Scripture is wholly silent" on questions of political authority. Clerical meddlers in political affairs should be ignored. As Mr. Freeman declares, "I do not much value the opinion of divines in matters of politics."[29]

Tyrrell was equally clear as to whom he hoped to influence. *Bibliotheca Politica* was dedicated "to all impartial and unprejudiced readers, especially those of our hopeful and ingenious nobility and gentry." Fame was not his objective in publishing the dialogues; rather, he wrote "for the publick good and happiness of my country," whose future resided in the hands of "our young nobility and gentry."[30] Tyrrell's dedication was probably sincere. Unlike Atwood, he had no political ambitions, spending most of his time in dusty archives and libraries. He considered *Bibliotheca Politica* a friendly dialogue between himself and men of similar backgrounds and interests—those who he believed made up England's political elite.

Yet Tyrrell also hoped to reach the widest possible audience. He wished to keep the price of each dialogue down for the sake of "common readers" and to use a dialogue format that he thought would "prove more pleasant" than the "old dry scholastic way of objection and solution." He also thought it was more fitting "for men of ordinary learning and capacities."[31] Several dialogues were published separately by Whig publisher Richard Baldwin in 1692 and 1693. Then in 1694, Baldwin put out the first complete edition of *Bibliotheca Politica* containing thirteen dialogues. In 1702, a fourteenth dialogue concerning the

---

28. Preface to the 1718 edition of *Bibliotheca Politica*, v–vi.
29. *Bibliotheca Politica*, 3, 188; Dialogue 4, 216; *A Brief Enquiry*, 4; *Bibliotheca Politica*, Dialogue 4, 292, for the quotations.
30. Epistle dedicatory to *Bibliotheca Politica*.
31. Epistle dedicatory to *Bibliotheca Politica*; "The Publisher's Preface to the Reader," in *A Brief Enquiry*, probably written by Tyrrell, pages unnumbered.

"murder of King Charles I" was published.[32] All fourteen dialogues were collected and issued again in 1718, the year of Tyrrell's death, with a slightly revised preface. A second edition was published nine years later.

Bibliotheca Politica reviewed all the major and controversial legal, historical, and political issues of the 1680s, along with several that arose in the aftermath of the Revolution of 1688–89. Two dialogues were concerned with refuting divine right and patriarchal theories of monarchy and succession. Three dialogues took up the issues of resistance and passive obedience, arguing in favor of the right of resistance to kings turned tyrants. The fifth dialogue attacked Filmer's and Hickes's opinion that the king could act as sole legislator, presenting instead a theory of mixed government. Three dialogues concerned the antiquity of the House of Commons and were aimed at destroying Robert Brady's vision of medieval England. Three more justified the Revolutionary Settlement of 1689, defending the measures taken by the convention, including the abdication/vacancy formula. The thirteenth dialogue argued for the legitimacy of the oaths of allegiance for William and Mary.

Bibliotheca Politica was a compendium of Whig politics. Tyrrell may have been more conservative than Thomas Hunt, who argued that legislative power could be placed in Parliament's hands alone. He was certainly not as vocal and infamous a polemicist as Samuel Johnson, who lambasted the convention for not acknowledging the people's part in the late Revolution. But in all its important component parts, Tyrrell's work upheld a radical Whig theory of the English government, both past and present. It was a theory that envisioned the English polity as an unbroken continuum with a far distant past, embodying the customary wisdom of the ages. The English government was a secular creation based on the consent of the governed. Should those entrusted with its safety violate that trust, they may be resisted in defense of the people and the constitution.

Tyrrell was concerned that all Englishmen understand and appreciate these political principles. Among the Whigs he was probably not unique in this regard, but he alone presented the radical ideology of the 1680s in a form specifically designed "to make every man (though of never so common a capacity) understand . . . what is the true, ancient

---

32. J. P. Kenyon discusses the early eighteenth-century context behind Tyrrell's Dialogue 14 in Chapter 5, "King Charles's head," of *Revolution Principles* (see p. 69 specifically).

and legal government of his kingdom." In *A Brief Enquiry into the Ancient Constitution and Government of England* (1695), a "Justice of the Peace" (a country gentleman) converses with "an understanding Freeholder," (a yeoman farmer), explaining to him the rights, liberties, and responsibilities of the average subject. All of the debates discussed in *A Brief Enquiry* echo the positions taken in *Bibliotheca Politica*, but in a simplified and abbreviated format. As the preface stated, "the principles here laid down are founded not only upon right reason, but the ancient constitution of the English government."[33] As in *Bibliotheca Politica*, Tyrrell constructed his arguments based on the principles of natural law and the lore of the ancient constitution.

In *A Brief Enquiry*, Tyrrell's patient justice of the peace kindly informs the earnest freeholder of the "ancient rights and liberties of the subject, set down in Magna Carta and other ancient statutes which were only declarative of the common law of England." The English constitution was not disturbed in 1066, the JP declares. William of Normandy did not make war "against the English nation." His quarrel was with Harold Godwinson alone "who had usurped the crown contrary to right." Furthermore, the coronation oath represents the "original contract" between king and people and is "constantly renewed every fresh succession to the crown." The JP also spends a considerable amount of time justifying the people's right of resistance and the conditions under which resistance is warranted. He informs the freeholder that to resist a law-breaking king is not only the duty of every gentleman but of "all orders and degrees of men." "Not only we gentlemen, buy you yeomen can judge (nay, are obliged at your perils to do it) when things are imposed upon you contrary to law." The JP assures the freeholder that such resistance is made not against the king, but "only the king's person, when he acts not as king but as a private man."[34]

With regard to the Revolutionary Settlement of 1689, Tyrrell reiterated the theories of Ferguson and Atwood in *A Brief Enquiry*. Once again James II was guilty of abdicating his throne. But the JP assures the freeholder that James's self-abdication was not simply a matter of "his desertion of the throne by going away." James had violated the "original contract" and endeavored to subvert the constitution. "If kingship be a trust for the preservation of the rights and liberties of the people," the

33. Preface to *A Brief Enquiry*.
34. *A Brief Enquiry*, preface, 33, 22, 51, 47, 49.

JP exclaims, echoing the words of Ferguson, "than such actings contrary to that trust as plainly strike at the very fundamentals of the constitution are not only a breach of that trust, but a tacit renunciation of it also." James II's abdication should be understood as both a "renunciation and also a forfeiture of royal power."[35]

With *Bibliotheca Politica* and *A Brief Enquiry* Tyrrell had reached out to a wide spectrum of the reading public and, with his dialogues, reiterated and propagated all of the principles of radical Whiggism. Still he was not satisfied. Between 1696 and 1704, he began publishing the same ideas in yet another form. This time Tyrrell chose history, which, like Atwood and Johnson before him, he saw as the natural ally of Whig constitutionalism. In the preface to his *General History of England*, Tyrrell explained that his purpose was to demolish the work of Dr. Robert Brady, who "takes all occasions . . . to show his partiality, whilst he endeavors to represent the English nations as slaves by conquest thereby to advance an arbitrary power to unreasonable height."[36]

Tyrrell accused Brady of being a poor historian, writing for a party, and concealing and altering evidence "that makes against the cause he maintains or else he wrests and misconstrues the words that chiefly make against him." Further, Tyrrell claimed that Brady never fairly represented "the errors, failings, and violence of princes" and thus "will never be able to render his History so useful to prosperity." For if the people do not "receive any notice or warning how to avoid the like mismanagement for the time to come," they cannot "learn what breaches have been formerly made upon their ancient rights and liberties so that they may not think it a thing strange and unheard of if the like should happen again in their times."[37] Tyrrell aspired to continuing his history up to the reign of William III, but the volumes published in 1695, 1700, and 1704 only reached as far as the reign of Richard II. He worked on his history up to the time of his death in 1718, meeting occasionally with fellow antiquarian Thomas Hearne. Hearne noted the news of Tyrrell's death in his journal, describing him as "a good scholar and well versed in our history, but tied to a party and writ to serve a turn."[38]

35. *A Brief Enquiry*, 60–62.
36. *The General History of England*, 1:xix.
37. *The General History of England*, 1:xix.
38. *Remarks and Collections of Thomas Hearne*, 11 vols., ed. Charles Doble, et. al. (Oxford:

Tyrrell was the ideal spokesman for the radical Whigs in the 1690s and early eighteenth century. Like Ferguson, he synthesized the ideas of the rationalists (Thomas Hunt and John Locke) with those of the constitutionalists (William Atwood and Samuel Johnson). Yet unlike Ferguson or Johnson, Tyrrell was untainted by the conspiratorial politics of the 1680s. As a gentleman and a scholar, complete with a most distinguished ancestry, Tyrrell brought a respectability to radical Whig ideology just as the Williamite Whigs of the 1690s brought new respectability to the party as a whole. Most important, Tyrrell wished to reach the widest possible audience—a feature of his work that has been ignored by modern scholars. He was concerned with the common reader. The freeholders as well as the gentlemen needed to understand their political rights and responsibilities, as the Whigs perceived them. Tyrrell took the politics developed in the combative years of the 1680s and transformed the ideas of the radical theorists into a synthetic whole. *Bibliotheca Politica* and *A Brief Enquiry* turned the politics of rebellion into casual conversations, reference works for the young nobleman and the yeoman farmer alike.

Legacies

Tyrrell was the last of the radical Whig propagandists to die (in 1718). In the early decades of the eighteenth century, he witnessed the rise of a second generation of radical theorists, including the deist and free-thinker John Toland; the Whig bishop Benjamin Hoadly; the pamphleteer and journalist John Trenchard; and the novelist, poet, and spy Daniel Defoe.[39] Tyrrell would also have noticed that both the politics of

---

Clarendon Press, 1885–1922), 7:19. Hearne noted on September 14, 1731, that Tyrrell had left another volume of his history with his publisher at the time of his death (10:455).

39. On John Toland (1670–1722), see Stephen Daniels, *John Toland: His Methods, Manners, and Mind* (Toronto: McGill-Queen's University Press, 1984); on Benjamin Hoadly (1676–1761), see Reed Browning, *The Political and Constitutional Ideas of the Whigs* (Baton Rouge: Louisiana State University Press, 1982), Chapter 3, "Benjamin Hoadly (1676–1761): The Court Whig as Controversialist," 67–88; on John Trenchard (1662–1723), the son of Whig radical Henry Trenchard and nephew of Sir John Trenchard, see Charles B. Realey, *The London Journal and Its Authors, 1720–23* (Lawrence: University of Kansas Press, 1936); and on Daniel Defoe (1660–1731), see John Robert Moore, "Daniel Defoe: King William's Pamphleteer and

his generation and its promoters were not forgotten. Even Thomas
Hunt, who died in exile in 1688, was remembered and celebrated by
Defoe in 1703, who called him a man of "unspotted honesty . . .
learning, wit, and sense / And more than most men have had since."[40]
    William Atwood died in 1712.[41] His career did not turn out to be all
that he had wished. In the 1690s, he published frequently, not only
Whig propaganda but also tracts on trade, empire, and coinage reform.
Then in June 1700, Atwood finally received the reward for which he had
been working and waiting. He was appointed lord chief justice of New
York, "a place of considerable profit," in Luttrell's words.[42] Atwood went
to New York with his son, who was also a lawyer, and immediately fell
afoul with the local politicians for "taking too much upon himself."[43] He
was accused of corruption and recalled. In his defense, Atwood published a pamphlet describing the lawlessness and factionalism with
which he had had to deal in the colonies, and with much drama
described how he and his son had to race back to England in fear of
their lives. He concluded stating that it was a "hazardous post of no
profit."[44]
    Though his career in public service ended in disappointment, the
principles Atwood had propagated in the 1680s and 1690s lived on. His
ideas, along with those of the other Whig constitutionalists, were
echoed by the second generation of polemicists. Copies of his tracts
were stored in the libraries of eighteenth-century gentlemen both in
England and America.[45] Yet Atwood was never a notorious public figure

Intelligence Agent," *Huntington Library Quarterly* 34 (1971): 251–60, and Paula Backscheider,
Daniel Defoe: His Life (Baltimore: John's Hopkins University Press, 1989).

    40. *Hymn to the Pillory* (1703), 4. Hunt's *Defense of the Charter* was registered at the stationer's
office during the Glorious Revolution in January 1689. A treatise by Hunt entitled, "The
Character of Popery: in Two Parts," which was probably written while he was in exile, was
transcribed by one John Donley and can be found at the British Library (Add. 23,619, fols.
1–183).

    41. The *DNB* and *BDBR* articles on Atwood state that he died in 1705. This is incorrect.
Atwood stopped publishing in 1705, but he lived until 1712. Thomas Hearne recorded
Atwood's death on October 22, 1712, noting that Atwood was "a learned antiquary and a very
curious man" (Hearne, *Remarks*, 3:475).

    42. Luttrell, 4:657.

    43. Nicolson, *The London Diaries*, 172–73.

    44. *The Case of William Atwood, esq.* (1700), 17.

    45. Atwood's books can be found in the listings of the following libraries: the Reverend
John Tilloston (*A Collection of Excellent English Books . . . being the Library of the Reverend Father
in God, Dr. Tilloston*, 1695); Lord Ford Grey, earl of Tankerville ("A Catalogue of Books," PRO

like the Plotter, Robert Ferguson, or the Protestant martyr, Samuel Johnson, both of whom left the strongest impressions upon their contemporaries as well as the next generation of Whigs and Whig sympathizers.

Robert Ferguson's occupation as a professional plotter did not cease with the Glorious Revolution. In his new incarnation as a Jacobite, Ferguson published tract after tract of propaganda in the service of James II and was involved in plot after plot against the life of William III. He was ever before the public consciousness. Weeklies recorded every tidbit of news about his doings and whereabouts; satirical literature, poems, dialogues, and invectives concerning Ferguson's strange career and the twists and turns of his politics flooded the public reading market.[46] In the end, the man who had plotted against so many lives, who was considered by so many as responsible for the deaths of Russell, Sidney, and Monmouth, died in his own bed, a pauper, eking out a living with his pen.[47]

Ferguson was an embarrassment to the Whigs in the 1690s. It is hardly surprising that, considering Ferguson's Jacobite politics, he was left out of the Whig martyrologies. Secretary of state, Sir John Trenchard, and his friends Aaron Smith and Hugh Speke (all Ferguson's fellow conspirators during the 1680s), did their utmost to track him down and incarcerate him.[48] Yet others recognized the value of Ferguson's earlier

c.104/82); Sir William Temple (Huntington Library, Stowe Collection, vol. 365); John Locke's Library (John Harrison and Peter Laslett, eds., *The Library of John Locke* (Oxford: Oxford University Press, 1971); and Thomas Jefferson's Library (*A Catalogue of the Library of Thomas Jefferson,* 5 vols. [Washington: Library of Congress, 1955]).

46. News of Ferguson's Jacobite activities can be found in nearly all the major diaries and correspondence collections of the time. See, for example, HMC: *Finch,* vol. 3, and the *Portledge Papers being extracts from the letters of Richard Lapthorne,* eds. Russell J. Kerr and Ida Coffine Duncan (London, 1928). Among the plentiful anti-Ferguson satirical works, see *A Dialogue Between Sir Roger L'Estrange and Mr. Rob. Ferguson* (1696); *Robert against Ferguson: or a New Dialogue between Robert an Old Independent Whig and Ferguson a New Pretended Jacobite* (1704); and *Who Plot Best: The Whigs or the Tories . . . in a Letter to Mr. Ferguson* (1710).

47. Robert Wodrow wrote in 1713 of Ferguson, "He is yet alive, in great want and upwards of ninety years, and hath nothing but what he begs" (*Analecta,* 2:271). Ferguson was writing up to the time of his death (his last tract had to be finished by another "hand"). He had a wife and two children to whom he wrote throughout his exile in the 1680s. His wife, Hanna, died in 1710.

48. See Ferguson's fiery attacks upon his former allies (Trenchard, Smith, and Speke) in his *Letter to the Lord Chief Justice Holt* (1694), and *Letter to Mr. Secretary Trenchard, discovering a Conspiracy against the laws . . . of England* (1694).

Whig propaganda, especially as it was articulated in *A Brief Justification*. An anonymous Whig tract entitled *Vox populi, vox dei*, first published in 1709, plagiarized word for word the first seventeen pages of *A Brief Justification*. Those pages contain Ferguson's most important political conceptions: they describe the origins of government, the obligations of the prince and the people, the historical evidence for the ancient constitution, the functions of Parliament, and the right of popular resistance. *Vox populi, vox dei* went into eight editions in 1709 alone and six more in 1710. It was also published under a second title in 1710, *The Judgement of the Whole Kingdoms and Nations concerning the Rights, Powers and Prerogatives of Kings and the Rights, Privileges and Properties of the People*, which went into eleven editions in four years.[49] Separated from his person and hence the eccentric career of the infamous Plotter, Ferguson's Whig principles reached yet another generation of the reading public. *A Brief Justification* was not simply the manifesto of the Glorious Revolution. In its second coming as *Vox populi, vox dei* and *The Judgement of the Whole Kingdoms*, it was the manifesto of early eighteenth-century Whiggism, read alongside the works of another member of the radical network, the Reverend Samuel Johnson. J. P. Kenyon has described *Vox populi, vox dei* as the most important Whig tract of the post-Revolution era.[50]

Unlike Ferguson, Johnson's image was untainted by his later activities. In fact, the legacy of both the man and his work only grew in the years after his death in 1703. Johnson's unyielding spirit and determination to judge the Revolution and William III's policies by the Whig tenets developed in the 1680s earned him both considerable respect and amity. Nor did the suffering that Johnson endured for his principles end with the Revolution. On the night of November 27, 1692, seven men broke into Johnson's house near Piccadilly and assaulted him. He was beaten with clubs and cut with swords. One of his assailants shouted, "Pistol him, kill him, kill him for the book he wrote."[51] The book was *An Argument Proving*, Johnson's uncompromising interpretation of the

49. Information on *Vox populi, vox dei* can be found in Richard Ashcraft and M. M. Goldsmith, "Locke, Revolution Principles, and the Formation of Whig Ideology," *HJ* 26 (1983): 773–800, and Kenyon, *Revolution Principles*, appendix, "Vox Populi, Vox Dei," 209–10.

50. "The Revolution of 1688: Resistance and Contract," in Neil McKendrick, ed., *Historical Perspectives in English Thought and Society in Honour of J. H. Plumb* (London: Europa, 1974), 62–64.

51. *A True and Faithful Relation of the Horrid and Barbarous Attempt to Assassinate the Reverend Mr. Samuel Johnson* (1692). Also see Luttrell, 2:627.

Revolution, which had angered James II's supporters. The martyr lived a martyr's life.

Although Johnson accumulated enemies, he also had many politically like-minded admirers, including Lady Rachel Russell, Sir Robert Howard, John Hampden, the younger, the Reverend John Tillotson, and Edward Fowler, bishop of Gloucester.[52] John Hampden, who spent time with Johnson in King's Bench Prison, later stated that he "never knew a man of greater sense, of a more innocent life, nor of greater virtue." Hampden published an open letter to Johnson in 1692, calling his *Julian [the Apostate]*, the next best book to the Bible."[53]

In the early eighteenth century, Johnson received favorable portraits from Whig historian White Kennett and biographers Samuel Knight and Francis Lee. Though Lee was a nonjuror, the subject of his biography, John Kettlewell, knew Johnson through Lord Russell's family, the Bedfords. Lee wrote of Johnson's work, "In his books written before and after the Revolution, the principles which he espoused are better and more consistently explained, then perhaps in any one writer whatsoever."[54] Whig journalist Richard Steele evoked Johnson's name in his weekly, *The Englishman*, during the Jacobite rising of 1715, to remind readers of those who had fought and suffered for the Protestant cause. Steele concluded the October 10, 1715 issue with a stirring excerpt from Johnson's *Humble and Hearty Address to all the English Protestants in this Present Army*.[55]

Johnson was the only early Whig propagandist to have his writings published together in a single volume. His complete works were first published in 1710, with a second edition issued in 1713. The 1710 edition was prefaced by a hagiographic memorial to the Whig divine. It also contained an impressive list of 319 subscribers, fourteen of whom were peers who had served the governments of William III and Queen Anne in various positions. They were supporters of the Union with Scotland and the Hanoverian Succession, and, if able, fought for the government in 1715. Some of the subscribers, such as Anthony Ashley

---

52. Fowler and Tilloston sent Johnson money when he was in prison in the 1680s (*DNB*, s.v. "Johnson, Samuel" and "Fowler, Edward"). Howard wrote a laudatory letter to Johnson in 1692, entitled *A Letter to Mr. Johnson*.

53. *A Letter to Mr Samuel Johnson, occasioned by his Argument Proving* (1692), 2.

54. White Kennet, *A Complete History of England* (1706), 3:414; Samuel Knight, *The Life of John Colot* (1724), 411–12; Francis Lee, *The Life of John Kettlewell* (1718), 331, for the quotation.

55. Rae Blanchard, ed., *The Englishman: A Political Journal by Richard Steele* (Oxford: Clarendon Press, 1955), 468.

Cooper, the third earl of Shaftesbury, and Wriothesly Russell, duke of Bedford (Lord William Russell's son), were members of the earliest Whig families. At least a dozen subscribers were nonconformist ministers, including the Reverend Thomas Bradbury who wrote various political tracts defending the Revolution and the right of resistance. Others were booksellers, journalists, and men of letters. The Scot George Ridpath published the stridently Whig weekly, the *Flying Post*; Sir William Benson was a literary critic and Whig politician famous for his diatribe against divine right kingship. James Tyrrell subscribed to Johnson's works, as did three other friends and admirers of John Locke: Anthony Collins, a committed Whig and Locke's intimate in the last years of the philosopher's life; Awnsham Churchill, Locke's publisher and a Whig MP; and John Shute, later Viscount Barrington, a Whig writer and Locke protégé.[56]

The list of Johnson's subscribers demonstrates that the ideas of the first generation of Whig radicals had become incorporated into mainstream Whig political theory. These eighteenth-century Whigs were no longer members of a conspiratorial network. Rather, they were members of Parliament, office holders, naval officers, men of letters, science, art, and divinity. Unlike the previous generation of plotters, who met in darkened rooms and hid in haylofts, they met in boardrooms and parlors. The popularity of Ferguson's and Johnson's works not only suggests that early eighteenth-century Whiggism was far less conservative than it has often been portrayed by historians, but that the political principles developed during the conspiratorial politics of the 1680s were incorporated into the political liberalism of the following generation.

While many of the individuals of the radical network were forgotten, the ideas they had propagated continued to have a lasting influence on

---

56. The list of subscribers is found in Johnson, *Works*, xxv–xxviii. The fourteen nobles were Lords Raby and Russell; Viscount Barrington; the earls of Haddington, Leven, Oxford, Portland, Rochfort, Shaftesbury, Stramford, Sunderland, and Torrington; and the dukes of Devonshire and Roxburghe. Only Lord Raby (created earl of Strafford in 1711) was a Tory, though he served in various positions under William III. Thomas Bradbury wrote *The Lawfulness of Resisting Tyrants* (1714). His sermons were often violently critical of kingship. When Queen Anne died, he reportedly preached on 4 Kings 9.34, "Go, see now this cursed woman and bury her, for she is a King's daughter" (*DNB*). William Benson's diatribe is entitled, *A Letter to Sir Jacob Banks* (1711) (*DNB*). On the connections among Collins, Churchill, Shute, and Locke, see Locke, *The Correspondence of John Locke*, 8 vols., E. S. De Beer, ed. (Oxford: Oxford University Press, 1989), vol. 8.

English political culture and ideology in the 1690s and early eighteenth century. Members of the network had made the manipulation of the royal succession a viable and an acceptable alternative to a Catholic monarchy. They had justified the use of violence and attempted to use force to accomplish their ends. The Glorious Revolution was certainly not their revolution alone. But their ideas, their tropes, and their slogans were central to it: they were incorporated in the prince of Orange's *Declaration of Reasons*, debated at the convention and inscribed in *The Declaration of Rights*. The network's propagandists had vindicated the Revolution, and its plotters and rebels had landed at Torbay with the prince, greeted his marching army, sat at the convention, and participated in his government. Revolution, the young John Hampden declared in 1689, "was the way which our ancestors always took when the sovereign authority came to so great a height. . . . [C]ustom had made this the law of England."[57] For many, the Glorious Revolution was the victory of the "old English government" as re-created and propagated by the radical Whig exclusion movement.

The Whig conspirators and propagandists of the 1680s left to the next generation of like-minded men and women a pantheon of martyr-heroes and a set of political principles from which to draw for inspiration and indoctrination. In the early eighteenth century, works that were once subversive, scribbled in rented rooms, left on church pews, and read in smoke-filled taverns, were now patronized by members of the newly established order. Although the names of most of the Whig exclusionists of the 1680s would eventually be forgotten, the constitutionalist principles they propagated and the stories they told in the 1680s and 1690s would help to construct the liberal political vision and the Whig interpretation of history for centuries to come. "O' that we had now an SJ to fight the Tories," an excited Samuel Taylor Coleridge scribbled in the margin of Johnson's complete works in 1833.[58] For like Samuel Johnson's contemporaries, Coleridge knew that the conspirators and propagandists of the exclusion movement were the combatants on the front lines of ideological conflict in the first age of party. The revolutionary principles that had helped to justify the events of 1688–89

---

57. Report to the House of Lords on the 20th of December 1689 from the Committee for Inspections of Examinations, concerning the Murders of Lord Russell, Colonel Sidney, etc., *State Trials*, 9:960.

58. Coleridge's marginalia is found in the 1710 edition of Samuel Johnson's *Works* held at the British Library, 305 (emphasis his).

had not been crafted in the philosopher's study but forged in taverns and coffeehouses, transmitted through the popular press, raucously celebrated on the streets, and defended on the battlefield and the scaffold. When contemporaries read Hunt, Atwood, Johnson, Ferguson, or Tyrrell, they were present at the creation.

Appendix: Radical Whig Careers

Radical	GRC	PI	P2	E	RHP	Exile 1	MR/AI	Exile 2	GR	Fate
Armstrong, Sir Thomas (1633–84)		X		X	X	X				Executed for outlawry, 1684
Arnold, John (c. 1635–1702)	X			X					X	Imprisoned for *scandulum magnatum*, 1682–86
Atwood, William (d. 1705)		X		X					X	
Ayloffe, John (1645–85)	X		X	X	X	X	AI			Executed for Argyle's Invasion, 1685
Barnardiston, Sir Samuel (1620–1707)			X	X						Imprisoned for seditious libel, 1684–88; rewarded post-1688
Barnardiston, Samuel			X?		X	X	MR			Exempted from the Pardon of 1686; pardoned, 1687
Bateman, Charles	X		X		X					Executed for the Rye House Plot, 1685
Bethel, Slingsby (1617–97)	X		X	X						In exile, 1682–89; rewarded post-1688
Betiscomb, Christopher	X	X			X	X	MR			Executed for Monmouth's Rebellion, 1685
Blaney, Robert	X		X		X					Turned king's evidence, 1683; rewarded post-1688
Blount, Charles (1654–93)	X		X	X					X	Suicide, 1693
Booth, Henry Lord Delamere (1652–94)	X		X	X	X				X	Imprisoned in 1683, 1684, and 1685–86; rewarded post-1688
Bourne, Zachary	X		X		X					Turned king's evidence, 1683; rewarded post-1688
Burnet, Bishop Gilbert (1643–1715)		X				X			X	In exile, 1683–88; rewarded post-1688
Burton, James			X?		X	X	MR			Turned king's evidence, 1685

Radical	GRC	PI	P2	E	RHP	Exile 1	MR/AI	Exile 2	GR	Fate
Capel, Arthur, earl of Essex (1631–83)	X			X	X					Suicide, 1683
Care, Henry (1646–88)			X	X						
Charlton, Francis			X	X	X	X	MR			Excepted from the Pardons of 1686 and 1688
Clayton, Sir Robert (1629–1707)		X		X					X	Rewarded post-1688
Colledge, Stephen			X	X	X					Executed for sedition, 1681
Cooke, Edward			X?	X	X					
Cooper, Anthony Ashley, earl of Shaftesbury (1621–83)		X		X	X	X				Died in exile, 1683
Cornish, Henry			X	X						Executed for the Rye House Plot, 1685
Danvers, Henry (c. 1622–87)			X		X?	X		X		Died in exile, 1687
Dare, Thomas	X	X			X		MR			Killed, 1685
Disney, William			X	X	X	X	MR			Executed for sedition, 1685
Ferguson, Robert			X	X	X	X	MR	X	X	Exempted from the 1688 Pardon; rewarded post-1688
Foulkes, John			X	X			MR	X	X	Exempted from the 1688 Pardon
Freke, John	X	X		X	X					Killed in battle, 1685
Goodenough, Francis	X	X			X	X	MR			Turned king's evidence, 1685
Goodenough, Richard (d. 1689)	X	X		X	X	X	MR			
Grey, Ford, baron Grey of Werk (d. 1701)	X	X		X	X	X	MR			Turned king's evidence, 1685
Hampden, John, Junior (1653–96)		X?	X	X	X?				X	Imprisoned, 1683–86; turned king's evidence, 1686

Radical	GRC	PI	P2	E	RHP	Exile 1	MR/AI	Exile 2	GR	Fate
Hicks, John (1633–85)		X			X		MR			Executed for Monmouth's Rebellion, 1685
Holloway, James			X		X	X				Executed for the Rye House Plot, 1684
Holmes, Major Abraham		X			X	X	MR			Turned king's evidence, 1683; executed for Monmouth's Rebellion, 1685
Hone, William	X		X		X					Executed for the Rye House Plot, 1683
Hooke, Nathaniel (1664–1738)		X				X	MR			Pardoned, 1688
Hooper, James	X		X	X						Pardoned, 1686
Howard, William, Baron Howard of Escrick (d. 1694)	X	X		X	X		MR			Turned king's evidence, 1683
Hunt, Thomas			X?	X	X?	X				Died in exile, 1688
Ireton, Henry	X	X	X?		X?	X	MR			Pardoned, 1686; rewarded post-1688
Jenks, Francis	X				X	X				Imprisoned, 1683–89; rewarded post-1688
Johnson, Samuel (1649–1703)			X?	X						
Lee, Thomas	X		X?		X	X				Turned king's evidence, 1683; rewarded post-1688
Lobb, Stephen (d. 1699)		X	X?	X	X	X	MR	X	X	Pardoned, 1686
Locke, John (1632–1704)			X?			X	MR?	X	X	Exempted from the 1688 Pardon
Manley, Major John (d. 1699)			X?		X	X	MR			
Matthews, Captain Edward			X?		X	X	MR	X	X	Exempted from the 1688 Pardon

Radical	GRC	PI	P2	E	RHP	Exile 1	MR/AI	Exile 2	GR	Fate
Mead, Matthew (d. 1699)		X			X	X			X	Pardoned 1687
Nelthorpe, Richard	X		X	X	X	X	MR			Executed for Monmouth's Rebellion, 1685
Norton, Edward (1654–1702)	X	X		X	X	X		X	X	Pardoned, 1686; rewarded post-1688
Papillon, Thomas (1623–1702)		X		X	X	X			X	In exile, 1685–88; rewarded post-1688
Partridge, John (1644–1715)			X	X?	X	X	MR	X	X	
Petyt, William (d. 1707)		X	X	X						Rewarded post-1688
Peyton, Sir Robert (d. 1689)	X	X		X				X	X	Exempted from the 1688 Pardon
Pilkington, Thomas (d. 1691)			X	X					X	Imprisoned for seditious words, 1683–85; rewarded post-1688
Player, Sir Thomas (d. 1686)		X		X						
Prideaux, Edmund (1634–1702)	X	X		X	X?		MR			Fined for Monmouth's Rebellion, 1685; rewarded post-1688
Rouse, John			X		X					Executed for the Rye House Plot, 1683
Row, John	X	X			X	X				Rewarded post-1688
Rumbold, Richard		X	X	X	X	X	AI			Executed for Argyle's Invasion, 1685
Rumbold, William			X	X	X	X	MR			Pardoned, 1688
Rumsey, Colonel John	X		X	X	X		MR			Turned king's evidence, 1683 and 1685
Russell, Lord William (1639–83)	X			X	X					Executed for the Rye House Plot, 1683

Radical	GRC	PI	P2	E	RHP	Exile 1	MR/AI	Exile 2	GR	Fate
Scott, James, duke of Monmouth (1649–85)	X				X	X	MR			Executed for Monmouth's Rebellion, 1685
Shepherd, Thomas			X?		X			X		Turned king's evidence, 1683
Shower, John (1657–1715)		X		X		X	MR	X		
Sidney, Colonel Algernon (1622–83)			X	X	X					Executed for the Rye House Plot, 1683
Smith, Aaron (d. 1699)	X		X		X					Imprisoned, 1683–88
Smith, Francis (d. 1688)	X		X?	X		X	MR			Rewarded post-1688
Speke, Charles	X	X								Executed for Monmouth's Rebellion, 1685
Speke, George (1623–89)	X	X	X	X			MR	X	X	Pardoned, 1687
Speke, Hugh (b. 1656)	X	X		X					X	Imprisoned, 1683–88; rewarded post-1688
Speke, John (d. 1728)	X	X		X			MR	X		Pardoned, 1687; rewarded post-1688
Starkey, John (d. 1699)	X	X		X	X	X	MR			In exile, 1683–88
Strode, Edward	X		X	X	X?	X	MR			Pardoned, 1686
Strode, William			X	X	X	X	MR			Pardoned, 1686
Tily, Joseph	X			X	X?			X		
Trenchard, Henry (d. 1694)	X	X		X	X		MR		X	Pardoned, 1687
Trenchard, Sir John (1649–95)	X	X		X	X	X		X	X	Pardoned, 1687; rewarded post-1688
Trenchard, William (d. 1713)	X	X		X					X	
Tutchin, John (d. 1707)	X						MR		X	Imprisoned, 1685–86; rewarded post-1688

Radical	GRC	P1	P2	E	RHP	Exile 1	MR/AI	Exile 2	GR	Fate
Tyrrell, James (1642–1718)		X		X					X	
Wade, Nathaniel (d. 1718)		X			X	X	MR			Turned king's evidence, 1685
Wade, William			X		X					
Walcott, Captain Thomas		X			X					Executed for the Rye House Plot, 1683
Waller, Edmund (1652–1700)	X	X			X?				X	
Waller, Sir William (d. 1699)	X	X	X?	X	X?	X			X	Rewarded post-1688
Ward, Sir Patience (1629–96)			X	X	X	X	MR		X	Rewarded post-1688
Weeks, Thomas			X		X		MR			
West, Robert	X		X		X					Turned king's evidence, 1683
Wildman, Major John (1623–93)	X				X		MR	X	X	Exempted from the 1688 Pardon; rewarded post-1688
Yonge, Sir Walter (1653–1713)	X		X	X						Rewarded post-1688

GRC, member of the Green Ribbon Club; P1, signatory of the 1679 petition calling for Parliament; P2, signatory of the 1680 Monster Petition calling for Parliament; E, active promoter of the Exclusion Bill; RHP, participant in the Whig conspiracy of 1682–83 known as the Rye House Plot; Exile 1, in exile following the discovery of the Rye House Plot; MR, participant or promoter in Monmouth's Rebellion of 1685; AI, participant in Argyle's invasion of 1685; Exile 2, in exile following Monmouth's Rebellion; GR, participant or promoter of the Glorious Revolution of 1688–89; Fate, rewards, punishments, and the last acts of radical careers.

Bibliography

Manuscript Sources

British Library, London

Additional 4,460   Birch Manuscript
17,677   John Hampden's Confession
21,094   Political Poems
22,589   Tracts on the Succession Crisis
23,619   "The Character of Popery" by Thomas Hunt
27,440   Charles Allestree Memoirs
28,092   Political Tracts
28,875   Ellis Papers
28,930   Ellis Papers
28,938   Ellis Papers
29,497   Political Poems
29,910   Swynjen Correspondence
30,077   Concerning Monmouth's Rebellion
30,084   Pelham Papers
30,277   Correspondence of Lord Caryll
32,518–20   Papers of Lord Keeper North
34,508   Mackintosh Collection, vol. 22
34,510   Mackintosh Collection, vol. 24
34,512   Mackintosh Collection, vol. 26
35,104   Conway Letter-Book, 1681–83
35,508   Rumbold's arrest, fol.17
35,852   Hardwicke Papers, 1681–88
37,980   Chuleigh Letters to Conway
37,981   Dispatches of William Carr
37,982   Wyche Letters, 1681–82
37,983–84   Skelton Letters, vols. 1–2
37,986   Poley Letters, 1681–82, vol. 1
38,847   Hodgkin Papers, vol. 2
40,060   Political Poems
41,568   Newsletters, 1675–79

41,804   Middleton Collection, vol. 2
41,809–21   Middleton Collection, vols. 7–20
61,651   Blenheim Papers, vol. DLI
Harleian   6,845   Wade's Confession, fols. 266–72v
           7,006   Concerning Monmouth's Rebellion
           7,319   Political Poems
Sloane   3,929   Muddiman and Randall's Newsletters
Stowe   185   Historical Papers, vol. 2
            305   Witnesses against Burnet, fol. 40
Lansdowne 1,152A   Bridgman's Collection

Public Records Office, Chancery Lane, London

Sp 29   State Papers Charles II
Sp 44   State Papers Entry Books
Sp 84   State Papers Holland
PRO 30/24   Shaftesbury Papers
PRO c.104/82 Tankerville Papers (3 boxes)

Dr. William's Library, London

Roger Morrice. "Ent'ring Book, Being a Historical Register of Occurrences From April, Anno. 1677 to April 1691." 4 vols. I have used a photocopy of the original from the library of the late Douglas R. Lacey now in the possession of Lois G. Schwoerer.

Bodleian Library, Oxford

Ballard   27   Letters to Dr. Charlett
Carte   39   Ormonde Correspondence, 1679–82
         219   Ormonde Correspondence, 1660–82
         228   Wharton and Huntingdon Papers
Firth   c.16   Political Poems

Cambridge University Library, Cambridge

Sel. 2. 114–26   The Verney Collection, 13 vols.

Magdelene College, Cambridge

PL   2,875/456-91 Pepys Library, Journal of the Green Ribbon Club

Folger Shakespeare Library, Washington, DC

L.c.   1,168–1,402 Newdigate Newsletters, 673/74–1715

Henry E. Huntington Library, California

Stowe Collection   Temple Papers, vol. 365
Hastings   Inventories (box 2)

Printed Diaries, Memoirs, Letters

(The place of publication is London unless otherwise indicated.)

Ailesbury, Thomas Bruce. *Memoirs of Thomas Bruce, Earl of Ailesbury, written by himself.* 2 vols. W. E. Buckley, ed. Roxburghe Club. 1890.
Bramston, John. *Autobiography.* Lord Braybrooke, ed. 1845.
Browning, Andrew, ed. *Memoirs of Sir John Reresby.* Glasgow, 1936.
Burnet, Gilbert. *History of His Own Time.* 6 vols. Oxford, 1823.
Bulstrode, Richard. *Memoirs and Reflections on the Reign and Government of King Charles I and King Charles II.* 1721.
Dalrymple, John. *Memoirs of Great Britain and Ireland.* 2 vols. London and Edinburgh, 1771–73.
De la Pryme, Abraham. *The Diary.* Edinburgh, 1870.
Diaries of the Popish Plot. Douglas C. Greene, comp. Delmar, NY, 1977.
Dunton, John. *The Life and Errors of John Dunton.* 1705.
Collections of the Massachusetts Historical Society: The Mather Papers. 4th ser., vol. 3. Boston, 1846.
The Ellis Correspondence, 1686–1688. 2 vols. G. A. Ellis, ed. 1831.
Evelyn, John. *The Diary of John Evelyn.* 6 vols. E. S. de Beer, ed. Oxford, 1955.
Fountainhall, Sir John Lauder. *Chronological Notes of Scottish Affairs from 1680 till 1701, being chiefly taken from the Diary of Lord Fountainhall.* Sir Walter Scott, ed. Edinburgh, 1822.
Foxcroft, H. C., ed. *The Life and Letters of Sir George Savile, Bart. First Marquis of Halifax.* 2 vols. London, 1898.
Grey, Anchitell. *Debates of the House of Commons from the Year 1667 to the Year 1694.* 10 vols. 1763.
Hearne, Thomas. *Remarks and Collections of Thomas Hearne.* 11 vols. Charles Doble, et al., eds. Oxford, 1885–1921.
Horwitz, Henry, ed. *The Parliamentary Diary of Narcissus Luttrell, 1691–1693.* Oxford, 1972.
Locke, John. *The Correspondence of John Locke.* 8 vols. E. S. de Beer, ed. Oxford, 1989.
Luttrell, Narcissus. *A Brief Historical Relation of State Affairs from September 1678 to April 1714.* 6 vols. Oxford, 1857.
Nicolson, William. *The London Diaries of William Nicolson, Bishop of Carlisle.* Clyve Jones and Geoffrey Holmes, eds. Oxford, 1985.
Noble, Mark, ed. *Memoirs of the Proctoral House of Cromwell.* 2 vols. 1787.
Original Letters of John Locke, Algernon Sidney, and Anthony, Lord Shaftesbury. T. Forster, ed. 1847.
Papillon, Alexander. *Memoirs of Thomas Papillon.* 1887.

Parker, Samuel. *Bishop Parker's History of His Own Time.* 1728.
Pinney, John. *The Letters of John Pinney.* Geoffrey F. Nuttall, ed. Oxford, 1939.
The Portledge Papers, being extracts from the letters of Richard Lapthorne. Russell J. Kerr and Ida Coffine Duncan, eds. 1928.
Russell, Rachel. *The Letters of Lady Rachel Russell.* 1854.
Shower, John. *Memoirs.* 1716.
Sidney, Henry, earl of Romney. *Diary of the Times of Charles II by the Honourable Henry Sidney (afterwards Earl of Romney).* 2 vols. R. W. Blencowe, ed. 1843.
Smith, Matthew. *Private Memoirs Relating to his Grace the Late Duke of Shrewsbury.* 1718.
Stout, William. *The Autobiography of William Stout of Lancaster, 1665–1752.* J. D. Marshall, ed. New York, 1967.
Thoresby, Ralph. *The Diary.* 2 vols. Joseph Hunter, ed. 1830.
Trosse, George. *The Life of the Reverend George Trosse Written by Himself.* A. W. Brink, ed. Montreal, 1974.
Wood, Anthony. *The Life and Times of Anthony Wood, Antiquary of Oxford, 1632–1695, Described by Himself.* 5 vols. Andrew Clark, ed. Oxford, 1891–1900.

Periodicals

(The place of publication is London.)

Heraclitus Ridens: Or, a Discourse between Jest and Earnest, 1681–1682, 2 vols., 1713. By Edward Rawlins.
The Domestick Intelligence, 1679. By Benjamin Harris.
The Impartial Protestant Mercury, 1681. By Richard Janeway.
The Independent Whig, 1721–1732. By John Trenchard and Thomas Gordon.
The London Gazette.
Observator, 1679–1686. By Roger L'Estrange.
Observator, 1702–1707. By John Tutchin.
The True Domestick Intelligence, 1680. By Nathaniel Thompson.
The Weekly Pacquet of Advice from Rome, or the History of Popery, 1679–1683. By Henry Care.

Other Primary Material

(The place of publication is London unless otherwise indicated.)

Abstracts of Somerset Wills. 6 ser., 4th ser. Copied by Reverend Frederick Brown. 1889.
A Biographical Dictionary of British Radicals in the Seventeenth Century. 3 vols. Richard L. Greaves and Robert Zaller, eds. Brighton, 1982.
A Catalogue of the Library of Thomas Jefferson. 5 vols. Washington, DC, 1955.
A Collection of Scarce and Valuable Tracts. 13 vols. Sir Walter Scott, ed. 1809–15.

A Complete Collection of Papers in Twelve Parts. 1689.

A Complete Collection of State Trials. 22 vols. T. B. Howell, ed. 1816.

A Dictionary of Booksellers and Printers Who Were at Work in England, Scotland and Ireland, 1641 to 1725. Henry R. Plomer, ed. London, 1922.

English Historical Documents, 1660–1714. Andrew Browning, ed. New York, 1953.

A Genealogy and Heraldic History of the Landed Gentry of Great Britain and Ireland. 2 vols. Bernard Burke, ed. 1886.

The General Biographical Dictionary. 32 vols. Alexander Chalmers, ed. 1812.

Harleian Miscellany. 12 vols. J. Malham, ed. 1808–10.

The History of Parliament: The House of Commons, 1660–1690. 3 vols. B. D. Henning, ed. The History of Parliament Trust, 1983.

Journals of the House of Commons.

Journals of the House of Lords.

Middlesex County Records (Old Series). 4 vols. John Cordy Jeaffreson, ed. London, 1972.

Original Records of Early Nonconformity Under Persecution and Indulgence. 3 vols. G. Lyon Turner, ed. 1911.

Poems on the Affairs of State: Augustan Satirical Verse, 1660–1714. 7 vols. George de F. Lord, general ed. New Haven, 1963–75.

Royal Families of England, Scotland and Wales. 2 vols. John Burke, ed. 1851.

The Stuart Constitution, 1603–1688. J. P. Kenyon, ed. Cambridge, 1966.

A Transcript of the Registers of the Worshipful Company of Stationers from 1640–1708. 3 vols. 1913.

Historical Manuscript Commission

Downshire. 2 vols.

Finch. 4 vols.

Seventh Report, part 1.

Exeter.

Stopford Sackville. vol 1.

Hastings.

Calendar of State Papers, Domestic Series

Vol. 21, January 1, 1679 to August 31, 1680

Vol. 22, September 1, 1680 to December 31, 1681

Vol. 23, January 1 to December 31, 1682

Vol. 24, January 1 to June 30, 1683

Vol. 25, July 1 to September 30, 1683

Vol. 26, October 1, 1683 to April 30, 1684

Charles II, May 1, 1684 to February 5, 1685

Charles II, Addenda

James II, vol. 1., February–December 1685

James II, vol. 2., January–May 1687

James II, vol. 3, June 1687 to February 1689

William & Mary, May 1690 to October 1691

William & Mary, February 13 to April 1690

The Works of the Five Major Propagandists

(The place of publication is London unless otherwise indicated.)

William Atwood

A Poetical Essay towards an Epitome of the Gospel of the Blessed Jesus. 1678.

Jani Anglorum facies nova: or, Several Monuments of Antiquity touching the Great Councils of the Kingdom. 1680.

Jus Anglorum ab antiquo: or, A Confutation of an important libel against the Government . . . under the Pretense of Answering Mr. Petyt and the Author of Jani Anglorum facies nova. 1681.

Lord Hollis [sic], His Remains which contains, *Reflections on Antidotum Britannicum and Mr. Hunt's Late Book and Postscript as far as concerns the controversy between Dr. Brady and the author of Jani Anglorum facies nova.* 1682.

A Letter of Remarks upon Jovian, or, An Answer to Julian the Apostate. 1683.

Letters Concerning Church Communion. 1683.

A Seasonable Vindication of the Truly Catholic Doctrine of the Church of England in a Reply to Dr. Sherlock's Answer to Anonymous. 1683.

Grotius His Arguments For the Truth of the Christian Religion rendered in plain English verse. 1686.

Wonderful Predictions of Nostredamus, Grebner, David Pareus and Antonius Torquaturs. Wherein the grandeur of their present Majesties, the happiness of England . . . are foretold. 1689.

The Chief Justice Herbert's Account Examined. 1689.

An Apology for the East India Company: with an account of some large prerogatives of the Crown of England . . . in relation to foreign trade and foreign parts. 1690.

The Fundamental Constitution of the English Government. 1690.

The Antiquity and Justice of the Oath of Abjuration. 1694.

A Safe and Easy Method for Supplying the want of Coin. 1695.

The Case of William Atwood, esq. 1703.

The Superiority and Direct Dominion of the Imperial Crown of England over the Crown and Kingdom of Scotland. 1704.

The Scotch Patriot Unmasked in Animadversions upon a Seditious Pamphlet. 1705.

[Atwood, William]. *Dr. Sherlock's Two Kings of Brainford brought upon the stage in a Congratulatory Letter to Mr. Johnson.* 1691.

[Atwood, William]. *Reflections upon a Treasonable opinion, industriously promoted against the Signing the National Association.* 1696.

Robert Ferguson

Justification onely [sic] upon a Satisfaction. 1668.

A Sober Enquiry into the Nature, Measure, and Principle of Moral Virtue. 1673.

The Interest of Reason in Religion. 1675.

The East-India Trade, a most Profitable Trade to the Kingdom. 1677.

The Narrative of Mr. John Smith . . . containing to a Further Discovery of the late Horrid and Polish Plot. 1679.

A Letter to a Person of Honour, Concerning the Black Box. 1680.

A Letter to a Person of Honour, Concerning the King's own Disavowing the having been Married to the Duke of Monmouth's mother. 1680.

No Protestant Plot, or the Pretended Conspiracy of Protestant against the King and Government. 1681.

The Second Part of No Protestant Plot. 1682.

The Third Part of No Protestant Plot. 1682.

The Declaration of James, duke of Monmouth. 1685.

A Representation of the Threatening Dangers, impending over the Protestants in Great Britain. 1687.

Reflexions of Monsieur Fagel's Letter. 1688.

A Brief Justification of the Prince of Orange's Descent into England. 1689.

A Brief Vindication of the Parliamentary Proceedings against the Late King James II. 1689.

The Design for Enslaving England discovered in the Incroachments upon the Powers and Privileges of Parliament by Charles II. 1689.

An Enquiry into and Detection of the Barbarous Murther of the late Earl of Essex. 1689.

The Late Proceedings and Votes of the Parliament of Scotland, contained in an address delivered to the King. 1689.

A Letter to the Lord Chief Justice Holt. 1694.

A Letter to Mr. Secretary Trenchard, discovering a Conspiracy against the laws . . . of England. 1694.

A Brief Account of the late incroachments . . . of the Dutch upon the English. 1695.

Whether Parliament be not in Law dissolved by the death of the Princess of Orange. 1695.

Whether Preserving the Protestant Religion was the motive . . . the late Revolution. 1695.

A Just and Modest Vindication of the Scots Design. 1699.

The History of all Mobs, Tumults and Insurrections in Great Britain. 1715.

[Ferguson, Robert]. *An Impartial Enquiry into the Administration of the Affairs of England.* 1684.

"Concerning the Rye House Business," ms. published in James Ferguson, *Robert Ferguson: The Plotter.* 409–37.

Thomas Hunt

The Honours of the Lords Spiritual Asserted. 1679.

The Great and Weighty Considerations Relating to the Duke of York or the Succession of the Crown . . . Considered. 1680.

The Rights of the Bishops to Judge in Capital Cases in Parliament Cleared. 1680.

Two Books in Defense of the Bishops Voting in Capital Cases. 1680.

An Apology for the Government of England and the Reason and Structure thereof declared out of the Ancient Records Introduced: Upon a Question of the Bishops Right of Judging Capital Cases. 1682.

An Argument for the Bishops Right in Judging Capital Cases in Parliament. 1682.

Mr. Hunt's Argument for the Bishops Rights . . . Upon a Question of the Bishops Right of Judging Capital Cases. 1682.

210 Bibliography

A Defense of the Charter and the Municipal Rights of the City of London. 1683.
Mr. Hunt's Postscript for rectifying some mistakes in some of the inferior clergy. 1682.

Samuel Johnson

Julian the Apostate. 1682.
A Sermon Preached before the Lord-Mayor and Alderman at Guildhall Chappel, on Palm-Sunday, 1679. 1684.
Several Reasons for the Establishment of a Standing Army and the Dissolving the Militia. 1685.
The Absolute Impossibility of Transubstantiation Demonstrated. 1688.
The Grounds and Reasons for the Laws against Popery. 1688.
Purgatory proved by Miracles: Collected out of Roman Catholick Authors. 1688.
The True Mother Church. 1688?
The Way to Peace Amongst all Protestants; being a Letter of Reconciliation sent by Bishop Ridley to Bishop Hooper with some Observations upon it. 1688.
A Humble and Hearty Address to all the English Protestants in this Present Army. 1689 (no surviving copies from 1686).
Julian's Arts to Undermine and Extirpate Christianity. 1689.
A Letter from a Freeholder to the Rest of the Freeholders of England. 1689.
A Letter of Advice to all Protestant Soldiers and Seamen (repr. of *A Humble and Hearty Address*). 1689.
Of Magistracy. 1689.
Reflections on the History of Passive Obedience. 1689.
Remarks upon Dr. Sherlock's Book intitled [sic] the Case of Resistance of the Supreme Powers Stated and Resolved. 1689.
A Second Five Year's Struggle against Popery and Tyranny. 1689.
The Trial and Examination of a Late Libel, intitled [sic] A New Test of the Church of England's Loyalty. 1689.
Remarks upon Dr. Sherlock's Book, intitled [sic] The Case of Allegiance due to Sovereign Princes, Stated and Resolved. 1690.
An Argument Proving that the Abrogation of King James by the People of England . . . was according to the Constitution of the English Government. 1692.
An Essay Concerning Parliaments at a Certainty; or The Kalenders of May. 1693.
Notes upon the Phoenix Edition of the Pastoral Letter. 1694.
A Confutation of a late Pamphlet intitled [sic] A Letter Ballancing the Necessity of Keeping of Land Force. 1698.
The Second Part of the Confutation of the Ballancing Letter: Containing an Occasional Discourse in Vindication of Magna Carta. 1700.
A Vindication of Magna Carta as a Summary of English Rights and Liberties. 1702.
The Works of the Late Reverend Samuel Johnson. 1710, 1713, 2d ed.

James Tyrrell

Mr. John Milton's Character of the Long Parliament. 1681.
Patriarcha non Monarcha, The Patriarch Unmonarched. 1681.

"A Dedication to Charles II," in James Ussher, *The Power Communicated by God to the Prince and the Obedience Required of the Subject,* 2d ed. 1683.

A Vindication of His [Ussher's] Opinions and Actions, in Richard Parr, *The Life of the Most Reverend Father in God, Late Lord Archbishop of Armagh.* 1686.

Bibliotheca Politica: An Enquiry into the Ancient Constitution . . . in Thirteen Dialogues. 1694.

A Brief Enquiry into the Ancient Constitution and Government of England. 1695.

The General History of England . . . to the reign of William III. 1698–1704.

Other Books, Pamphlets, Broadsides

(The place of publication is London unless otherwise indicted.)

An Account of How the Earl of Essex Killed Himself in the Tower of London. 1683.

The Account of the Life of Julian the Apostate Vindicated and the Truth of the Assertions therein. 1682.

An Account of the Pretended Prince of Wales . . . [and] A Short Account of the murther of the earl of Essex. 1688.

An Account of the Proceedings against Samuel Johnson at the King's Bench Bar. 1686.

Animadversions on the Last Speech and Confession of the late William, Lord Russell. 1683.

Animadversions upon a Paper entitled, The Speech of the late Lord Russell. 1683.

Antidotum Britannicum, or a Counter-Pest against the Destructive Principles of Plato Redivivus. 1681.

The Arraignment, Trial and Condemnation of Algernon Sidney. Esq., for High-Treason. 1684.

The Arraignment, Tryal and Condemnation of Stephen Colledge for High-Treason, in Conspiring the Death of the King, the Levying of War, and the Subversion of Government. 1681.

A Brief Discourse Between A Sober Tory and a Moderate Whig. 1682.

The Bully Whig or, The Poor Whores Lamentation for the Apprehending of Sir Thomas Armstrong. 1684.

The Case of William Strode and John Speke. 1679.

The Charter : A Comical Satyr. 1682.

The Citizens Loss, when the Charter of London is forfeited, or given up. 1683.

A Collection of Excellent English Books . . . being the Library of the Reverend Father in God, John Tilloston. 1695.

Colonel Algernon Sidney's Speech, delivered to the Sheriff on the Scaffold. 1684.

The Declaration of Archibald, earl of Argyle, Lord Kintyre, Cowall, Campbell and Lorne. 1685.

The Declaration of His Highness William Henry, Prince of Orange, of the Reasons Inducing Him to Appear in Arms in the Kingdom of England. 1688.

The Declaration of James, Duke of Monmouth, and the Noblemen, Gentlemen, and others, now in Arms for the Defense and Vindication of the Protestant Religion, and the Laws, Rights and Privileges of England from the Invasion made upon them and for delivering the Kingdom from the Usurpation and Tyranny of James Duke of York. 1685.

A Dialogue between Sir Roger L'Estrange and Mr. Rob. Ferguson. 1696.

A Dialogue between Tom and Dick over a Dish of Coffee, Concerning Religion and the Government. 1680.

The Duke of Monmouth's Case. 1682.

The Dying Speeches, Letters, and Prayers of Several Excellent Persons who suffered for their Zeal against Popery and Arbitrary Government. 1689.

The Dying Speeches of those Eminent Protestants who suffered in the West. 1689.

Ecclesiastica, The Book of Remembrance of the Independent Congregations of Axminster and Chard. Barnstaple, 1874.

An Exact Account of the Trial of Algernon Sidney, esq., who was tryed at the King's Bench-Bar. 1683.

The Examination and Confession with the Behavior and Speeches of Captain Walcot, William Hone and John Rouse. 1683.

Mr. Ferguson's Letter to his Friends. 1683.

The Free and Voluntary Confession and Narrative of James Holloway. 1684.

An Historical Account of the Heroick Life and Magnamimous Actions of the Most Illustrious Prince, James, duke of Monmouth. 1683.

The Imposter Exposed, in a Dissection of a Villinous Libel, entitled No Protestant Plot. 1681.

Intrigues of the Popish Plot Laid Open. 1685.

The Judgement and Decree of the University of Oxford, pass'd in their Convocation, July, 21, 1683, against certain Pernicious Books and Damnable Doctrines, Destructive to the Sacred Persons of Princes, their State and Government, and of all Human Society. 1683.

The Judgement of the Whole Kingdoms and Nations concerning the Rights, Powers and Prerogatives of Kings and the Rights, Privileges and Properties of the People. 1710.

The Last Legacy or Affectionate and Pious Exhortations of the Late W. Lord Russell to his Lady and Children. 1683.

The Last Speech and Behavior of William, Lord Russell, upon the Scaffold in London's-Inn Fields. Edinburgh, 1683.

The Last Speech and Carriage of Lord Russell upon the Scaffold. 1683.

The Last Speech and Confession of Mr. Stephen Colledge, Who was Executed at Oxford, 2d ed. 1681.

The Last Words of Richard Rumbold. 1685.

The Last Will and Testament of the City Charter of London. 1683.

The Life of Boetius. 1683.

Massinello: or, A Satyr Against the Guild-hall Riot. 1683.

Memoirs of the Life of the Earl of Shaftesbury. 1683.

A Modest Reply to the too hasty and malicious Libel entitled An Elegy upon Mr. Stephen College. 1682.

Mrs. Gaunt's Last Speech who was burnt at London, October 23, 1685. 1685.

The Muses Farewell to Popery and Slavery. 1689.

A New Song on the Death of College. 1681.

A Poem by way of Elegie upon Mr. Stephen College. 1681.

The Proceedings at the Tryal of Sir Patience Ward, Kt. 1683.

The Proceedings upon the Second Trial of Titus Oates. 1685.

The Processsion: or, The Burning of the Pope in effigie in Smithfield-Rounds on 17 November 1681. 1681.

The Protestant Martyrs, or the Bloody Assizes. 1689.

Rebellious Antidote: Or A Dialogue Between Coffee and Tea. 1685.

Robert against Ferguson: or a New Dialogue between Robert an Old Independent Whig and Ferguson a New Pretended Jacobite. 1704.

Sidney Redivius. 1689.

Some Animadversions on the Paper Delivered to the Sheriffs . . . by Algernon Sidney. 1683.

Some Remarques Upon a Late Piece of Nonsense called Julian the Apostate. 1682.

The Speech and Carriage of Stephen Colledge at Oxford. 1681.

The Speech and Confession of William, Lord Russell, Who was Executed for High Treason against His Majesty. 1683.

The Speech of . . . Sir Patience Ward, Lord Major Elect, at Guildhall, London, September 29, 1680. 1680.

The Speech of the Late Lord Russel [sic], To the Sheriffs: Together with the Paper delivered by him to them, at the Place of Execution, on July 21, 1683. 1683.

The Speech of the Right Honourable Sir Patience Ward, Kt., The Present Lord Major of London. 1681.

Stephen Colledge's Ghost to the Fanatical Cabal. 1681.

Strange News from Newgate. 1683.

The Trials of Henry Cornish for conspiring the death of the King . . . and Elizabeth Gaunt . . . for harboring and maintaining Rebels. 1685.

The True Account of the Behavior and Confession of William Disney, esq., . . . His Last Dying Words. 1685.

A True Account of the Proceedings against John Ayloffe and Richard Nelthorp. 1685.

A True and Faithful Relation of the Horrid and Barbarous Attempt to Assassinate the Reverend Mr. Samuel Johnson. 1692.

A True Copy of the Dying Speech of Mr. Stephen Colledge. 1681.

A True Narrative of the Sentence of Titus Oates for Perjury. 1685.

The Tryal of Benjamin Harris on an Information for Printing an Appeal from the Country to the City. 1680.

The Tryal and Conviction of John Hampden upon an indictment of high misdemeanour. 1684.

The Tryal and Conviction of Sir Samuel Barnardiston, bt. for High Misdemeanor. 1684.

The Tryal of Francis Smith on an Information. 1680.

The Tryal of Laurence Braddon and Hugh Speke, gent. upon an information of high-misdemeanor. 1684.

A Very Copy of a Paper Delivered to the Sheriffs. 1683.

A Vindication of the Lord Russell's Speech and Innocence. 1683.

A Vindication of the Lord Russell's Speech and Paper . . . from the foul imputations of falsehood. 1683.

A Vindication of the Royal Family of the Stuarts. 1734.

Vox populi, vox dei. 1709.

The Whigs Lamentation for the Death of their Dear Brother College, The Protestant Joiner. 1681.

Who Plot Best: The Whigs or the Tories . . . in a Letter to Mr. Ferguson. 1710.

A Word of Advice to the Author of the Scurrilous and Seditious Libel, entitled No Protestant Plot. 1681.

Assherton, William. *The Royal Apology.* 1684.

Atkyns, Richard. *The late Lord Russell's Innocency further defended.* 1689.

Ayloffe, John. "Britannia and Raleigh" (1674–75), in *Poems on the Affairs of State,* 1:228–35.

————. "Marvell's Ghost" (1678), in *Poems on the Affairs of State*, 1:285.

————. "Oceana and Britannia" (1681), in *Poems on the Affairs of State*, 1:395–405.

[Ayloffe, John]. "A Dialogue between Two Horses" (1676), in *Poems on the Affairs of State*, 1:275–83.

Barlow, Thomas. *A Discourse of the Peerage and Jurisdiction of the Lords Spiritual in Parliament.* 1679.

Barrington, John Shute. *The Revolution and Anti-Revolution Principles Stated and Compared.* 1714.

Behn, Aphra. *The Roundheads.* 1681.

————. *The Second Part of the Rover.* 1681.

————. *Love Letters Between a Nobleman and His Sister.* New York, 1987.

————. *Aphra Behn Poems—A Selection.* Janet Todd, ed. New York, 1994.

Bennet, John. *Constantius the Apostate.* 1683.

Benson, William. *A Letter to Sir Jacob Banks.* 1711.

Bernard, Nicholas. *The Life and Death of . . . Dr. James Ussher.* 1656.

Blount, Charles. *William and Mary, Conquerors.* 1694.

[Blount, Charles]. *An Appeal to the Country from the City.* 1679.

Booth, Henry, Lord Delamere. *Lord Delamere's Speech.* 1688.

————. *The Late Lord Russell's Case.* 1689.

Bradbury, Thomas. *The Lawfulness of Resisting Tyrannts.* 1714.

Braddon, Laurence. *Essex Innocency and Honour Vindicated.* 1690.

————. *Bishop Burnet's late History charged with great Partiality and Misrepresentations to make the present and future Ages believe that Arthur, Earl of Essex, in 1683, killed himself.* 1725.

[Braddon, Laurence]. *A True and Impartial Narrative of the Murder of Arthur, Earl of Essex.* 1729.

Brady, Robert. *A Full and Clear Answer to a Book written by William Petit . . . together with some animadversions upon a Book, called Jani Anglorum facies nova.* 1681.

————. *A True and Exact History of the Succession of the Crown of England.* 1681.

————. *Introduction to Old English History.* 1684.

Briggs, Henry. *Considerations touching that question, whether prelates have the right to sit among the Lords and vote with them in Parliament in capital cases.* 1682.

Burnet, Gilbert. *An Enquiry into the Measures of Submission.* 1688.

————. *A Pastoral Letter Writ by the Right Reverend Father In God Gilbert, Lord Bishop of Sarum.* 1689.

Calamy, Edmund. *The Nonconformists Memorial, being an Account of the Lives, Sufferings and Printed Works of Two Hundred Ministers.* 1775.

Care, Henry. *English Liberties: or, The Freeborn Subject's Inheritance.* 1682.

Carstares, William. *State Papers and Letters Addressed to William Carstares . . . to which is prefixed the Life of Mr. Carstares.* Edinburgh, 1774.

Coke, Roger. *A Detection of the Court and State of England during the Last Four Reigns and Interregnum.* 2 vols. 1694.

Colledge, Stephen. *A Raree Show.* 1681.

————. *Truth Brought to Life, or Murder Will Out.* 1679.

Cooke, Edward. *Magna Carta, made in the ninth year of King Henry the Third . . . faithfully translated for the benefit of those that do not understand the Latin.* 1680.

————. *A True Narrative of the Inhumane Positions and Practices of the Jesuits and Papists, towards all good Protestants.* 1680.

———. *Argumentum Anti-Normannicum or, an Argument Proving from Ancient Histories and Records that William, Duke of Normandy made no absolute Conquest of England by the Sword.* 1682.

———. *The History of the Successions of the Kings of England.* 1682.

———. *A Seasonable Treatise: wherein it is proved that King William, commonly called the Conqueror did not get the Imperial Crown of England by Sword.* 1689.

Dangerfield, Thomas. *A Particular Narrative of the Late Popish Design to Charge those of the Presbyterian Party with the Pretended Conspiracy.* 1679.

Danvers, Henry. *Murder Will Out; or a Clear and Full Discovery that the Earl of Essex did not Murder Himself, but was murdered by others.* 1684.

Defoe, Daniel. *Hymn to the Pillory.* 1703.

———. *An Account of the Proceedings against the Rebels and other Prisoners tried before the Lord Chief Justice Jefferies.* 1716.

Disney, William. *Nil Dictum quod non Dictum Prius.* 1681.

[Doddridge, Sir John]. *The Antiquity and Power of Parlaiments in England.* 1658, repr. 1679.

Dowell, John. *The Triumph of Christianity.* 1683.

Dryden, John. *Absalom and Achitophel.* 1681.

———. *Satire against Sedition.* 1682.

———. *The Second Part of Absalom and Achitophel.* 1682.

———. *The Vindication: or Parallel of the French Holy League and the English League and Covenant Turn'd into a Seditious Libel against the King and His Royal Highness by Thomas Hunt.* 1683.

———. *The Vindication: or, the Parallel of the Holy-League and the English League and Covenant turn'd a seditious libel against the King and his Royal Highness by Thomas Hunt.* 1683.

Dryden, John, and Nathaniel Lee. *The Duke of Guise.* 1683.

Dugdale, William. *The Baronage of England.* 1675.

———. *A Short View of the Late Troubles in England.* Oxford, 1681.

Dunton, John. *The Merciful Assizes.* 1701.

Echard, Laurence. *The History of England.* 3 vols. 1707–18.

Ellesby, James. *The Doctrine of Passive Obedience Stated in a Sermon.* 1685.

Fagel, Casper. *A Letter Writ by Mijn Heer Fagel, Pensioner of Holland . . . giving an Account of the Prince and Princess of Orange's Thought concerning the Repeal of the Test and the Penal Laws.* 1687.

Filmer, Robert. *Patriarcha and Other Writings.* J. P. Sommerville, ed. Cambridge, 1991.

Galloway, William. *Reflections upon Mr. Johnson's Notes on the Pastoral Letter.* 1694.

Goodman, J. *The Interest of Divine Providence in the Government of the World.* 1683.

Grey, Lord Ford. *The Secret History of the Rye House Plot and of Monmouth's Rebellion.* 1754.

Hampden, John. *A Letter to Mr. Samuel Johnson, occassioned by his Argument Proving.* 1692.

Hawles, John. *Remarks on the Tryals of . . . Stephen Colledge, . . . The Lord Russel, Collonel Sidney, Henry Cornish.* 1689.

Hickes, George. *Jovian, or an Answer to Julian the Apostate.* 1683.

Hoadly, Benjamin. *The Original and Institution of Civil Government Discussed.* 1709.

Holles, Denzil. *Letter of a Gentleman to His Friend shewing that the Bishops are not to be Judges in Parliament in Capital Cases.* 1679.

Hopkins, William. *Animadversions on Mr. Johnson's Answer to Jovian.* 1691.

Howard, Robert. *A Letter to Samuel Johnson.* 1692.

Hume, Patrick. *Narrative of Occurrences in the Expedition of the Earl of Argyle in 1685,* in *Observations on the Historical work of the Right Honorable Charles James Fox,* by George Rose. 1809.

[Jones, William]. *A Just and Modest Vindication of the Last Two Parliaments.* 1679. Possibly written in collaboration with Algernon Sidney and John Somers. Also attributed to Sidney alone and to Robert Ferguson alone.

Kennett, White. *A Complete History of England.* 3 vols. 1706.

Knight, Samuel. *The Life of John Colet, Dean of St. Paul's.* 1724.

Lanthom, Paul. *The Power of Kings from God.* 1683.

Lee, Francis. *The Life of John Kettlewell.* 1718.

L'Estrange, Roger. *Citt and Bumpkin in a Dialogue over a Pot of Ale, Concerning matters of Religion and Government.* 1680.

———. *Notes upon Stephen College.* 1681.

———. *Considerations Upon a Printed Sheet entitled the Speech of the Late Lord Russell.* 1683.

———. *The Lawyer Outlaw'd Or, a A Brief Answer to Mr. Hunt's Defense of the Charter.* 1683.

———. *Mr. Sidney His Self Conviction: Or His Dying Paper Condemned to Live.* 1684.

Locke, John. *Essay Concerning Human Understanding.* 1690.

———. *Two Treatises of Government.* Peter Laslett, ed. Cambridge, 1991.

Long, Thomas. *A Vindication of the Primitive Christians . . . with an Appendix being a more full and distinct Answer to Mr. Hunt's Preface and Postscript.* 1683.

May, Thomas. *A Breviary of the History of Parliament.* 1650, repr. 1680.

Marvell, Andrew. *Account of the Growth of Popery and Arbitrary Government.* Amsterdam, 1677.

Meredith, Edward. *Some Remarques upon . . . Julian the Apostate.* 1682.

Moore, John. *Of Patience and Submission to Authority.* 1684.

N.N. *A Letter from Oxford concerning Mr. Samuel Johnson's Late Book.* 1693.

[Nalson, John]. *Reflections on Coll. Sidney's Arcadia, the Old Cause, Being Some Observations Upon his Last Paper.* 1684.

Neville, Henry. *Plato Redivivus, or a Dialogue Concerning Government* in *Two English Republican Tracts.* Caroline Robbins, ed. Cambridge, 1969.

Nicholas, Bernard. *The Life and Death of . . . Dr James Ussher.* 1654.

North, Roger. *Examen: or an Enquiry into the Credit and Veracity of a Pretended Complete History.* 1740.

———. *Lives of the Norths.* 3 vols. Augustus Jessopp, ed. 1890.

Northleigh, John. *The Parallel: or, the New Specious Association an Old Rebellious Covenant.* 1682.

———. *Remarks upon the Most Eminent of our Late Antimonarchical Authors and their Writings.* 1685.

Oldmixon, John. *The History of England, during the reigns of King William and Queen Mary.* 1735.

Oates, Titus. *The Discovery of the Popish Plot.* 1679.

———. *A True Narrative of the Horrid Plot and Conspiracy of the Popish Plot and Conspiracy against the Life of his Sacred Magisty.* 1679.

———. *A Display of Tyranny; or Remarks upon the Illegal and Arbitrary Proceedings in the Courts of Westminster and Guild-hall.* 1689.

Parr, Richard. *The Life of the Most Reverend Father in God, the Late Lord Archbishop of Armagh, Primate and Metropolitan of all Ireland.* 1686.

Parsons, Robert. *A Conference About the Next Succession to the Crown of England.* repr. 1681.

Partridge, John. *Merlinus Liberatus: Being an Almanack for the year of our Redemption, 1686.* 1686.

Pelling, Edward. *The Apostate Protestant.* 1682.

Petit, Edward. *The Visions of Government, wherein the Antimonarchical Principles and Practices of all Fanatical and Commonwealthsmen . . . are discovered, confuted and exposed.* 1684.

Petyt, William. *The Ancient Right of Commons of England Asserted.* 1680.

———. *Britannia Languens, or a Discourse on Trade.* 1680.

———. *Miscellanea Parliamentaria.* 1680.

———. *The Pillars of Parliament struck at by the Hands of a Cambridge Doctor.* 1681.

Pomfret, Thomas. *Passive Obedience stated and asserted.* 1683.

Ralph, James. *The History of England during the Reigns of King William, Queen Anne, and King George I.* 2 vols. 1744–46.

Ravenscroft, Edward. *The London Cockolds.* 1681.

Rushworth, John. *Historical Collections. Private Papers of State.* 1691.

Salmon, Nathaniel. *Lives of the English Bishops from the Restauration to the Revolution.* 1733.

Salmon, Thomas. *The Chronological Historian.* 1733.

Seller, Abednigo. *A History of Passive Obedience.* Amsterdam, 1689.

Settle, Elkanah. *The Character of the Popish Successor.* 1681.

[Settle, Elkanah]. *Remarks upon Algernon Sidney's Paper Delivered to the Sheriffs.* 1683.

Shadwell, Thomas. *Some Reflections upon the Pretended Parallel in the Play called the Duke of Guise.* 1683.

Sherlock, William. *A Letter to Anonymous [William Atwood] in Answer to his Three Letters.* 1683.

———. *Observations upon Mr. Johnson's Remarks upon Dr. Sherlock's Book of Non-Resistance.* 1689.

Shower, Bartholemew. *An Antidote Against Poison: composed of some remarks upon the Paper printed by the direction of Lady Russell.* 1683.

Sidney, Algernon. *Discourses Concerning Government.* Thomas G. West, ed. Indianapolis, 1990.

———. *The Very Copy of a Paper Delivered to the Sheriffs, Upon the Scaffold on Tower-Hill.* 1683.

Smith, William. *Intrigues of the Popish Plot Laid Open.* 1685.

Speke, Hugh. *Some Memoirs of the Late Happy Revolution.* Dublin, 1709.

———. *The Secret History of the Happy Revolution in 1688.* 1715.

———. *The Case of Hugh Speke, esq. and Family.* 1716.

[Speke, Hugh] *The Prince of Orange his Third Declaration.* 1688.

Sprat, Thomas. *A True Account and Declaration of the Horrid Conspiracy against the Late King.* 1685.

Stillingfleet, Edward. *Irenicum.* 1659.

————. *The Grand Question concerning the Bishops Right to Vote in Parliament in Capital Cases*. 1680.

Strong, James. *Lydia's Heart Opened*. 1675.

T.S. *The Perplexed Prince*. 1682.

Thompson, Nathaniel. *A Collection of Eighty-Six Loyal Poems*. 1685.

Trenchard, John. *A Collection of all the Political Letters in the London Journal*. 1721.

[Tutchin, John]. *The Bloody Assizes, or the Compleat History of the Life of George, Lord Jefferies*. 1689.

[Tutchin, John]. *A New Martyrology, or The Bloody Assizes*. 1693.

[Tutchin, John]. *The Western Martyrology, or The Bloody Assizes*. 1705.

Ussher, James. *The Power Communicated by God to the Prince and the Obedience Required of the Subject*. 1683.

Ward, S. *The Animadversions and Reflections upon Col. Sydney's Paper Answered*. 1684.

Whiting, John. *Persecution Exposed in Some Memoirs relating to the Suffering of John Whiting, and many others called Quakers*. 1715.

Wildman, John. *London Liberties: or, A Learned Argument of Law and Reason*. 1651, repr. 1682.

Williams, Walter. *An Answer to Sundry Matters contained in Mr. Hunt's Postscript*. 1682.

Wodrow, Robert. *The History of the Sufferings of the Church of Scotland from the Restoration to the Revolution*. 4 vols. Glasgow, 1828.

————. *Analecta, or Materials for a History of Remarkable Providences*. 4 vols. M. Leishman, ed. Edinburgh, 1842–43.

Wood, Anthony. *Athenae Oxonienes*. 2 vols. 1721.

Secondary Works

Adair, Douglas. "Rumbold's Dying Speech, 1685, and Jefferson's Last Words on Democracy," *William and Mary Quarterly* 9 (1952): 520–31.

Alexander, Gorden. *Freedom after Ejection*. London, 1917.

Allen, David F. "The Role of the London Trained Bands in the Exclusion Crisis, 1678–1681," *English Historical Review* 87 (1972): 287–303.

————. "Political Clubs in Restoration London," *Historical Journal* 19 (1976): 561–80.

Ashcraft, Richard. "On the Problem of Methodology and the Nature of Political Theory," *Political Theory* 3 (1975): 5–25.

————. "*The Two Treatises* and the Exclusion Crisis: The Problem of Lockean Political Theory as Bourgeois Ideology," in J, G. A. Pocock and Richard Ashcraft, eds., *John Locke: Papers Read at a Clark Seminar.* William Andrews Clark Memorial Library, University of California, Los Angeles, 1980, 27–83.

————. *Revolutionary Politics and Locke's Two Treatises of Government*. Princeton: Princeton University Press, 1986.

Ashcraft, Richard, and M. M. Goldsmith. "Locke, Revolution Principles and the Formation of Whig Ideology," *Historical Journal* 26 (1983): 773–800.

Ashley, Maurice. *John Wildman, Plotter and Postmaster: A Study of the English Republican Movement in the Seventeenth Century*. London: Jonathan Cape, 1947.

Backscheider, Paula. *Daniel Defoe: His Life.* Baltimore: John's Hopkins University Press, 1989.

Barnes, Thomas G. *Somerset, 1625–1640.* Cambridge: Harvard University Press, 1961.

Beaven, Alfred B. *The Alderman of the City of London.* London, 1908.

Beaver, Dan. "Conscience and Context: The Popish Plot and the Politics of Ritual," *Historical Journal* 34 (1991): 297–327.

Beddard, R. "Anti-Popery and the London Mob, 1688," *History Today* 38 (1988): 36–39.

Behrens, B. "The Whig Theory of Constitution in the Reign of Charles II," *Cambridge Historical Journal* 7 (1941): 42–71.

Bell, Maureen. "Women and the Opposition Press after the Restoration," in John Lucas, ed., *Writing and Radicalism.* London: Longman, 1996, 39–60.

Bennett, G. V. "Conflict in the Church," in G. Holmes, ed., *Britain after the Glorious Revolution.* New York: St. Martin's, 1969, 155–75.

Blanchard, Rae, ed. *The Englishman: A Political Journal by Richard Steele.* Oxford: Clarendon Press, 1955.

Burgess, Glenn. *The Politics of the Ancient Constitution.* University Park: Pennsylvania State University Press, 1992.

Bremer, Francis. "Increase Mather's Friends: The Trans-Atlantic Congregational Network of the Seventeenth Century," *Proceedings of the American Antiquarian Society* 94 (1984): 59–96.

Brown, F. C. *Elkanah Settle, His Life and Works.* Chicago: Chicago University Press, 1910.

Browning, Andrew. "Parties and Party Organization in the Reign of Charles II," *Transactions of the Royal Historical Society,* 4th ser., 30 (1948): 21–36.

———. *Thomas Osborne, Earl of Danby and Duke of Leeds, 1632–1712.* 3 vols. Glasgow: Jackson, Son & Co., 1951.

Browning, Reed. *The Political and Constitutional Ideas of the Whigs.* Baton Rouge: Louisiana State University Press, 1982.

Cameron, Vivian. "Political Exposures: Sexuality and Caricature in the French Revolution," in Lynn Hunt, ed., *Eroticism and the Body Politic.* Baltimore: The John's Hopkins University Press, 1991, 90–107.

Carswell, John. *The Porcupine: The Life of Algernon Sidney.* London: John Murray, 1989.

Cassen, Stephen. *Lives of the Bishops of Bath and Wells.* London, 1829.

Claydon, Tony. *William III and the Godly Revolution.* Cambridge: Cambridge University Press, 1995.

Clifton, Robin. *The Last Popular Rebellion: The Western Rising of 1685.* New York: St. Martin's Press, 1984.

Collinson, John. *History and Antiquities of Somerset.* 3 vols. London, 1791.

Condren, Conal. *The Language of Politics in Seventeenth-Century England.* New York: St. Martin's Press, 1995.

Conniff, James. "Reason and History in Early Whig Thought: The Case of Algernon Sidney." *Journal of the History of Ideas* 43 (1982): 397–416.

Cranston, Maurice. *John Locke: A Biography.* London: Longmans, Green and Co., 1957.

Cressy, David. *Literacy and the Social Order: Reading and Writing in Tudor and Stuart England.* Cambridge: Cambridge University Press, 1980.

Crist, Timothy. "Government Control of the Press After the Expiration of the Printing Act in 1679," *Publishing History* 5 (1979): 49–77.

Cruickshanks, Eveline, ed. *By Force or by Default? The Revolution of 1688–89.* Edinburgh: John Donaldson Publishers, Ltd., 1989.

Daly, James. *Sir Robert Filmer and English Political Thought.* Toronto: University of Toronto Press, 1979.

Daniels, Stephen. *John Toland: His Methods, Manners, and Mind.* Toronto: McGill-Queen's University Press, 1984.

Davis, J. C. "Radicalism in a Traditional Society: The Evaluation of Radical Thought in the English Commonwealth, 1649–1660," *History of Political Thought* 3 (1982): 193–213.

De Krey, Gary S. *Fractured Society: The Politics of London in the First Age of Party, 1688–1715.* Oxford: Oxford University Press, 1985.

———. "The London Whigs and the Exclusion Crisis Reconsidered," in A. L. Beier, D. Cannadine, and J. M. Rosenheim, eds., *The First Modern Society: Essays in English History in Honour of Lawrence Stone.* Cambridge: Cambridge University Press, 1989, 457–82.

———. "Revolution *Redivivus:* 1688–1689 and the Radical Tradition in Seventeenth-Century London Politics," in Lois G. Schwoerer, ed., *The Revolution of 1688–1689: Changing Perspectives.* Cambridge: Cambridge University Press, 1992, 198–217.

———. "Rethinking the Restoration: Dissenting Cases for Conscience, 1667–1672," *Historical Journal* 38 (1995): 53–83.

Dunn, John. *The Political Thought of John Locke.* Cambridge: Cambridge University Press, 1969.

Earl, D.W. L. "Procrustean Feudalism: An Interpretative Dilemma in English Historical Narrative," *Historical Journal* 19 (1976): 33–51.

Earle, Peter. *Monmouth's Rebels: The Road to Sedgemoor, 1685.* New York: St. Martin's Press, 1977.

Edie, C. A. "Succession and Monarchy: The Controversy of 1679–1681," *American Historical Review* 70 (1964–65): 350–70.

Evans, A. M. "The Imprisonment of Lord Danby in the Tower, 1679–1684," *Transactions of the Royal Historical Society,* 4th ser., 12 (1929): 105–35.

Feiling, Keith. *A History of the Tory Party, 1640–1714.* Oxford: Clarendon Press, 1924.

Ferguson, James. *Robert Ferguson, the Plotter.* Edinburgh, 1887.

Fox, James. *A History of the Early Part of the Reign of James the Second.* London, 1808.

Foxcroft, H. C. and T. E. S. Clark. *A Life of Gilbert Burnet, Bishop of Salisbury.* Cambridge: Cambridge University Press, 1907.

Fraser, Peter. *The Intelligence of the Secretaries of State and Their Monopoly of Licensed News, 1660–1688.* Cambridge: Cambridge University Press, 1956.

Fry, F. M. *The Pictures of the Merchant Taylor's Company.* London: Chapman & Hall Ltd., 1907.

Furley, O. W. "The Whig Exclusionists: Pamphlet Literature in the Exclusion Campaign, 1979–81," *Cambridge Historical Journal* 13 (1957): 19–36.

———. "Pope-Burning Processions of the Late Seventeenth Century," *History* 44 (1959): 16–23.

Glat, Mark. "John Locke's Historical Sense," *Review of Politics* 43 (1981): 3–21.

Goldie, Mark. "Charles Blount's Intention in Writing 'King William and Queen Mary Conquerors' (1693)," *Notes and Queries* 223 (1978): 527–32.

———. "The Revolution of 1689 and the Structure of Political Argument," *Bulletin of Research in the Humanities* 83 (1980): 473–564.

———. "The Roots of True Whiggism, 1688–94," *History of Political Thought* 1 (1980): 195–236.

———. "John Locke and Anglican Royalism," *Political Studies* 31 (1983): 61–85.

———. "Obligations, Utopias, and Their Historical Context," *Historical Journal* 26 (1983): 727–46.

———. "Danby, the Bishops and the Whigs," in Tim Harris, Paul Seaward, and Mark Goldie, eds., *The Politics of Religion in Restoration England.* Oxford: Basil Blackwood, 1990, 76–105.

———. "John Locke's Circle and James II," *Historical Journal* 35 (1992): 557–86.

———. "James II and the Dissenters' Revenge: the Commission of Enquiry of 1688," *The Bulletin of Historical Research* 66 (1993): 53–88.

———. "Priestcraft and the Birth of Whiggism," in Nicholas Phillipson and Quentin Skinner, eds., *Political Discourse in Early Modern Britain.* Cambridge: Cambridge University Press, 1993, 209–31.

Goldie, Mark, and John Spurr. "Politics and the Restoration Parish: Edward Fowler and the Struggle over St. Giles Cripplegate," *English Histoical Review* 109 (1994): 572–96.

Gough, J. W. "James Tyrrell, Whig Historian, and Friend of John Locke," *Historical Journal* 19 (1976): 581–610.

Gray, H. St. George. "Whitelackington and the Duke of Monmouth in 1680," *Somerset Archaeological and Natural History Society* 73 (1927): 35–39.

Greaves, Richard. "The Tangled Careers of Two Stuart Radicals: Henry and Robert Danvers," *Baptist Quarterly* 29 (1981): 32–43.

———. *Deliver Us from Evil: The Radical Underground in Britain 1660–1663.* Oxford: Oxford University Press, 1986.

———. *Enemies Under His Feet: Radicals and Nonconformists in Britain 1664–1677.* Stanford: Stanford University Press, 1990.

———. *Secrets of the Kingdom: British Radicals from the Popish Plot to the Revolution of 1688–89.* Stanford: Stanford University Press, 1992.

Green, Emanuel. *The March of William of Orange through Somerset and a Notice of Other Local Events in the Time of James II.* London, 1882.

Greenberg, Janelle. "The Confessor's Laws and the Radical Face of the Ancient Constitution," *English Historical Review* 104 (1989): 611–37.

Haley, K. H. D. *The First Earl of Shaftesbury.* Oxford: Clarendon Press, 1968.

Harris, Tim. *London Crowds in the Reign of Charles II.* Cambridge: Cambridge University Press, 1987.

———. "Was the Tory Reaction Popular? Attitudes of Londoners towards the Persecution of Dissent, 1681–6," *London Journal* 13 (1988): 106–20.

———. "The Problem of 'Popular Political Culture' in Seventeenth-Century London," *History of European Ideas* 10 (1989): 43–58.

———. "Introduction: Revising the Restoration," in Tim Harris, Paul Seward, and Mark Goldie, eds., *The Politics of Religion in Restoration England.* Oxford: Basil Blackwood, 1990, 1–28.

————. *Politics Under the Later Stuarts: Party Conflict in a Divided Society, 1660–1715.* New York: Longman Group Ltd., 1993.

————. "Tories and the Rule of Law in the Reign of Charles II," *The Seventeenth Century* 8 (1993): 9–27.

Harrison, John, and Peter Laslett, eds. *The Library of John Locke.* Oxford: Oxford University Press, 1971.

Harth, Phillip. *Pen for a Party: Dryden's Tory Propaganda in Its Contexts.* Princeton: Princeton University Press, 1993.

Hinton, R. W. K. "English Constitutional Theories from Sir John Fortsecue to Sir John Eliot," *English Historical Review* 75 (1969): 410–25.

Hoftijzer, Paul. "'Such only as are very honest, Loyall and Active': English Spies in the Low Countries, 1660–1688," in Paul Hoftijzer and C. C. Barfoot, eds. *Fabric and Fabrications: The Myth and Making of William and Mary.* Amsterdam: DQR Studies in Literature 6, 1990, 73–92.

Horwitz, Henry. "Protestant Reconciliation During the Exclusion Crisis," *Journal of Ecclesiastical History* 15 (1964): 201–17.

————. "Party in a Civic Context: London from the Exclusion Crisis to the Fall of Walpole," in Clyve Jones, ed. *Britain in the First Age of Party.* London: Hambledon Press, 1978, 173–94.

Houston, Alan Craig. *Algernon Sidney and the Republican Heritage in England and America.* Princeton: Princeton University Press, 1991.

Hume, Robert. *The Development of English Drama in the Late Seventeenth Century.* Oxford: Clarendon Press, 1976.

Hunt, Lynn. *Politics, Culture, and Class in the French Revolution.* Berkeley and Los Angeles: University of California Press, 1984.

Israel, Jonathan I. "General Introduction," in Jonathan I. Israel, ed. *The Anglo-Dutch Moment: Essays on the Glorious Revolution and Its World Impact.* Cambridge: Cambridge University Press, 1991, 1–43.

Jones, J. R. "The Green Ribbon Club," *Durham University Journal* 49 (1956): 17–20.

————. "James II's Whig Collaborators," *Historical Journal* 3 (1960): 65–70.

————. *The First Whigs: The Politics of the Exclusion Crisis, 1678–1683.* Oxford: Oxford University Press, 1961.

————. *The Revolution of 1688 in England.* New York: St. Martin's Press, 1972.

————. "James II's Revolution: Royal Policies, 1686–92," in Jonathan I. Israel, ed. *The Anglo-Dutch Moment.* Cambridge: Cambridge University Press, 1991, 47–71.

Kenyon, J. P. *The Popish Plot.* Harmondsworth: Pelican Books, 1974.

————. "The Revolution of 1688: Resistance and Contract," in Neil McKendrick, ed., *Historical Perspectives in English Thought and Society in Honour of J. H. Plumb.* London: Europa, 1974, 43–70.

————. *Revolution Principles: The Politics of Party, 1689–1720.* Cambridge: Cambridge University Press, 1977.

Kitchin, George. *Sir Roger L'Estrange: A Contribution to the History of the Press in the Seventeenth Century.* London: Kegan Paul, Trench, Trubner & Co., 1913.

Knights, Mark. "London Petitions and Parliamentary Politics in 1679," *Parliamentary History* 12 (1993): 29–46.

————. "London's 'Monster' Petition of 1680," *Historical Journal* 36 (1993): 39–67.

————. "Petitioning and the Political Theorists: John Locke, Algernon Sidney and London's 'Monster Petition,'" *Past and Present* 138 (1993): 94–111.

————. *Politics and Opinion in Crisis, 1678–81*. Cambridge: Cambridge University Press, 1994.

Knott, David. "The Booksellers and the Plot," *The Book Collector* 23 (1974): 194–206.

Knott, John. *Discourses of Martyrdom in English Literature*. Cambridge: Cambridge University Press, 1993.

Knox, R. Buick. *James Ussher, Archbishop of Armagh*. Cardiff: University of Wales Press, 1967.

Landon, Michael. *The Triumph of the Lawyers: Their Role in English Politics, 1678–89*. Tuscaloosa: University of Alabama Press, 1970.

Laslett, Peter. "Sir Robert Filmer: The Man Versus the Whig Myth," *The William and Mary Quarterly* 5 (1948): 522–46.

————. "Introduction" to *Patriarcha and other Political Works by Robert Filmer*. Oxford: Basil Blackwood, 1949.

Lathbury, T. *A History of the Nonjurors*. London, 1845.

Lemmings, David. *Gentlemen and Barristers: The Inns of Court and the English Bar, 1680–1730*. Oxford: Clarendon Press, 1990.

Levin, Jennifer. *The Charter Controversy in the City of London, 1660–1688, and Its Consequences*. London: The Anthlone Press, 1969.

————. Lillywhite, Bryant. *London Coffee Houses: A Reference Book of Coffee Houses of the Seventeenth, Eighteenth, and Nineteenth Centuries*. London: Allen & Unwin, 1963.

Macaulay, Thomas Babington. *History of England from the Accession of James II*. 6 vols. C. H. Firth, ed. London: Macmillan & Co., 1913–15.

MacDonald, Michael. "The Strange Death of the Earl of Essex, 1683," *History Today* 41 (1991): 13–18.

MacDonald, Michael, and Terrance Murphy. *Sleepless Souls: Suicide in Early Modern England*. Oxford: Clarendon Press, 1993.

Marsh, J. B. *For Liberty's Sake*. London, 1873.

Marshall, John. *John Locke: Resistance, Religion, and Responsibility*. Cambridge: Cambridge University Press, 1994.

Marshall, Lydia. "The Levying of the Hearth Tax, 1662–1688," *English Historical Review* 51 (1936): 628–46.

Matthews, A. G. *Calamy Revised*. Oxford: Clarendon Press, 1988.

Mayhew, George P. "The Early Life of John Partridge," *Studies in English Literature* 1 (1961): 31–42.

Mendle, Michael. *Dangerous Positions: Mixed Government, the Estates of the Realm, and the Making of the Answer to xix Propositions*. Tuscaloosa: University of Alabama Press, 1985.

Meadly, George. *Memoirs of Algernon Sidney*. London, 1813.

Milne, D. J. "The Results of the Rye House Plot and Their Influence on the Revolution of 1688," *Transactions of the Royal Historical Society*, 5th Ser., 1 (1951): 19–108.

Miller, John. *Popery and Politics in England, 1660–1688*. Cambridge: Cambridge University Press, 1973.

————. *James II: A Study in Kingship*. London: Wayland Publishers, 1978.

————. "The Crown and the Borough Charters in the Reign of Charles II," *English Historical Review* 100 (1985): 53–84.

————. "Public Opinion in Charles II's Reign," *History* 80 (1995): 359–81.

Monod, Paul K. *Jacobitism and the English People, 1688–1788*. Cambridge: Cambridge University Press, 1989.

Moore, Robert John. "Daniel Defoe: King William's Pamphleteer and Intelligence Agent," *Huntington Library Quarterly* 34 (1971): 251–60.

Muddiman, J. G., ed. *The Bloody Assizes*. London: William Hodge & Co., 1929.

Nenner, Howard. *By Colour of Law: Legal Culture and Constitutional Politics in England, 1660–1689*. Chicago: Chicago University Press, 1977.

Ogg, David. *England in the Reign of Charles II*. 2 vols. Oxford: Clarendon Press, 1955.

Oliver, H. J. *Sir Robert Howard*. Durham: Duke University Press, 1963.

Orme, William. *Memoirs of the Life, Writings, and Religious Connexions of John Owen, D.D.* London, 1826.

Ormond, David. "Puritanism and Patriarchy: The Career and Spiritual Writings of Thomas Papillon, 1623–1702," in *Studies in Modern Kentish History*. Maidstone: Kent Archaeological Society, 1983, 123–37.

Ozouf, Mona. *Festivals and the French Revolution*. Alan Sheridan, trans. Cambridge: Harvard University Press, 1988.

Parry, Edward. *The Bloody Assize*. New York: Dobb, Mead, Co., 1929.

Pincus, Steve. "'Coffee Politician Does Create': Coffeehouses and Restoration Political Culture," *Journal of Modern History* 67 (1995): 807–34.

Plumptre, E. H. *The Life of Thomas Ken, D.D.* London, 1890.

Pocock, J. G. A. "Robert Brady, 1627–1700, A Cambridge Historian of the Restoration," *Cambridge Historical Journal* 10 (1951): 186–204.

———. "The Myth of John Locke and the Obsession with Liberalism," in J. G. A. Pocock and Richard Ashcraft, eds., *John Locke: Papers read at a Clark Library Seminar*. William Andrews Clark Memorial Library, University of California, Los Angeles,1980, 1–24.

———. *The Ancient Constitution and the Feudal Law*. Reissue. Cambridge: Cambridge University Press, 1987.

———. "The Concept of a Language and the *Metier d'Historien*: Some Considerations on Practice," in Anthony Pagden, ed., *The Languages of Political Theory in Early Modern Europe*. Cambridge: Cambridge University Press, 1987, 19–38.

Price, Cecil. *Cold Caleb: The Scandalous Life of Ford Grey, first Earl of Tankerville, 1655–1701*. London: Andrew Melrose, 1956

Priestly, Margaret. "London Merchants and Opposition Politics in Charles II's Reign," *Bulletin for the Institute of Historical Research* 29 (1956): 205–19.

Rahn, B. J. "*A Ra-Ree Show*—A Rare Cartoon: Revolutionary Propaganda in the Treason Trial of Stephen College," in Paul J. Korshin, ed., *Studies in Change and Revolution*. Menston: Scolar Press, 1972, 77–97.

Ramsbottom, John D. "Presbyterians and 'Partial Conformity' in the Restoration Church of England," *Journal of Ecclesiastical History* 43 (1992): 249–70.

Realey, Charles B. *The London Journal and Its Authors, 1720–23*. Lawerence: University of Kansas, 1956.

Richards, Judith, Lotte Mulligan, and John K. Graham. "'Property' and 'People': Political Usages of Locke and Some Contemporaries," *Journal of the History of Ideas* 42 (1981): 29–51.

Roberts, George. *The Life, Progresses and Rebellion of James, Duke of Monmouth*. London, 1844.

Robbins, Caroline. *The Eighteenth-Century Commonwealthman*. Cambridge: Harvard University Press, 1959.

Rogers, Henry. *Life and Character of John Howe*. London, 1836.

Rose, George. *Observations on the Historical Works of . . . Fox*. London, 1809.

Salmon, J. H. M. "Algernon Sidney and the Rye House Plot," *History Today* 4 (1954): 698–705.

Schochet, Gordon. *Patriarchalism in Political Thought*. Oxford: Basil Blackwell, 1975.

Schwoerer, Lois G. "Propaganda in the Revolution of 1688," *American Historical Review* 82 (1977): 843–74.

———. *The Declaration of Rights, 1689*. Baltimore: Johns Hopkins University Press, 1981.

———. "William, Lord Russell: The Making of a Martyr, 1683–1983," *Journal of British Studies* 24 (1985): 41–71.

———. "The Role of Lawyers in the Revolution of 1688–89," *Fortsetzung Umschlagseite* 3 (1987): 473–98.

———. *Lady Rachel Russell: "One of the Best Women."* Baltimore: Johns Hopkins University Press, 1988.

———. "The Trial of Lord William Russell: Judicial Murder?" *Journal of Legal History* 9 (1988): 142–68.

———. "Liberty of Press and Public Opinion, 1660–1695," in J. R. Jones, ed., *Liberty Secured? Britain Before and After 1688*. Stanford: Stanford University Press, 1992, 199–230.

———, ed. *The Revolution of 1688–89: Changing Perspectives*. Cambridge: Cambridge University Press, 1992.

Scott, Jonathan. "England's Troubles: Exhuming the Popish Plot," in Tim Harris, Paul Seaward, and Mark Goldie, eds., *The Politics of Religion in Restoration England*. Oxford: Basil Blackwood, 1990, 108–31.

———. *Algernon Sidney and the Restoration Crisis, 1677–1683*. Cambridge: Cambridge University Press, 1991.

Sewell, Thomas. "On the Strodes of Somersetshire," *Somerset Journal* 13 (1865–66): 7–20.

Sharpe, Reginald R. *London and the Kingdom*. 3 vols. London, 1894–95.

Sitwell, George. *The First Whig*. Scarborough, 1894.

Skinner, Quentin. "Meaning and Understanding in the History of Ideas," *History and Theory* 8 (1969): 3–53.

———. "Some Problems in the Analysis of Political Thought and Action," *Political Theory* 2 (1974): 277–303.

Sommerville, J. P. *Politics and Ideology in England, 1603–1640*. New York: Longman, 1986.

———. "Introduction" to *Patriarcha and Other Writings*. Cambridge: Cambridge University Press, 1991.

Snyder, Henry L. "Newsletters in England, 1689–1715, with Special Reference to John Dyer—A Byway to the History of England," in Donovan H. Bond and Reyonds McLeod, eds., *Newsletters to Newspapers: Eighteenth-Century Journalism*. Charlottesville: West Virginia University Press, 1977, 3–19.

Staves, Susan. *Players' Scepters: Fictions of Authority in the Restoration*. Lincoln: University of Nebraska Press, 1977.

Sutherland, James. *The Restoration Newspaper and Its Development*. Cambridge: Cambridge University Press, 1985.

Tarlton, Charles. "The Exclusion Controversy Pamphleteering and Locke's *Two Treatises*," *Historical Journal* 24 (1981): 49–68.

———. "'Rulers Now on Earth': Locke's *Two Treatises* and the Revolution of 1688," *Historical Journal* 28 (1985): 279–98.

Thompson, Martyn. "A Note on 'Reason' and 'History' in Late Seventeenth-Century Political Thought," *Political Theory* 4 (1976): 491–503.

———. "The Reception of Locke's *Two Treatises of Government*, 1690–1705," *Political Studies* 24 (1976): 184–91.

———. "The Idea of Conquest in the Controversies over the 1688 Revolution," *Journal of the History of Ideas* 38 (1977): 33–46.

———. "Significant Silences in Locke's *Two Treatises of Government*: Constitutionalism, History, Contract, and Law," *Historical Journal* 31 (1987): 275–94.

Thompson, Martyn, and Harro Hopfl. "The History of Contract as a Motif in Political Thought," *American Historical Journal* 84 (1979): 919–44.

Toon, Peter. *God's Statesman: The Life and Work of John Owen*. Exeter: Paternoster Press, 1971.

Tully, James. "Placing the *Two Treatises*," in Nicholas Phillipson and Quentin Skinner, eds., *Political Discourse in Early Modern Britain*. Cambridge: Cambridge University Press, 1993, 253–80.

Von Ranke, Leopold. *A History of England, principally in the seventeenth century*. Oxford, 1875.

Walker, J. "English Exiles in Holland during the Reigns of Charles II and James II," *Transactions of the Royal Historical Society*, 5th Ser., 30 (1948): 111–25.

———. "Censorship of the Press During the Reign of Charles II," *History* 35 (1950): 219–38.

Walker, R. B. "The Newspaper Press in the Reign of William III," *Historical Journal* 17 (1974): 691–709.

Weston, Corrine. "The Theory of Mixed Monarchy Under Charles I and After," *English Historical Review* 75 (1960): 426–43.

Weston, Corrine, and Janelle Greenberg. *Subjects and Sovereigns: The Grand Controversy over Legal Sovereignty in Stuart England*. Cambridge: Cambridge University Press, 1981.

Western, J. R. *Monarchy and Revolution: The English State in the 1680s*. London: Blanford Press, 1972.

Whiting, C. E. "Sir Patience Ward of Tanshelf," *Yorkshire Archaeological Journal* 34 (1939): 245–72.

Whiting, George W. "Political Satire in London State Plays," *Modern Philology* 28 (1930): 29–43.

Wigfield, W. MacDonald. *The Monmouth Rebels, 1685*. New York: St. Martin's Press, 1985.

Williams, Shelia. "The Pope-Burning Processions of 1679, 1680, and 1681," *Journal of the Warburg and Courtauld Institutes* 21 (1958): 104–18.

Willcock, John. *A Scot's Earl in Covenanting Times: Being the Life and Times of Archibald, the Ninth Earl of Argyle*. Edinburgh: Andrew Elliot, 1907.

Wilson, Walter. *The History and Antiquities of Dissenting Churches and Meeting Houses*. 5 vols. London, 1808.

Woodhead, J. R. *The Rulers of London, 1660–1689*. London: London and Middlesex Archaeological Society, 1965.

Worden, Blair. "The Commonwealth Kidney of Algernon Sidney," *Journal of British Studies* 24 (1985): 1–40.

Zook, Melinda. "Early Whig Ideology, Ancient Constitutionalism, and the Reverend Samuel Johnson," *Journal of British Studies* 32 (1993): 139–65.

———. "The Bloody Assizes: Whig Martyrdom and Memory After the Glorious Revolution," *Albion* 27 (1995): 373–96.

Zwicker, Steven. *Lines of Authority: Politics and English Literary Culture, 1649–1689*. Ithaca: Cornell University Press, 1993.

Unpublished Dissertations

Colquhoun, Kathleen Mary. " 'Issue of the Late Civill Wars': James, Duke of York and the Government of Scotland, 1679–1689," University of Illinois at Urbana-Champaign, PhD Thesis, 1992.

Crist, Tim. "Francis Smith and the Opposition Press in England, 1660–1688," Cambridge University, PhD Thesis, 1977.

Zook, Melinda. "Propagators of Revolution: Conspiratorial Politics and Radical Whig Culture in Late Stuart England," Georgetown University, PhD Thesis, 1993.

Index

Ailesbury, Thomas, earl of, 110
America (or New England), 88, 95, 173, 119, 125, 188
Amsterdam, xx, 19, 24, 27, 23, 29, 35, 45, 61, 95, 99, 104, 113, 119, 129, 149, 151
ancient constitution, xv, xviii, xxii, xxiii, 24, 62, 64–73, 80–85, 100, 132, 134, 153–54, 161–64, 166–70, 181–87
Andrews, Lancelot, 48
Anglican Church, xix, 64, 91, 135
   and Atwood, 73–74
   the bishops' rights, 40–42, 54, 75–76
   the clergy, xvii, 2, 24, 46, 48, 51, 56n, 64, 66, 78n, 84, 107–8, 108, 91, 95, 134, 145–46, 157, 160, 182–83
   and James II, 145–46, 151
Anne (Queen of England), 107, 191
Antipopery, xiii, xix, xxiii, xv, 7, 12, 14, 16, 24, 31, 49, 82, 90, 99–100, 101–2, 119, 121, 133–34, 142–43, 150–51
Argyle, Archibald Campbell, earl of, 128–30, 111n
   his execution, 139
   Argyle's invasion, 2, 7n, 25, 33, 35, 137
Armstrong, Katherine, 35
Armstrong, Sir Thomas, 8n, 21, 22n, 35, 103, 110, 144n, 196
Arnold, John, 9, 12n, 196
Ashcraft, Richard, xvi n, xvii–xviii, 8, 94, 103n, 131n, 132n, 163, 181
Atkyns, Sir Robert, 25, 159n
Atwood, William, xx, xxi, xxiii, 24, 25, 65–86, 155, 146n, 196

and the Glorious Revolution, 159–65, 167, 171, 173, 174, 175, 178–83, 185, 186, 187
   last years and legacy, 188–89, 194
   Fundamental Constitution, 161–64, 171
   Jus Anglorum, 71–72
   Letter of Remarks, 73
   Seasonable Vindication, 74
Axminster, 135
Ayloffe, John, 7n, 9, 25, 103, 106, 128n, 141n, 196

Bacon, Nathaniel, 27
Baldwin, Richard, 44, 165, 183
Barnardiston, Sir Samuel, 17, 19, 29, 91, 110, 196
Barnardiston, Samuel, 145n, 196
Barrington, John Shute, earl of, 192
Bateman, Charles, 12, 141, 196
Behn, Aphra, 1, 6, 16, 90, 127, 130n, 139
Behrens, B., 39n
Benson, William, 192
Bethel, Slingsby, 8, 9, 13, 16, 17, 19, 45, 89, 145n, 196
Bettiscomb, Christopher, 9, 196
Blaney, Robert, 9, 25, 196
Blood, Colonel Thomas, 8
Bloody Assizes, xxiii, 30, 34, 112, 137, 141, 173
Blount, Charles, 9, 178–79
   An Appeal, xiii, 28, 178, 196
Boden, Jean, 47
Booth, Henry Lord Delamere, 9, 115, 146–47, 170, 196

Bourne, Zachary, 7, 9, 102, 170, 196
Bradbury, Reverend Thomas
Braddon, Lawrence, 29, 117–19
Brady, Dr. Robert, 43, 71–72, 75–77, 79, 82,
    83, 182, 184, 186
    A Full and Clear, 70, 83
Bristol, 8, 93
Buchanan, George, 38
Buckingham, George, earl of, 8, 39
Buckinghamshire, 30, 177
Burgess, Glenn, xviii note
Burnet, Gilbert (bishop of Salisbury) 13,
    121, 130–31, 158, 167, 196
Burton, James, 140n, 146n, 196

Cambridge, 39
Cameronians, 128
Canterbury, 101
Care, Henry, 7n, 81–82, 83, 97n, 100,
    146n, 197
    English Liberties, 81, 142
    Weekly Pacquet, 100
Carstares, William, 105
Charles I, 48, 49n, 52, 99, 121, 175, 184
Charles II, xiii, xiv, xv, 4, 12, 13, 15, 27, 31,
    40, 41, 46, 50, 53, 89, 92, 97, 103, 126,
    128, 146
Charlton, Francis, 197
Chester, 126
Cheshire, 146
Churchill, Awnsham, 192
Claydon, Tony, xvi note
Clayton, Sir Robert, 15, 17, 19, 108, 197
Coke, Sir Edward, 67
Coleridge, Samuel Taylor, 193
Colledge, Stephen, 15, 25, 29, 89–91, 107,
    118, 122, 134, 174, 197
Collins, Anthony, 192
Condren, Conal, xxii, 65
Conway, Edward, earl of, 13
Cooke, Edward, 25, 72n, 81–83, 155, 177–
    78, 180, 182, 197
    Introduction to Old English History, 82
    A True Narrative, 82–83
    Anti-Normannicum, 81, 82–83, 161
Cornish, Henry, 16, 17, 19, 89, 107, 141,
    197
Corringham, 165
Cornwall, 101
Cromwell, Oliver, xxi, 30, 35, 96, 124

Curtis, Jane, 2, 28, 34
Curtis, Langely, 28

Dalrymple, Sir John, 23, 130, 134
Danby, Thomas Osborne, earl of, 40–41,
    159n
Dangerfield, Thomas, 7n, 8n
Danvers, Henry, 118, 144n, 197
Darby, John, 122
Dare, Thomas, 9, 131, 132, 134, 197
Defoe, Daniel, iii, 187–88
Derby, 102
Devon, 135
Devizes, Wiltshire, 128
Disney, William, 29, 35, 141n, 197
Dorset, 135
Dorsetshire, 30, 101
Dryden, John, 44, 63, 100, 127
    Duke of Guise, 44
    Absalom and Achitophel, 65, 98
Dublin, 102, 122
Dubois, John, 17
Dugdale, Sir William, 68, 71
Dunn, John, xvii
Dunton, John, 27, 137

Edinburgh, 122, 139
Edward the Confessor, 82, 83, 161, 153, 168
Elizabeth I, 50, 102
Essex, 159
Essex, Arthur Capel, earl of, 8n, 21n, 22,
    23, 29, 30, 56, 66, 99, 197
    and the Rye House Plot, 104–5, 110–13
    his death and martyrdom, 115–20, 123,
    126, 133, 174
Evelyn, John, 110, 122
Exclusion Crisis, xiv, xv, xvi, xx, xxiii, 2, 3,
    30, 38, 55, 78, 83–86, 120, 155, 156, 173
Exeter, 91, 145

Fagel, Caspar (pensionary of Holland),
    150–51
Ferguson, Robert, xvi, xx, xxi, 13, 21n, 22,
    23, 24, 29, 30, 45, 55, 81, 93–113, 118,
    129, 131, 138, 197
    and the Glorious Revolution and after,
    149–56, 169, 173, 174, 178, 179, 181,
    185, 187
    his legacy, 189–90, 192

Ferguson, Robert (*continued*)
   A Brief Justification, xvi, 152, 56, 161,
      163, 171
   An Enquiry, 118–19
   Interest of Reason, 23
   Monmouth's *Declaration*, 23, 130–37, 152
   No Protestant Plot series, 97–98
   Representation of the Dangers, 150–51

Filmer, Sir Robert, xvii, xx, 43, 45–48, 56,
      60, 62, 64, 65, 71, 124, 145, 177, 182,
      184
   Freeholder, 68–69, 70
   Patriacha, xvii, 47, 55, 64, 123
Fortescue, Sir John, 66, 81
Foulkes, John, 197
Fowler, Edward (bishop of Gloucester),
      60n, 191
Fox, John, 100, 125n
France, 31, 173
French Revolution, xvii, 108
Freke, John, 9, 25, 146n, 197
Frome, 135

Gaunt, Elizabeth, 2, 35, 137
   her execution, 140
Gaunt, William, 35
Germany, 45, 61, 144
Glat, Mark, 72n
Glorious Revolution, xvi, xvii, xviii, xx,
      xxiii, 2, 3, 19, 24, 65, 82, 93, 112–13,
      118, 122, 125, 136, 137, 144, 151–52,
      155, 159, 165–70, 173, 184, 189, 190,
      193
   The Revolutionary Settlement, xx, 152,
      155–59, 159–63, 184, 185
Godfrey, Sir Edmundbury, 16, 99, 118
Goldie, Mark, 64
Goodenough, Francis, 9, 17, 19, 25, 32,
      33, 100, 128, 131, 197
Goodenough, Richard, 9, 16, 17, 25, 32,
      33, 103, 128, 131, 141, 146n, 197
Gouge, William, 95n
Greaves, Richard, xvi note, xxi note, 103n
Greenberg, Janelle, 65, 94
Green Ribbon Club, 2, 3, 7–12, 30, 103,
      89, 117
   Green Ribbon Brothers, 1, 9–11, 27, 141

Grey of Werk, Ford, lord, 7, 8n, 9, 16, 31n,
      103–05, 111, 115, 129, 131, 141–42,
      146n, 147n, 170, 197
Gun Powder Plot (1605), 99, 100

Haley, K.H.D., 103n
Hampden, John, the younger, 34, 56, 96n,
      105, 112–15, 123n, 146n, 197
   his treatment by James II, 141–42, 155
   after the Glorious Revolution, 156–57,
      191, 193
Hampden, Sarah, 34
Hampden family of Buckinghamshire, 30
Hancock, Giles, 6
Harris, Benjamin, 26, 27, 29, 142
Hague, The, 126
Hearne, Thomas, 186
Henry II, 82
Henry III, 68
Hewling, Benjamin, 35, 137
Hewling, William, 35, 137
Hickes, George, 57, 60, 73–74, 160, 164,
      178, 182, 184
Hicks, John, 12n, 30, 141n, 198
Hoadly, Benjamin, 187
Hobbes, Thomas, 38
Holland (or the Netherlands), 19, 24, 45,
      95, 99, 131, 142, 144, 149, 150, 151
Holloway, James, 123n, 198
Holles, Lord Denzil, 40, 75
Holmes, Major Abraham, 33, 141, 198
Holmes, Blake, 33
Hopkins, William, 160n
Hone, William, 7, 9, 111, 198
Hooke, Nathaniel, 13, 29, 146n, 171n, 198
Hooper, James, 9, 198
Horwitz, Henry, 13
Howard, Sir Robert, 191
Howard, of Escrick, William, baron, 7, 10,
      104, 123, 142, 146n, 198
Howe, John, 30
Hume, Sir Patrick (of Polwarth), 128–30
Hunt, Thomas, xx, xxi, 25, 37–56, 49n,
      57–8, 59–60, 62, 63, 65, 74–80, 85, 92,
      93, 101, 102, 125, 132, 155, 160n, 164,
      168, 173, 181, 187, 188, 194, 198
   An Argument for Bishops, 54
   An Apology, 75–79
   Defense of the Charter, 44–45

Great and Weighty, 42, 54, 49–50, 54, 75
Postscript, 37–39, 42–46, 54, 58, 58, 74–76,
  79
Hunton, Philip, 38

Illminster, 30, 32, 117
Ireland, xiii
Ireton, Henry, 10, 25, 198
Islington, 96

Jackson, Thomas, 48
Jacobites, 3, 156, 158, 171n, 189, 191
James I, 48, 175
James II, as duke of York, xiii, xiv, xv, xxii,
  2, 14–16, 28, 32, 42, 50, 53, 57, 83, 84,
  88, 99, 101, 107, 119, 126, 128, 133
  as King, 2, 4, 13, 32, 34, 35, 39, 45, 119,
  136, 138, 142–46, 147n, 151, 153,
  155–59, 161, 162, 164, 166, 170, 171,
  185–86, 189, 191
James Edward (Prince of Wales), 136, 151
Janeway, Richard, 27
Jefferys, Sir George, xv, 30, 34, 35, 61, 112,
  137, 138, 140–41, 174
Jenkins, Leoline, 34, 38, 43, 91, 103, 109
Jenks, Francis, 10, 16, 17, 198
Jennings, Mary, 34
Johnson, Reverend Samuel, xviii, xx, xxi,
  xxiii, 13, 22, 29, 33, 37–39, 43, 55–63,
  73, 74, 81, 85, 91, 93, 101, 110, 121,
  125, 198
  treatment under James II, 143–44
  and the Glorious Revolution, 155, 158–
  59, 160, 164–70, 171, 173, 174, 178,
  180, 181, 182, 186, 187, 189
  his last years & legacy, 190–94
  Humble & Hearty Address, 143–44, 191
  Julian the Apostate, 23, 28, 37–38, 57–62,
  73, 143, 165, 191
  Julian's Arts, 165, 168
Jones, J.R., xiv note, xvi note, xxi note, 31n
Jones, Sir William, 56, 57, 96n

Keeling, Josiah, 109
Kent, 96
Kenyon, John, 100
Kennett, White, 191
Kick, Abraham, 95n
Knights, Mark, xiv note, xxi note, 8, 12n,
  13, 26

Laslett, Peter, xvii
Lee, Francis, 191
Lee, Thomas, 10, 198
L'Estrange, Sir Roger, 28, 38, 42–43, 89,
  91–92, 98–99, 107, 122, 125, 165n
Leveller, xxi, 95
Liberalism, xvii, xxiii
Lisle, Lady Elizabeth, 140, 141n
Lobb, Stephen, 29, 30, 146n, 198
Locke, John, xvii–xviii, xix, 22, 55–56, 72n,
  94–95, 97n, 132n, 163–64, 173, 177,
  179–80, 181, 182, 183, 187, 192, 198
  The Two Treatises, xvii, 80, 94–95, 163–
  64, 173, 177, 179, 180
London City Charter, 19, 20, 28, 43–45,
  87–88, 92–93, 99
Long, Thomas, 58
Louis XIV, 49, 99
Love, William, 17
Luttrell, Narcissus, 109, 188
Lyme Regis, 32, 101

Macaulay, Thomas Babington, 131, 152
Magna Carta (1215), 81, 83, 100, 153, 157,
  168, 185
Manley, Major John, 33, 198
Manley, Izack, 33, 144n, 155
Marvell, Andrew, 100
Mary I, 99, 101, 150
Mather, Increase, 95n
Mather, Nathaniel, 88
Matthews, Captain Edward, 21, 22n, 25,
  144, 198
Matthews, Jane, 35
Mead, Matthew, 13, 29, 146n, 199
Mews, Peter (bishop of Bath and Wells), 34
Miller, John, 92
Milne, D. J., 103n
Milton, John, 38
Moore, Sir John, 15, 106
Monmouth, James, duke of, xv, xxiii, 8n,
  12n, 21, 23, 24, 27–30, 32, 44, 97,
  101–3, 105, 110–13, 115, 119, 126–37,
  130n, 144, 151, 189, 200
  his execution, 138–39
Monmouth's Rebellion, xv, xvi, xx, 2, 3,
  4, 7, 13, 23, 24, 29–35, 45, 93, 94,
  126–37, 156, 157, 174
Monmouth rebels, 9–10, 26, 155, 156,
  157, 170

Monmouth, James, duke of (*continued*)
  Monmouth's *Declaration*, 29, 35, 119,
    130–37, 138

Nelthorpe, Richard, 25, 26, 131, 141n, 199
New York, 188
Nicolson, William (bishop of Carlisle),
    178n
Norfolk, duke of, 39
Norman Conquest (1066), 71, 77, 79–84,
    153, 161, 185
North, Sir Francis, 35
North, Roger, 25
Northleigh, John, 15
Norton, Edward, 10, 103, 145n, 170, 199

Oates, Titus, 16, 35, 99, 112
  treatment under James II, 142–43, 174
Oldmixion, John, 110
Owen, John, 96
Oxford, xiii, 37, 60, 96, 108, 177
Oxford Book Burning (July 1683), xviii, 5,
    37–38, 55, 62
Oxford Parliament (March 1681), xiv, xxii,
    4, 5, 20, 23, 36, 86, 89–90, 103, 107

Papillon, Thomas, 17, 19, 23, 30, 107, 155,
    199
Parkinson, Reverend James, 60n
Partridge, John, 129, 199
Pelling, Edward, 54, 57
petitions (calls for Parliament to sit, 1679,
    1680, 1681), xxiii, 2, 3, 5, 6, 8, 12–13,
    20, 27
Petyt, William, 21n, 22, 24, 25, 43, 66, 69–
    72, 75, 76, 80–83, 85, 155, 161, 177,
    180, 182, 199
  Ancient Right, 22, 83
Peyton, Sir Robert, 10, 17, 19, 145n, 199
Pilkington, Thomas, 15, 16, 17, 19n, 91,
    155, 199
Player, Sir Thomas, 16, 18, 85, 199
Pocock, J.G.A., xviii, xxi, 39n, 65, 72n, 82,
    167
Popish Plot (1679), xiii, 2, 5, 12, 13, 26,
    30, 43, 54, 90, 99, 119, 120, 142
Prideaux, Edmund, 10, 25, 31, 199
Prideaux family of Devon, 31, 32
Protestant Dissent (or nonconformity),
    xix, 4, 14, 17–18, 26, 29–31, 33–34,

41, 43, 64, 84, 87, 95, 97, 106, 120–21,
    128, 133–35, 140, 145–46, 150–51
Pye family of Berkshire, 31
Pym, John, xxi

Ravenscroft, Edward, 13
Republican, xxi, 95, 118, 124–25, 134
Ridpath, George, 192
Richard III, 186
right of resistance, xx, 59, 62, 100–101,
    153–54, 155, 162, 174
Robbins, Caroline, xxi note, 180
Roberts, George, 131n
Rochester, earl of, 130
Rome, 31, 90, 150
Rouse, John, 15, 116, 199
Row, John, 10, 199
Rumbold, Richard, 32, 33, 103, 105, 128
    152, 170
  his execution, 139–40, 199
Rumbold, William, 32, 33, 146n, 199
Rumsey, Colonel John, 10, 21, 95n, 103,
    104, 109, 111, 116, 141, 146n, 199
Russell, Lord William, 12n, 22, 28, 30, 37–
    39, 56–57, 60–61, 99, 199
  and the Rye House Plot, 103–5, 110–13
  his execution and martyrdom, 115–23,
    125–27, 133, 138, 139, 156, 173–74,
    189, 191
Russell, Lady Rachel, 30, 33, 120, 144,
    165, 166n, 191
Rye House Plot (1682–83), xiv, xvi, xx, 2,
    3, 4, 12, 13, 19, 23, 25, 26, 29, 38–39,
    60, 93, 101–113, 115–26, 128, 135,
    142, 156, 157
  the plotters, 9–11, 24, 25, 32, 45, 94,
    128, 131, 133, 141, 152, 155–57, 170
Russell, Wriothesly, duke of Bedford, 192

Salmon, J.H.M., 111
Sancroft, William (archbishop of Canter-
    bury), 73
Sawyer, Sir Robert, 123–24
Schochet, Gordon, 48
Schwoerer, Lois, 33
Scotland, 33, 95, 96, 151, 191, 127, 128, 137,
    139, 151, 191
Scott, Jonathan, xxi, 4, 12n, 38n, 110n
Scroggs, Sir William (lord chief justice),
    89

Sedgemoor (Battle of, 1685), xv, xxiii, 19,
    30, 94, 138, 141, 149, 152
Settle, Elkanah, 97n
Shaftesbury, Anthony Ashley Cooper, earl
    of, xiv note, 8n, 12, 15, 19, 21n, 22,
    23, 25, 26, 40, 81–83, 91, 95n, 96–98,
    115, 121, 126, 127, 140n, 141, 174,
    177–78, 197
    and the Rye House Plot, 103–4
Shaftesbury, Anthony Ashley Cooper, third
    earl of, 192
Sherlock, William, 74, 96, 160, 164–65
Shepherd, Thomas, 200
Shower, Bartholomew, 61, 122
Shower, John, 29, 200
Shute, Samuel, 16, 18
Sidney, Colonel Algernon, 40, 55, 96n, 99,
    200
    and the Rye House Plot, 103–5, 110–13
    his execution and martyrdom, 115–18,
    120, 123–26, 133, 138, 156, 173–74,
    189
    Discourses, 123, 126
Sitwell, George, 7n
Skelton, Bevil, 129–30
Smith, Aaron, 10, 25, 103, 106, 170, 189,
    200
Smith, Elinore, 28
Smith, Francis, 26–29, 92, 200
Sommerville, J.P., 67
Spanish Armada (1588), 99, 100
Steele, Richard, 191
Speke, Charles, 32, 34, 200
Speke, George, 10, 34, 117–19, 200
Speke, Hugh, 10, 25, 29, 34, 117, 143–44,
    189, 200
Speke, John, 10,25, 32, 34, 144, 145n,
    146n, 200
Speke, Mary, 33–34
Speke family of Illminster, 30–32, 134
Stephen (King of England), 82
Steward, James (of Coltness), 130
Starkey, John, 11, 18, 27, 29, 200
Stout, John, 146
Strode, Edward, 32, 146n, 200
Strode, William, 32, 146n, 200
Strode family of Somerset, 32, 134
Sunderland, earl of, 166n
Switzerland, 144

Taunton, 93, 101
Thompson, Martin, xviii
Thompson, Mary, 28
Thompson, Nathaniel, 28
Thoresby, Ralph, 146
Tillotson, Reverend John, 165, 166n
Tily, Joseph, 11, 25, 131, 141n, 145n,
    146n, 200
Toland, John, 187
Torbay, 94, 146, 151, 193
Trenchard, Henry, 11, 25, 146n, 200
Trenchard, Sir John, 11, 21, 25, 32, 34–35,
    85, 103, 112, 115, 144, 145n, 146n,
    155, 170, 189, 200
Trenchard, John (journalist), 187
Trenchard, Phillipa, 34–35
Trenchard, William, 11, 31, 200
Trenchard family of Dorset, 30, 31
Trosse, George, 145–46
Tutchin, John, 123, 136, 165, 170, 200
Tyrrell, James, xx, xxi, xxiii, 55, 82, 200
    post-Glorious Revolution, 174–87, 192,
    194
    Bibliotheca Politica, 180, 181–85, 186, 187
    Brief Enquiry, 181, 185–86, 187
    General History of England, 186
    Patriarcha non Monarcha, 55, 64, 81, 176–
    77, 182

Ussher, James (archbishop of Aramagh),
    175–76
Utrecht, 45, 61, 133

von Ranke, Leopold, xix
Vox populi, vox dei, 190

Wade, Nathaniel, 25, 32, 33, 103, 104, 109,
    128, 131, 141, 146n, 200
Wade, William, 32, 33, 200
Walcott, Captian Thomas, 22, 103, 104, 106,
    111, 200
Waller, Edmund, 11, 25, 200
Waller, Sir William, 8n, 11, 200
Wallop, Richard, 25, 159n
Warcup, Edmund, 21n
Ward, Sir Patience, xv, 16, 18, 19, 27, 30,
    107, 155, 200
Weeks, Thomas, 200
Wellington, 101

West, Robert, 11, 25, 102, 103, 105, 110,
   200
Weston, Corrine, 94
Wildman, Major John, 25, 81, 95n, 103,
   104, 111, 112, 155, 200
William I, 82, 83, 84
William III, as Prince of Orange, xv, xxiii,
   4, 32, 45, 84, 130, 136, 145, 154–56
   as King, 156, 165, 166, 167, 168, 170,
   186, 189, 190, 191

his *Declaration of Reasons*, 136, 146, 149–
   52, 167
William and Mary, 2, 142, 154, 156, 157,
   158, 161, 161, 162, 166, 167, 179
Williams, Walter, 43, 51, 54
Williams, Sir William, 25, 159n
Wood, Anthony, 39, 60

Yonge, Sir Walter, 11, 32, 200
Yonge family of Devon, 32, 134

Printed in the United States
204408BV00001B/367/P